BUCCANEER

Also by Dudley Pope

BUCCANEER

A novel by
DUDLEY POPE

Walker and Company
New York

Oz Editions

First published in the United States of America
in 1984 by the Walker Publishing Company, Inc.

ISBN: 0-8027-0783-1

Library of Congress Catalog Card Number: 83-40575

Printed in the United States of America

10 9 8 7 6 5 4 3 2 1

For Jane: with love

Author's Note

The Caribbean at the time of the buccaneers nourished some bizarre characters, of whom Sir Thomas Whetstone is the most intriguing. He did exist in real life and he was the Royalist nephew of Oliver Cromwell. As readers of my biography of Sir Henry Morgan know, Whetstone was eventually captured and imprisoned by the Spanish and nothing was ever heard of him again.

Dudley Pope
Yacht Ramage
Sint Maarten/St. Martin
West Indies

Chapter One

Now the wind had died, the cloying smell of charcoal once again covered the island and soaked into the folds of his jerkin so that every movement provoked puffs, like pumping a blacksmith's bellows. Yorke wished that his father had bought a plantation on the windward side where the Trade winds arrived cool and fresh after crossing the Atlantic, free of wood smoke and the warm, damp stench of the dung of the cattle, hogs, horses and mules which ranged the length of the ropes tethering their hind legs.

Clearing the island of the Brazil wood forests sufficiently to farm it properly was going to take years, he thought irritably. Thirty years ago the first few settlers had been hard put to find an acre clear of trees and later arrivals began buying so-called plantations comprising either flat sandy scrub or woods which they had to clear, felling the trees and digging up the roots.

Some of the poorer planters with only a few white indentured servants had tried various ways of killing the roots instead of digging (the dry season made the trees go wide or deep searching for water) but usually ended up ploughing round them. Gouging a basin-like depression in the top of the root and filling it with turpentine did not work very well; nor did Stockholm tar, because the heat of the tropical sun dried up the liquors before they soaked deep enough into the sap-sodden wood to kill it.

Yorke's method, which he was still using on the tiny corner of the estate yet to be cleared, was simpler and more effective, although provoking the scorn of his neighbours. He had the servants strip a foot-wide band of bark from just above ground level, and within a few weeks the tree was obviously dying. In a year or so the burrowing termites would reduce it to a riddled shell, but a sudden gale of wind often saved the bother of cutting it down, so the trunk could be burned where it fell or sawn up for the cooking ovens, while the root was soon dry enough to burn out.

Yorke felt drained of energy. He had slept badly, worried about the ship just arrived from England and now at anchor in the bay off Bridgetown. God only knew what letters her master had brought out; what fresh orders, proclamations and proscriptions from the Parliamentarians for the governor. Cromwell and the Council of State sniffed out and harried Royalists with the same tenacity that the Spanish Inquisition rooted out heretics. The only difference, it seemed to Ned, was that the Parliamentarians lacked the rack.

Yorke knew for certain that whatever news or instructions she was carrying, the arrival of the sloop – the *William and Mary,* taken from John Alston last year for some alleged plotting on behalf of the King – could mean only new penal taxes for the Royalists remaining in Barbados and the latest news from their relatives of what more the Lord Protector had confiscated in England.

He paused, watching one of the indentured servants filing at a saw blade to sharpen it before resuming his task of squaring up a block of coral stone, needed to extend a wing of the house. It was extraordinary that the coral block was comparatively soft when dragged from the sea and easily worked with saw, mason's chisel and maul: yet within a few months the air so hardened it that newcomers would inquire the whereabouts of the local quarry. He had heard of a similar material used in Italy. *Tuffa,* that was the name. It was sawn out of quarries just as a farm labourer would cut hay from a rick, but a few months later became as hard as a good mortar.

He thought for a moment. Was it worth sending for a horse, saddling up and riding into Bridgetown to see what letters the *William and Mary*'s master had brought from brother George in joyless Puritan England?

He would meet fellow planters riding in for the same purpose and three quarters of them, Roundheads to a man,

2

would be sneering, some even viciously pleased, at any orders enforcing new regulations and proscriptions on the Royalists. The few Cavaliers left, harassed by the governor, knowing that nothing short of a miracle could save them from having to sell out their plantations at ridiculous prices to Parliamentarians, would be even more maudlin than usual and, if there had been time, drunk as well. Finally he told himself that the news would be as good or bad tomorrow as today, with the advantage that tomorrow many fewer planters would be at the landing stage and in the taverns. He would be able to collect his mail and hear the news without some drunken neighbour trying to provoke him into drawing his sword – or, for that matter some raddled trull offering to console him.

A man was well advised to bear the label of a coward these days. Being the only Cavalier in a roistering group of a dozen Roundheads, at least one of whom was likely to be a regular duellist, was to invite a fight with three, the other nine ready to swear before the magistrate that the Royalist had drawn first.

Wilson would certainly be in Bridgetown; he would be expecting mail and drafts for the sugar and tobacco that he had sent home in the *William and Mary*. Any orders from London could only be to the advantage of such a staunch Parliamentarian. He would have arrived at the quayside early and drunk – he rarely mounted his horse sober – and would stay in town drinking with his cronies until dusk. By then he would be so sodden that mosquitoes and sandflies made no impression. The indentured servant whose task it was to find him would hoist him on to the horse and, as usual, he would fall off the other side and the servant would have to get help to sling him athwart the horse's back, with head and arms hanging down one side and legs the other, and the body periodically jerking in spasms as Wilson vomited.

In that fashion, besotted master, perspiring servant and besmeared horse would walk the five miles out to the plantation in St James's parish. By this time Wilson would have vomited himself into a semblance of sobriety: enough to jog the last mile or two swaying upright in the saddle; enough to abuse Aurelia when he arrived and probably hit her a few times but, Yorke hoped, still too drunk to be potent; more concerned with ordering tankards of rumbullion to be put on the table than ordering Aurelia to bed.

Yorke tried daily to drive this picture from his mind: his body would tauten like a rope under strain; he would see Wilson's closely-spaced, bloodshot eyes flicking from side to side like a boar inspecting a trough; then that piggish mouth (with the sloping chin jutting from bulging cheeks one realized it lacked only the ring through the nose) would sneer some insult in a strangely high-pitched voice.

Yorke admitted that this was not the man that Aurelia had married. When Wilson had taken the French girl as a bride in England he had been a wide-shouldered and stocky young man, black-haired and passing for handsome, his only slight physical faults the receding chin and closely-spaced eyes. At least, that was what Aurelia said, and if one looked carefully there were still traces, like the puddles left after a thunderstorm.

Four years in the tropics, four years of drinking rumbullion like water, four years of a life when it was unlikely he was sober for a total of seven hours in a week, and never two consecutive, had reduced his face to the likeness of a comical model made of unleavened bread and left out in the rain: bloated yet sodden, the features soft and blurred, the eyes like currants stuck in the dough, each with a red rim as though resting in a curl of bacon.

Wilson had made a bad start in the island: one had to make allowances for that. Arriving five years after the King's trial and execution, he had brought plenty of money and a weakness for hot liquors. Opinionated, wealthy, at first a Parliamentarian among a majority of Royalists, he had listened to no advice, asked no questions, had few guests to the house he rented – and sent most of those home disgusted at the way he belittled and abused his young and shy wife in public, drawing crude and vulgar comparison with her early life in France – she was from a Huguenot family hounded out of Poitou – and the rough existence of the island.

Then he had bought an estate. He had to buy it from a Royalist who, more farsighted than most and worried at the way events were going in England, had decided to sell up to try his luck in Virginia. And, disliking Wilson's politics and manners, he had charged him a high price – some said £200 an acre – for what was a large plantation but well known as an unlucky one: a river, one of the few on the island, flooded in the sudden storms, washing away the soil but leaving it a desert for the rest of the year, with no grass or scrub to stop the soil being scattered on the wind. One of the earliest plantations to be cleared of trees, it also taught the more observant planters the need for holding down the soil against the scorching sun and the strong winds so that the crops could take advantage of the rainy season.

At that time Cromwell and Parliament had complete power in England. For Yorke, aged twenty-one, it had been a time when he dreaded the arrival of each ship: every letter from his elder brother seemed to tell him that the Parliamentarians had seized yet another relative or his lands. Looking back on it was like remembering a recurrent nightmare: the King executed, the Prince escaped to France, most of the estates of the Royalists seized and their owners hunted down, churches stripped of ornaments or defaced, Catholic priests hunted like foxes. His own father and brother wounded at the battle of Marston Moor; and escaping only because they were left for dead on the battlefield. And he, the younger son, earlier ordered to look after the family plantation in Barbados, removed by a six-week sea voyage from news.

Then, slowly at the beginning, came the pressure on the island. The Cavaliers had at first been in the majority and the wilder ones tried to force out the Roundheads. The wiser Royalists protested, pointing out that they had to trade with England, and with it in Commonwealth hands the Caribbean islands were simply fruit that would shrivel and fall if the tree decided their time had come. The majority of the Assembly would not listen, and Cromwell's people, men like Wilson, sat in their homes, besotted with rumbullion – and waited.

The tree analogy had been a good one. The Royalist planters of course soon found they had no market for their produce in England – and England was no longer a source for all the things they needed to run a plantation, be it a horse or saddle, needles and thread, jerkins and hose for owners and servants, boots, spades and linen, silk and lace for the wives. Holland was the next choice – but Cromwell went to war with the Dutch for two years.

Swiftly the balance of power in the Barbados Assembly had changed: the Roundhead planters were bitter and resentful, but backed by renegade Royalists. Reinforced with Parliament's orders, they set out to break the Royalists. Some of them, like Wilson, saw it as a perfect opportunity to repair at practically no cost early mistakes in the choice of plantations or to buy, for next to nothing, well-run Royalist estates to replace or extend their own.

Now, Yorke thought bitterly, the island was divided: Cavalier and Roundhead clung to what they had. He was still standing in the heat of the sun and the indentured servant was beginning to look uncomfortable, thinking that the master was checking on his work.

He walked back to the house, glancing at the bronze sundial on its plinth in front of the stone steps leading up to the front door. Eight o'clock, and the sun strengthening.

"Henry," he called, "I'll have my horse!"

He walked through to his bedroom and went to the pewter handbasin which still held the water he had used for washing and shaving: the present drought made water as precious as imported brandy and it had to be used over and over again, until it stank. He wiped his face and washed his hands with soapberry, the flesh of the fruit sliced into a dish of water and making suds. He felt his chin and cheeks, although he had shaved carefully, as if knowing that eventually he would go into town. Then he straightened his hose, saw that the toes of his shoes were scratched and changed them for a newer pair.

Suddenly in the distance he heard hoofbeats drumming on the parched earth, as though on cobblestones, and Henry called:

"Mist' Alston sir, on his way from town."

It was easy to guess: John came along a lane from the south if calling on his return from Bridgetown; he rode along an opposite lane if coming from his own plantation to the north in St Lucy's Parish, surrounding Six Men Fort.

"Be ready to take his horse," Yorke said, less as an order than an indication he had heard, and went out to meet him.

His closest friend on the island, John Alston, was hot and angry, sliding off his horse with only a perfunctory nod to Henry. "'Lo Ned, I've just come from town." He waved a

6

worn leather satchel. "A single letter for you. Damned hot, this sun; let's go inside."

Alston was a slim, sallow-faced bachelor who seemed never to be affected by the heat. Certainly he was not a man to gallop eight miles unnecessarily on a hot day, having more respect for his horse. The all-too-casual "Let's go inside" hinted that his news from Bridgetown was private; not to be spoken aloud in front of the servants who would later gossip far into the night, talking in a dozen accents from Irish to Welsh, Scots to the quick twang of the city of London.

Yorke led the way into the house. It was large but sparsely furnished: back in England it would have been likened to a series of large cells fit for monks, but here in Barbados it was a bachelor's house, to become a married man's home with the addition of more chairs, extra shelves, a larger bed and perhaps some additional work in the kitchen.

Apart from that, it was a regular high-ceilinged plantation house with thick outer walls of coral stone, the inner walls being simply light wooden partitions seven feet high and leaving a space above so that a cooling wind from the windows blew through the house and into every room. The heavy double shutters, now clipped back, were made of bullet wood, fine-grained, heavy and tough, proof against musket balls and favoured for fiddle bows. Each half had a loophole cut in it, useful if the house was ever attacked by an enemy, and if it rained a source of a breeze, because the windows were not fitted with glass. The thick coral stone walls, the steeply-pitched roof and the open windows kept the house cool when there was a breeze.

"A drink?" Yorke asked as he gestured to one of the three rattan chairs.

"Lemon juice," Alston said, sitting down heavily, undoing the top buttons of his brown jerkin and using his wide-brimmed hat to fan himself. "Too hot and too early for rumbullion."

Yorke called to one of the servants: "Martha – lemon juice for the two of us, please." Turning back to Alston he took the letter handed to him, sat down and said: "And what do our friends have to say in Bridgetown?"

"We have no friends in Bridgetown *today*," Alston said bitterly. "We had some yesterday, but today – none."

7

"You're talking in riddles."

"I'm not, really. The news the ship brought in means some more of our Royalist friends will be quitting the island – but more will be joining Cromwell."

"Surely it can't be as bad as that, John."

"What is the worst news the *William and Mary* could bring?"

Yorke thought a few moments. "That the Commonwealth is sending out ships of war to take control of more of the islands."

"Exactly. A fleet is preparing at Spithead under Vice-Admiral Penn and General Venables. Or was, when the *William and Mary* sailed. It should be nearly here by now. It is going to strip the island of servants to provide troops, and then go on to capture Hispaniola from the Spanish. Or Trinidad. No one seems sure."

"So we'll lose all our men . . . and the Roundheads will raise taxes yet again."

"The governor will argue," Alston said, "but . . ."

"Now Cromwell's just signed a peace with the Dutch, he has a large navy with nothing to do. Attacking the Spanish out here seems an obvious move – and from the point of view of the islands, a welcome one. But for the last of us Royalists . . ."

Alston sighed. "So we'll lose our men, then we'll lose our plantations. The Assembly will take everything now, crippling us by taxation."

Martha brought in two pewter tankards of lemon juice and set them on the floor beside each man's chair. Alston waited until she left the room and said: "Read your letter, Ned, while I have my drink."

It was brief and from his father. The writing was hurried and the signature scrawled so that no one intercepting the letter could identify the writer.

Without preliminaries it said:

"Both estates have been seized and a Parliamentary general lives in the northern one while the southern one is abandoned except for the steward and his wife, who struggle to look after the place.

"Parliament finally called on me to compound. In

8

exchange for every penny I possess (and more: I would have had to mortgage the Barbados plantation) I could have kept the northern estate and, of course would have had to swear loyalty to Parliament and the Lord Protector.

"Were I not the sixth earl and father to you and your elder brother, I might have considered it, solely to keep our people employed on the estates after all their years of loyal service, but neither of you would have wished it and I value my sons' opinions of me too highly to risk their scorn should I compromise with Cromwell.

"So I have raised secretly what cash I can. I have secretly left sums which will look after our pensioners, and the rest we have taken with us – by the time you receive this we shall be with Prince Charles in France (or Spain – reports of his present whereabouts vary).

"Thus have we been forced to flee our own country, and it is a strange feeling. I am no longer an Englishman but a 'Cavalier', and Parliament will call me a traitor.

"I would have been persuaded to stay, despite conditions here during recent years, if I thought my departure would result in retaliation against you in Barbados, but this will happen anyway. The fleet under Penn and Venables is preparing to sail and will arrive off your coasts very soon after you receive this by the *William and Mary*. They will try to arrest you and a few others before going on to attack Spanish possessions with men pressed in the islands. As you have your *Griffin* sloop with you I know you can escape.

"Estates can be recovered in time – these scoundrels with their long faces, constant hymn-singing and hatred of laughter and happiness, concerned only with destroying what is beautiful, worthwhile or cheerful, cannot stay in power for ever. So remember, the important thing is to stay alive, even if it means fleeing now, to fight them on another day. The people of England will eventually throw out this tyranny.

"I do not wish to give you orders, merely to beg you not to take risks in trying to keep the plantation: orders have been given for General Venables to detain you and bring you back to England. I can give you no address and I presume you will have none for a year or two, but we have mutual friends with whom we can correspond. My prayers are for you."

For a few moments Ned felt like a man standing on a high wall watching his ladder crashing to the ground. Henry Sydney Broughton Yorke, sixth Earl of Ilex, and his heir George were fugitives and Ned himself was to be "detained". What his father had euphemistically called the "northern estate", which stretched from Godmersham to Molash, in the shadow of the North Downs, and the "southern estate", rich sheep country also in Kent surrounding Saltwood, and including the remains of the castle in which the three knights had slept the night on their way from France to Canterbury to murder Thomas à Becket, were abandoned to Cromwell. Cromwell, the Lord Protector, Parliament, the Roundheads, the Commonwealth: the hydra had many heads.

Where his father once sat at the head of his table at Godmersham, a Parliamentary favourite now claimed ownership: at Saltwood, a man and wife struggled with a thousand acres . . . And the small estate house at Ilex, across the county boundary in Sussex, was not even mentioned.

For a few moments he pictured the Godmersham house, with its tall, patterned red brick chimneys, where he had spent much of his childhood. If he relied on his memory, it was always either spring or autumn because the great beech trees protecting the house from the west and north, and scattered over the hills and valleys forming the estate, were bright green with fresh life or like beaten copper as autumn came. And he remembered the church in which (by coincidence) there was the oldest known image of St Thomas à Becket.

Then Saltwood came to his memory. He preferred it to Godmersham because the old castle had been his playground and as a child he frightened himself into hearing the clatter of hooves and clanking of armour as the knights rode off for Canterbury, to murder Becket at what they thought was the King's wish. When King Edward later claimed that he had been misunderstood, the Earl of Ilex was blamed for sheltering the knights, but the Earl replied indignantly. When three knights riding directly from the Court, then in France, banged on his door and demanded food and shelter "in the King's name", was he to refuse them entry and be accused of treason?

Now owls skimmed silently round the ruined walls of Saltwood castle, and no one cared about the house. No doubt the great flocks of sheep had been stolen, and Roundhead troops were probably living there and, unless exceptional men, using choice furniture for firewood and family portraits as pistol targets.

He refused to think of the house at Ilex. The estate was small, only a few hundred acres, but it had been a favourite home for the Yorke family. He and his brother had been born there, and his mother had used it during her last few years, dying in time to avoid seeing a civil war exile her family.

"Bad news?" Alston asked, and Yorke realized he must have been staring at the letter for a quarter of an hour or more.

He shrugged his shoulders. "No news from England can be good these days. My father tells me he refused to compound and has fled to France with my brother to join the Prince."

"So Parliament will be upon you," Alston said grimly. "Your father was lucky to be able to hold on for so long."

"I suppose so. Anyway, he also confirms that Cromwell's preparing a fleet to attack some Spanish possessions and will strip these islands of servants to provide men for its army."

Alston nodded and then asked quietly: "What are you going to do?"

"Leave, I think. At this moment my head is spinning, but really I have no choice."

"Ned, believe me," Alston said firmly, "more than any of us you have no choice. Your father has warned you. You have the finest estate, and thanks to you the best run –" he held up a hand, "– no, I am not flattering you. You have the best of the indentured servants and you and your father have invested a great deal of money in the place while most of the other planters have produced just enough sugar or cotton to pay their expenses and keep them in hot liquors. But you know of one man who will be even more powerful when Venables and Penn arrive and who for years has had his eye on this plantation . . ."

"Yes. Wilson wants to drive me out and buy the place for a few guineas."

"More likely he'll wait until a new Assembly confiscates all Royalist property and shares it among themselves. With a big fleet anchored here, they can decide that without worrying about the planters causing any trouble."

"No, Wilson is too cunning for that. He wants to *buy* it; then he has the deeds in his name, all properly executed, so that when the monarchy is restored Wilson will still own it: I could not claim the Parliamentarians confiscated it."

"That sounds like Wilson: full of cunning – and rumbullion. You'll leave the island in the *Griffin*?"

"Yes, I suppose so. It's hard to take in," he said, waving the letter. "I'll take any of my indentured servants who want to leave, and try my luck at one of the other islands. They say Antigua and St Christopher are still sympathetic to Royalists."

Alston again shrugged his shoulders. "If Venables goes on to pay them a visit and takes their servants . . ."

"There are other places," Yorke said vaguely, thinking of something else.

"And Ned . . ."

"Yes?"

"This is none of my affair, but I'm your oldest friend out here, and friendship has obligations which –"

"What do you want, John? Just ask and –"

"No," Alston interrupted, "I don't want anything: I will probably leave too, before Penn and Venables arrive. No, this concerns you and Wilson. Or, rather, you and Aurelia. Can you possibly leave her with that drunken pig?"

Yorke held out his hands in a helpless and hopeless gesture. "She won't leave him. The marriage vows . . ."

"Which he breaks regularly! At least three of his women servants claim to be his mistress and I've heard he's been trying to buy a mulatto woman for the same purpose."

"Yes, Aurelia knows. That fellow Hart is getting him another one from a Dutch sloop. Costing him twenty pounds – twice as much as a female slave normally sells for, but this one caught his eye."

He sipped his drink and then put the mug down. "Did anyone in the town know when Penn's fleet is expected?"

"Daily – it was nearly ready when the *William and Mary* sailed from Portland. Ships of war are bigger, so they can sail faster in strong winds, but I suppose keeping in some sort of formation slows them down. People – Wilson and other sycophants like Woods – say they'll be here in less than a week."

"A week!" Yorke exclaimed. "That doesn't give me much time."

"Where will you go, then? Montserrat?"

"It's too near. As you say, Venables will search all these islands, and he knows where to find the extra men he needs, although he's going to have trouble. Why, Cromwell's transportations alone have sent thousands of servants out here: the Irish after the fighting at Drogheda and Wexford, the Scots after Dunbar, and English after – well, after the King's execution. Those servants won't fight for Cromwell; they suffered enough as his prisoners in the Civil War."

"Aye, once Venables gets here the pillory, whipping post and ducking stool in St Michael's parish will be kept busy. And I don't suppose he'll be satisfied with this silly business here of charging a man a sucking pig for mentioning the words 'Cavalier' or 'Roundhead'."

"Under Venables or Penn I'm sure anyone using the word 'Royalist' will be arrested," Yorke said sourly. "And because the Lord Protector's foot soldiers cost Parliament only eight pence a day, I'm sure they'll have enough men to search all ten parishes on the island looking for 'recruits'. And they'll tax each plantation to supply horses – so many per dozen servants."

"Well, there are only six churches for his men to damage if they find 'graven images'. And who knows, the fleet might arrive at night and run ashore at Cuckold's Point in the darkness."

Yorke laughed mirthlessly. "Do you want to sail with me in the *Griffin*?"

Alston shook his head. "No, and I won't sail in company with you, because my *Lucy* is slow and needs careening. Neither of us can make plans or arrange a rendezvous because we don't know what we are going to do. But we'll meet somewhere . . ."

Alston stood up and held out his hand, and as Yorke shook

it he said: "Until then, Ned, unless you need a hand earlier. You can do something for Aurelia?"

Yorke looked bleak. "You have no idea how stubborn French Huguenot women can be."

"Stubborn? I'd put it down as misguided loyalty!"

"The effect is just the same," Yorke said ruefully, following Alston to the door and calling for his own horse, as well as his visitor's.

 *Chapter Two*

He watched Alston galloping away to the north, the sea glittering beyond him to the westward. The end, or simply a pause, in a five-year friendship? While a servant saddled his horse and brought it to the door, Yorke went back into the house and sat down again, suddenly overwhelmed by his father's letter, the news delivered by Alston, and his sudden decision to quit the island. The only thing missing, he thought bitterly, was a decision about Aurelia, and that did not rest with him.

Then his father's letter seemed almost to attack him, to drain his spirit and energy like some enormous leech. Apart from losing the Yorke estates in Kent, had George managed to take enough money or jewels? Or would his father become one of the motley crowd of penniless refugees traipsing after the exiled Court like itinerant tinkers?

The history of the Yorke family was turbulent, but never before had the government of the day labelled them traitors, driven them from their own lands. And, after being among the first to establish a plantation among the Caribbee islands, they were now being forced out of there as well.

To go where? Not, if his father's information was to be trusted, to Virginia, Antigua or Somers Island, and certainly not to any of the other Caribbee islands, because Penn and Venables would search them one after another.

In about half an hour, his world had collapsed because there was not the slightest question of being able to stay in Barbados. In Barbados the younger son of the sixth Earl of

Ilex was certainly an active Royalist in any Roundhead's list, quite apart from Wilson waiting in the shadows.

The sun's height and heat told him it was about ten o'clock. Wilson would stay roistering in Bridgetown until sunset and probably later, because today's news would be the best he had ever had; the steel that sharpened his greed.

Very well, he told himself, his father had sent him a warning about Penn's fleet and told him to quit; John Alston confirmed that it was due at any moment. If Edward Yorke was going to quit (flee, he corrected himself) the island in his sloop the *Griffin* for a completely unknown destination he needed her laden with provisions, and as much sugar and rum as possible to use as currency.

He went to the door and called his foreman, a stocky Lincolnshire man called Saxby. His name certainly was not Saxby, but he answered to no other. (Was it his surname or his Christian name? Ned had never asked.) As far as Ned knew he had deserted from the Navy many years ago, served in privateers along the coast of Brazil and the Main, and then come on shore when lameness made him, as he expressed it, "pitch and roll". Red of complexion and blue-eyed, his hair sprinkled with grey, he was famous for three qualities: a stentorian voice, a dislike of hot liquors (which made him one of the few men on the island who did not drink rumbullion or mobbie), and a great appetite for women, which the women indentured servants seemed quite happy to fulfil, even if pregnancy extended their indentures by two years and the father's (if he could be traced) by three.

It seemed that Saxby was out working in the field along the coast by Six Men Fort. Ned sent a lad to fetch him and took down the canvas-bound stock books from their shelves. They had nearly sixty tons of sugar in stock. He reflected over the current prices. A good horse fetched 3,000 pounds of sugar here in Barbados, more in the other islands. An anker of brandy wine was worth 300 pounds of sugar, a pair of shoes sixteen pounds, a yard of good white linen six pounds. The Dutch were selling sugar at the rate of a penny for a pound, and sugar was the currency of the Caribbee islands and the Main.

He nodded to himself satisfied. It was said a Dutch trading vessel with 100 guilders of commodities made 2,000 pounds of sugar, so the *Griffin*'s cargo could keep her crew for a long time.

He uncorked a bottle of ink, sharpened a fresh quill, took an empty page from the back of an account book and began writing.

"To stow in the *Griffin*.

Powder – all we have, 15 barrels.

Bullets – all we have, 12 barrels for pistols, 14 barrels for muskets.

Muskets – all we have, five matchlock, twenty wheel-lock.

Pistols – 10 wheel-lock, 10 matchlock.

Guns – those in the *Griffin*, viz:

> six minions of iron
> four minions of brass
> four three-pounders of brass
> all the shot for them.

Armour – 5 backs, 5 breasts, and 5 headpieces, from the saddleroom, with spare leather, needles, thread and sewing palms.

Sugar – all that she can stow, say 50 tons.

Horses – six, and their forage and harness.

Water – twelve casks.

Brandy – the ten ankers in the cellar.

Wine – the two barrels of madeira in the cellar.

Provisions – for ? people, to be arranged by Mr Saxby.

> Include fruit for juice, vegetables."

He wiped the pen and corked the ink. Provisions for how many people? There were Saxby and his assistant Simpson, forty male indentured servants and six female, and nine time-expired servants who after finishing their four years of indentured labour had asked to be allowed to stay on, even though paid their five pounds lump sum. Few plantations had such workers; John Alston's was the only other one he knew of. Most plantations, where servants were ill-treated, were plagued with them running away. The arrival of a Dutch trading sloop was usually the signal for such young men to try to board her – either as crew, to escape to another island or to join the cattle-killers. However, some plantations had good reputations and Kingsnorth was one of them.

17

How about those guns? He knew nothing of guns or gunnery and tried to remember what he had been told. A minion fired a shot weighing four pounds, about the size of a large orange. The gun itself was about seven feet long and the range was what? He seemed to remember a 'random range' of 1,500 paces. Anyway, Saxby would know.

A clatter of hooves and a bellowed "Saxby here, sorr!" told him the foreman had arrived. Apart from his other merits, Saxby could read, the only employee on the estate with that ability, and he could cast up accounts, and woe betide any tallyman who accidentally cut too many or too few notches on his tally stick.

Saxby came to the door and Yorke called him into the room. Seeing the stock books open on the table the foreman assumed there were questions to answer and put his broad-brimmed, high-crowned beaver hat on a chair and pulled open the top of his jerkin, hoping to cool off after his ride.

"You didn't go down to town then, sorr."

"No, but Mr Alston called in with the post on his way back, and brought the news."

Saxby glanced up at the intonation Yorke gave the word "news". He had already seen an opened letter (and thought he recognized the handwriting) and noticed the page torn from the accounts book and covered with what, even viewed upside-down, was obviously a list. He also knew that no ship came from England with good news for Royalists. Worse still, from a plantation's point of view, the Dutch, becoming wary, were putting up their prices in retaliation for Cromwell's Navigation Act. Saxby had bargained with Arabs in the bazaars of North Africa and with Levantines at the far end of the Mediterranean; he had haggled in the raucous markets of Bombay and Calcutta, but he had to admit a Dutchman drove the hardest bargain. Yet although the Hollander was clever enough to beat down a price and take every advantage of changing circumstances, he was too full of his own importance (and his own gin) to establish the trust that made him welcome back. Hollanders rarely had old and regular customers, merely new victims.

Saxby waited for Mr Yorke to speak. The youngster was under some terrible strain, that much was certain, and Saxby, more than twice and nearly three times his age, always thought of him with the same affection he would have for a favourite nephew.

Although an inch or two taller than himself, Saxby did not rate Mr Yorke as a tall man. He had wide shoulders, shown off to advantage by the jerkin, and his narrow hips were emphasized by the new fashion eagerly adopted out here in the tropics (and not new by now, Saxby realized) for breeches that were not padded.

The face was thin; Mrs Judd, the cook, always complained that the master did not eat enough and looked half-starved. The high cheekbones emphasized the thinness, of course, and the nose had very little flesh on it, so that the bone was prominent, like a bird's beak. Not a song bird, Saxby joked to himself; rather the beak of an osprey. The swarthy skin was a great help; it meant the sun turned him a deep golden brown, instead of the half-roasted beef that was the curse of Saxby's life, with the constant peeling and the nose as red as a pepper.

Then there was the hair, which any woman might envy: black and curly, though worn shorter than most other young Cavaliers, who liked it to brush their shoulders. Not as short as the Roundheads, though, who looked as though they were wearing basins on their heads – which, of course, was why they were called Roundheads. Pudden heads, it should be!

As Mrs Judd said, Mr Yorke was a man who walked alone without being lonely. He could be talkative in company and had a quick wit – that alone made him unpopular when he let fly at these dreary Puritans, who regarded laughter as a sin. But he lived out here in the big house and ran this great plantation for his father without apparently needing company of his own class – a cousin, say, or another young gentleman wanting to learn how to manage an estate. The exception was Mr Alston, who must have his own similar troubles.

Mrs Judd said the master should return to England for a season and bring back a young wife. Well, she'd stopped going on about that, what with the troubles, and she and Saxby now knew that the solution to it all – well, perhaps not the solution, but certainly the reason – was not above five miles away, in the next parish.

Saxby stopped scratching his head, a habit he had when thinking hard, as though his brains needed the stimulation of fingernails, and looked attentive as Yorke suddenly unfolded the letter on the table in front of him.

"What I am going to say, Saxby, is for your ears alone. My father has written. He has finally refused to compound with Parliament, so our two estates in Kent have been forfeited. There's a third one, smaller, in Sussex, and that will have gone, too. So he and my brother have fled to France, for their own safety."

"Aye," Saxby said, "they'd have had their blood, one way or t'other."

"And he warns me that Cromwell is sending out a fleet to attack Spanish possessions, but it will call here first to strip us of men to make up an army for them. How they'll train them, I don't know, but we'll lose our labour. And they'll 'detain' me. Mr Alston's news is that this fleet, commanded by Admiral Penn, is likely to arrive within a few days, carrying the army of General Venables."

Saxby could picture the fleet. Many years had passed since he deserted from the Navy, but he had spent just as many years at sea until that fateful day.

"How many men do you think will volunteer to serve with General Venables?"

Saxby did not have to think twice. "Five hundred scoundrels. The lazy rascals always trying to stow away in the Dutch sloops. But if the Assembly agrees to press men – well, I suppose there are three thousand servants available, now the Dutch are increasing the supply of negroes."

"Do you think many of our men will volunteer?"

"No, sir; don't forget Cromwell shipped 'em out as little more than slaves. They hate the Roundheads. Those that desert from other plantations do so because they are wild men; even in England they would not want regular work."

"So, if we don't want to be swept up by Cromwell's pressgangs, we must sail by tomorrow night," Yorke said, as though talking to himself. He slid the page from the stock book across to Saxby. "Can we have the *Griffin* loaded in time?"

"Providing the servants don't bolt."

"Do you think they will?"

Saxby scratched his head. "Some might. It depends."

"Depends on *what?*" Yorke asked irritably.

"Depends on them knowing *why* they're doing whatever it is, sir, and what the alternatives are."

Yorke suddenly realized that although he knew most things about every man, woman and boy indentured to him, as well as those who had stayed on after their indentures had expired, he had no real idea of their politics. Most men must regard Cromwell as the devil, because he had had them transported to the Caribbee islands after taking them prisoner in battles where they fought for the King. But a long time had passed since then, and did life in Barbados seem any better? The King for whom they had fought had been beheaded by this same Cromwell; the son who succeeded was said to be in France, paying too much court to the Papists, and apparently never likely to be powerful enough to overthrow Cromwell and his New Model Army. Could any of these indentured servants ever return to England, except as Parliament's reward for helping it?

Yorke looked out of the door and saw from the sun's shadow that it must be about eleven o'clock. "Have every person on the estate assemble by the well as soon as possible. Ring the bell, Saxby; this is as bad as a fire or an attack by the Spanish!"

They came hurrying from all parts of the estate, still holding hoes and shovels, faces shiny with perspiration and streaked with dust. Mrs Judd and her women from the kitchens still wore wide pinafores, their hair covered with scarves. All they knew was that the bell was an alarm; that when it tolled they were to assemble at the well (if one of the buildings was on fire) or otherwise at the main house. This time there was no fire, but Saxby's raucous voice called them to the well.

The well was surrounded by a four-foot-high circular wall made from red bricks the *Griffin* had brought out as ballast, and as soon as Saxby had counted heads and reported all the employees present, Ned scrambled on to the wall and told them all to gather round.

Then, speaking slowly and choosing his words with care, he explained that a Parliamentary fleet seeking troops was due to arrive at any moment, and that because it also had orders to arrest him, he intended to leave the island in the

Griffin to seek somewhere else to live that was free of politics, pressgangs, and the words Cavalier or Roundhead.

At the mention of the words one of the youngsters called out: "*Two* sucking pigs, sir!" and Yorke laughed with the crowd.

"To be eaten in the company of the people who heard the words," Yorke pointed out. "Which leads me to the next point. Forty-six of you are indentured to me, and your indentures do not say where you have to serve your time. I could take you to El Dorado or the empire of the Great Khan."

He waited for the laughter to die down. "However, you did not sign indentures to serve as sailors. The *Griffin* might be going on a voyage to one of the other islands; it might be longer. So I am giving you a choice, and I think a fair one. Either you can sail in the *Griffin* and take your chance with me – and obviously I can promise nothing – or you can stay here on the island, take your chance with the pressgangs, and I will pay each of you a part of the lump sum in proportion to the time you have served.

"You nine time-expired men who are on wages: you'll still be paid if you sail with me but if you stay in Barbados – well, you've received your lump sums and it will be up to you to find other jobs."

"What about us women, sir?" Mrs Judd called out. "Me an' six of the best!"

The men whistled and jeered good-naturedly. "Serve you right if we leaves you behind to poison the Roundheads with your cooking," Saxby growled.

"Dunno what a glutton like you would do without us!" Mrs Judd answered, and the other women giggled and blushed, well aware of the double meaning.

Yorke said: "The same offer is open to you women: be paid off a proportion or sail with me."

"What, all of us women?" demanded Mrs Judd.

"All seven of you – but you'll be responsible for their good behaviour!"

"Verree wise, sorr," Saxby commented loudly. "Let Martha keep them smart on parade."

The sun was blazing down on them by now and the wind had dropped. Yorke felt his jerkin slowly sticking to him, and his feet throbbed from the heat of the brick wall striking up through the soles of his shoes. The divi-divi trees pointed like signposts – to the westward, he noted, thinking of the significance, bent by the constant Trade wind blowing from the east. Westward – an omen, perhaps?

Yorke pulled down the brim of his hat and looked round. Fifty-six pairs of eyes were watching him.

"The decision is up to each of you, man or woman, and whatever you decide there will be no hard feelings. Mr Saxby will have your money ready by this evening for those deciding to stay. Now, those of us going in the *Griffin* have a lot to do. So, there's a divi-divi tree over there –" he pointed to the big shrub to the northwards, "– and another there, to the south. Will all of you who want to stay on the island go to that bush, the one to the north; those coming with me in the *Griffin* should go to the southerly one. And do it now."

With a loud "Humph!" Mrs Judd marched for the southern bush, head down, arms akimbo, striding with as long a step as her dress and petticoats would allow. The other six women giggled, hands to their mouths, chattering among themselves, and followed her.

For a few moments the seven women were the only ones to move and Yorke had a nightmarish picture of the *Griffin* sailing with himself, Saxby and a crew of women.

The men were far less sure. For a moment none moved to the northern tree but instead they stood talking with each other. Saxby and his tallow-haired assistant Simpson joined Mrs Judd and the women, and Saxby gave her a playful slap on the rump.

Finally the oldest of the nine time-expired men went to the southern tree, and a minute or two later his eight comrades joined him, although they all asked Saxby some question he obviously could not answer, so he came back to the well.

"The time-expired men, sorr: they're worried about their money, which they've hidden in various places. Would you look after it for them?"

"Yes, of course, and give them receipts."

"I reckoned as much, sorr; I'll tell 'em."

Three men were now walking towards the northern divi-divi, and Yorke saw they were a trio from the ship that arrived before the *William and Mary*; bad bargains, Saxby had called them, even by the standards of the Bridewell, which as far as jails went had London's finest selection of thieves, rogues, vagabonds and murderers, and which had been the men's home for some time before Cromwell's net swept them out to the West Indies.

Two more men followed, keeping a few yards behind them, as though indicating that although they had elected to stay, they were not associates of the trio. Five for Cromwell, Yorke noted. And two more – an unpopular pair, judging from the shrill abuse from two of the women.

Five men were walking towards Saxby and one of them made a rude gesture to Martha Judd and grinned. That made twenty-three for the *Griffin,* of whom seven were women. Twenty-six had still to make up their minds.

Three more left to join the northern group and Yorke realized they were being roundly abused by the twenty-three remaining, who had obviously been trying to persuade them to join the *Griffin* group. But when they saw they had failed, they all walked towards Saxby, talking among themselves.

So ten were staying and forty-six were coming in the *Griffin.* He had a larger ship's company than he expected, enough to handle the sails and weigh the anchor, but none too many when they started clearing a new plantation in some distant island.

"Well, I'm glad you are coming with me in the *Griffin.* I don't know where we're going, mind you, but I guarantee we'll all agree before we land!"

Then he walked to the northern group, who stood sheepishly, expecting the rough edge of Yorke's tongue. Instead he said simply: "Thank you for all you have done. Saxby will pay you what is due to you. I hope –"

"We should be paid orf in full," snarled one man. "Four years, five pun, that's what the paper says."

Knowing this was one of the troublemaking trio, Yorke asked quietly: "How long have you served, then?"

"That's not the point, I know my –"

"How long have you served?" Yorke persisted.

"Well, only three months, but I'd –"

"Three months out of four years. Well, you had the choice: you have terminated your indenture, not I, so anything paid you is a gift. Think about it."

One of the other men whispered: "Shut yore big mouff, Wedgewood. You 'aven't done a full day's work yet, let alone free months!"

Yorke turned away, knowing that Saxby would soon have the *Griffin* loaded, and walked back to the house, where his horse was still saddled and waiting patiently in the shade of the stable. Now for the hard part, he thought to himself.

Chapter
Three

Wilson's plantation was a few miles to the south towards
Bridgetown and, surrounding Valiant Fort on the coast, was
part of a large sandy area that made up much of St James's
Parish. It was plain irony that the next fort south along the
coast was called Royalist Fort (General Venables will soon
change that, Yorke thought), but plain stupidity had led
Wilson to buy the plantation in the first place.

By the time Wilson arrived on the island, there were few
large estates still available, but the one that wise men left well
alone was called the Bennery. The sandy soil and few trees
had led Wilson to conclude that it would be easier to clear the
land. This was true, of course, but once cleared, very little
would grow.

Wilson listened to no advice and planted tobacco. To be
sure, the Dutch would be eager to buy every leaf if the quality
was good, but it had been one of the first crops planted years
earlier in Barbados – and had never been a success.

Wilson's crop had been harvested and dried, and when
smoked even he had to admit its only use was to burn to
windward of a hammaco at night, or in a room to keep the
mosquitoes and sandflies away. Whether smoked in a pipe or
rolled into a cigar, it tasted dry and earthy; there was no
comparison between it and the rich tobacco being grown in
one area of the Spanish Main, and up in Virginia. No English
or Dutch merchant would think of buying it; even Wilson's
friends declined it as gifts.

Such a man was too stubborn and stupid to cut his losses and change to sugar or cotton. Older and wiser men suggested cotton, but Wilson again planted tobacco, producing a second crop that was, if anything, earthier.

Then, having wasted more than two years, he finally changed to cotton, an expensive crop to harvest with indentured servants, but initially even more expensive using negroes. A white servant cost only £5 and his keep for a four-year indenture, and a man as unscrupulous as Wilson usually claimed misbehaviour and extended it to five years and then finally made the man's life such a misery that he deserted before his £5 was due, having worked four years for only his keep. White men, however, were not good at the work because of the heat, which often affected their health, but they were cheap. The negroes were good at the work, when overseers watched them and threatened them with a whip, but a good black male bought from a Dutchman cost £20 and an overseer was also needed because negroes spoke no English and had curious customs.

So Yorke understood only too well why Wilson coveted Kingsnorth, one of the largest plantations on the island, already producing steadily both sugarcane and cotton, well supplied with water from wells, with a strongly built stone estate house, and belonging to a Royalist family.

The Civil War had made Wilson (and others like him) realize that the sooner its full effects came to Barbados the better: Roundhead friends of his in England were now the proud owners of large estates which, confiscated from their Royalist owners by Parliament, were sold off to Roundheads for nominal sums, or given as rewards. Why, Wilson never tired of saying, could not the same thing be done in Barbados? It was high time Cromwell and Parliament rewarded their supporters!

The sun was now directly overhead; Yorke could see his horse's shadow only by bending over sideways and looking beneath it. Wilson's estate house was large and pretentious but built of clapboard which the relentless termites and white ants were already destroying, so that even from a distance one could see dark stripes where planks had slipped down, the termites having eaten away the wood holding the nails. However, Wilson made little secret of why he did not bother to have the house repaired: the one he was determined to get was built of coral stone . . .

By now, Yorke anticipated, Wilson should be noisily inebriated in the St Stephen's Tavern, the largest (and shabbiest) on the waterfront overlooking the little port and generally reckoned to be the headquarters for the Parliamentarians. Years ago the island Assembly had its regular meetings there but the strict Puritans among them had complained, particularly because it was between two noisily cheerful brothels, so now the Assembly met at the governor's house and congratulated itself on the improvement.

As the Wilson house came in sight, Ned felt the usual excitement, but now there was also an underlying fear, an apprehension. He had to leave the island with the *Griffin* and servants: there was no question about that. To stay risked being shipped back to England as a prisoner of State, at best as a hostage for his now absent father and brother, at worst a prisoner on his own account because he would never join the Commonwealth cause. So leaving the island – escaping in fact – was necessary if he was going to keep his freedom.

Yet leaving Barbados was not so easy. He could leave a large plantation and an estate house which had been his home for the past four years and not feel the slightest regret: the estate was the same as any other, the house had been simply accommodation, a lonely building. The island itself was so flat that it was little more than an earthen dish, albeit skirted by some remarkable beaches. But most other Caribbee islands were more beautiful, mountainous and capped by rainforests.

The reason why Barbados was difficult to leave was contained in Wilson's house. He slid off his horse at the front door and gave the reins to a waiting servant.

"The mistress is in," the man said, and dropping his voice asked: "Be it true that Cromwell is sending a fleet against us, sir?"

Yorke knew the man well from scores of previous visits. "Yes – or at least," he added cautiously, "a Parliamentary fleet has left England bound for here."

The man, Bullock, paled under the deep tan. "They took

28

me at Edgehill and transported me; now they're coming again. 'Ow about you, sir?"

"I hope I'll be gone by the time they arrive."

"The mistress, sir. My wife and I worry a deal about 'er. He gets worse every day. Once he knows there's Cromwell's fleet anchored 'ere, I fear for 'er life. For all our lives, once he's got rumbullion inside him. Excuse me speaking out like this, sir; there ain't no one else we can trust to talk to and get advice."

Yorke saw sincerity in the man's eyes and became aware that the wife had come out from the front door and was red-eyed from weeping. The two of them waited for him to speak; there was a silence broken only by the snuffling of the horse and the sharp song of a grackle strutting a few yards away, a long-tailed version of an English blackbird, cheeky and unconcerned. He decided to trust them because they had proved their discretion.

"I'm leaving the island with my people. We sail tomorrow – secretly. You can guess why I've ridden over now."

They both nodded but a moment later the woman burst into tears again, sobbing to herself. "But she'll never leave him, sir; she just puts up with all his hittin' and cussin'. It's her being French, I suppose."

"T'ain't," the husband said grimly. "Leastways, t'is and t'ain't. She's got nowhere else to go; that's why she puts up with it."

The woman wiped away the tears and looked up at Yorke, a question in her eyes.

Yorke nodded and answered it. "Yes, if she'll agree. That's why I've ridden over."

"It'll be no sin, sir; the sin would be for her to stay, because that man is wicked to the marrow of his bones," the woman said. "All of us 'ere think the same, sir. If it goes on much longer 'e'll wake up one day to find 'isself dead."

"Hush up, Mary," her husband said hurriedly as Yorke went into the house.

He called her name as he went through the door. She was sitting on a high stool beside the window on the west side of the room, cooled by the breeze. When she looked up and saw Ned she smiled contentedly, put down her lace and the frame and wooden bobbins and stood up.

"I did not realize it was you," she said quietly, her voice husky, each word pronounced with the care of someone speaking a language not her own.

He reached out for her but she stepped back. "No, Edouard – the servants."

"They are outside – I've just been talking to them."

She smiled again and leaned her head forward. "In fact I was concerned for my lace. Kiss my cheek."

He kissed her and began collecting up the bobbins.

"Put this down. I have to talk to you."

"My lace hardly stops you talking," she said.

"Don't be so French and so practical."

"*Mon cher* Edouard, you look so fierce and stern I do not think I want to hear what you have to say."

She sat on the stool again. Her hair, fine ash-blonde, was combed back from her face and caught in a knot at the back, leaving long ringlets at the side that spiralled to her shoulders. She defied the Roundhead fashion of covering her hair in a scarf.

Her dress was a royal blue, made of stiff silk, the square neck cut low and edged with a fine white lace that matched the long cuffs. The front of the dress was drawn back in the current fashion to show a finely embroidered petticoat beneath. He remembered seeing her embroidering it a few weeks ago.

He liked her hair combed like this: it emphasized her profile. Her beauty was not classical; it was warmer than that. Her eyes were spaced just that much further apart than a pedantic portrait artist would specify, but would he capture the golden flecks in the grey which was always changing to reflect her mood, whether gay or sombre? And the cheekbones were high, joining a nose which the artist would say although perfectly shaped was too small. But the mouth, Ned thought for the thousandth time as he watched her securing the bobbins, was both generous and beautiful; the lips had colour and warmth; there was none of that narrowness that he saw in many women's faces, where the lips seemed specially formed for revealing jealousy or meanness.

"There," she said, putting the last of her lace work and the attached bobbins into a cloth bag and drawing the string closed. "For someone who has something to say, you are very quiet."

"I'm quite content to sit and watch you." This, said banteringly, was perfectly true, but he knew that this time he was only putting off a difficult task, something which she sensed and was obviously trying to reassure him.

"You did not go to Bridgetown?"

"No, but John Alston did and called in on his way back."

"You had letters from England?" She spoke the words lightly, but he knew she was trying to help him.

"My father wrote."

"He is well?"

"He is in France with my brother."

Her eyebrows lifted but otherwise she was motionless. "They have joined the Prince?"

"Probably, but that was not the main reason they fled."

"What happened?"

"You understand 'compounding'?"

"I think so. A Royalist is allowed to keep his property if he pays a large sum of money to Cromwell. To Parliament," she corrected herself.

"Yes, but there is also . . . well, paying it has a . . ."

"A stigma? Obviously a man who 'compounds' is buying his safety at the price of his honour, no?"

Yorke shrugged his shoulders in the face of such logic: she had a disconcerting way of going to the centre of a problem. "Well, I think so, and apparently my father does. But other Royalist landowners, some of the most powerful, have thought otherwise."

"They are wrong," Aurelia said firmly. "What happens when the King returns to the throne?"

Again, Ned shrugged his shoulders. "When will that be? We will be old folk by then."

Aurelia murmured an answer but as her face was turned away from him he asked her to repeat it, which she did, again without turning her head.

"Look at me, beloved," Ned said, "at the moment you are talking to the birds outside."

Then he remembered her hair had not been done in quite the usual style: it was slightly different on the right side.

"Look at me!"

She turned slightly so that he could see her eyes.

He stood up suddenly and walked over to her and, holding her gently by the shoulders, turned her so that he could see the right side of her face.

An angry, reddish-blue bruise covered the ear and part of the throat beneath it. She had tied the knot of her hair more to the right and left more ringlets dangling in an effort to hide it.

"When?" Ned demanded.

"It does not matter, *chéri*; it is nothing. I bruise easily – you know that."

"What happened?"

"I angered him: it was my fault."

"How did you anger him?"

"Oh Ned! Please, it is of no importance."

"Tell me, my love, or I shall ask the servants."

"You must do no such thing!"

Ned took his hands from her shoulders and turned towards the door.

"No, Ned. It was nothing. He was upset and – well, he had been drinking. He came back from the town, and supper was not ready. Yes, that was it. It made him angry. He was hungry after a busy day."

He held her shoulders again and forced her to meet his eyes. "Why was he upset?"

"Well, he was not upset at first; he was excited. What I said made him angry, and he hit me. I do not blame him."

"What did you say?"

"Oh, it is of no importance, *chéri*; please forget it."

"Was it about me?"

"No!"

She answered too quickly to be convincing. "About Kingsnorth, then?"

"*Peut-être,* but you give it an importance it does not have."

Ned could now guess what had happened and picture the scene. Wilson had been down at the town yesterday and heard rumours from the captain of the *William and Mary*. He had heard of Penn's fleet, and he had seen this as bringing him the chance of owning Kingsnorth within a few weeks. On his return home, drunk as usual, he had made some sneering remark to Aurelia.

He pushed her back gently so that she was again sitting on the stool, and said quietly: "I am leaving Kingsnorth tomorrow."

She went white, then her eyes seemed to be looking up at the beams of the roof, and then she slid to the floor.

Ned was about to shout for help when he realized that she had merely fainted and, he thought angrily, that was hardly surprising considering how crudely he had given her his news. He knelt and supported her head. Two or three minutes later her eyes opened and Ned thought of holding a frightened animal and seeing its eyes.

"Oh Ned, I am so sorry. I suddenly felt unwell. I – yes, help me up, I can stand." She kicked at a petticoat caught under her heel, and a moment later was again sitting on the stool, her hands clasped.

"Breathe deeply," he said.

After three or four minutes she said: "You were saying that you are leaving Kingsnorth tomorrow. Do you mean you are leaving the island?"

"Wilson must have told you last night that Cromwell is sending out a fleet against the Spanish. It is due any day, looking for recruits. It will send out pressgangs to force men to serve. And apart from all that, my father warns that they'll arrest me."

By now she was holding his hand and bending her head to hide tears.

"So I've asked my servants to sail with me and they are loading the *Griffin* with provisions."

"They agreed to come with you?"

"Most of the men and all the women."

"Led by the famous Martha."

He grinned. "Martha led them all, men and women."

"So now . . . now you come to say goodbye, Edouard. Or *au revoir*."

"No. I've come to ask you to pack a few clothes in a single bag, with any little treasures you have, and be ready for me to fetch you at noon tomorrow."

The silence in the house was so complete he could hear a beam creak from the heat of the sun. A finch perched on the window ledge, looking for sugar that Aurelia often sprinkled there. The bird found a few grains lodged in a split in the wood and pecked at them and the tapping alarmed a lizard nearby.

Finally Aurelia looked up at him, but her eyes were shut and brimming with tears. "No, my darling, I cannot come with you. I am married to another man. This you know. I cannot break my marriage vows. We have argued about that so often before."

"But darling heart, you know why he married you! Your money paid for this plantation and much more. He has broken his marriage vows. Why, even now he is probably with that creole whore of his. And he hits you."

"But I married him, Edouard. 'Until death us do part'."

Even as she spoke they both heard the jingle of harness followed a moment later by Wilson's harsh voice abusing his manservant Bullock for not being ready to help him from the saddle. At the same moment Mary Bullock ran into the room.

"Oh, ma'am, it's the master; we didn't see him coming. He's hours earlier than usual and —"

The thump of boots interrupted her and Wilson lurched into the room, his face streaming with the perspiration that always bothers heavy drinkers, and his eyes bloodshot.

"Ha, Yorke, here to caress your slut, eh? Or should I say *my* slut?"

He stood a couple of paces inside the door, swaying, looking from Yorke to Aurelia.

"Come, darling wife, kiss your dutiful husband."

Aurelia rose from the stool and walked towards him, and as she went to kiss him he slapped her viciously across the face, knocking her down. The violence of the blow and Aurelia's lightness meant he continued swinging unbalanced and sprawled flat on the floor himself.

Ned ran across the room to Aurelia just as the serving woman was kneeling beside her. The woman was muttering angrily to herself and tugging at something at her waistband, and Ned was appalled to see that she was drawing out a small carving knife.

Hurriedly Ned pressed her hand so that she pushed the knife back out of sight, then they both helped Aurelia to her feet. No sooner had they done that than Ned felt himself swung round by a hand on his shoulder and found himself facing an infuriated Wilson.

"Well, Yorke, cuckolding me in my own house, eh? Well, this time I demand satisfaction. The devil take appointing seconds, so choose your weapons and name a time."

Ned looked Wilson up and down. The man was swaying like a child's spinning top in the moments before it toppled. "I would duel only with a gentleman, Wilson, and a sober one at that."

"Fight, you cowardly cuckolder . . . cowardly cuckolder," Wilson repeated drunkenly. "Brave in front of the women, you are, but faced with a real man, you shelter behind their skirts. Now then, sword or pistol? I have a splendid pair of wheel-locks; you can choose which you want and load 'em both. That's fair, isn't it?"

His speech was blurred and now almost wheedling, but Ned watched the eyes. They belonged to a man who had been drinking heavily, but they were not the eyes of a drunken man. The eyes of a cunning man, yes; of a man laying a trap.

"Refuse to meet in fair fight, eh? Wait until the island hears about that! Planters don't like cowards, you know, especially cowards caught in adultery. You don't think she's worth you risking your skin, eh?"

He turned to Aurelia. "Well, my dear, perhaps you'll believe me now. You are a worthless French slut: worthless to me as a wife and worthless to your lover as a mistress. Pardon me, a *former* mistress."

Aurelia watched, her eyes frightened and moving back and forth from her husband to Ned, who was trying to keep a watch on the serving woman, half expecting any moment to see a flash of steel.

Ned waited because he knew Wilson was by no means finished. The challenge was only the beginning of whatever idea had formed in that cunning brain, and probably the least important part of it. Ned guessed that if he had accepted, naming a weapon, time and place, Wilson would have found a reason at the last moment why he would not fight. Ned knew nothing of the man's ability as a swordsman, but he had heard that he was such a bad shot that none of his neighbours who valued their lives would invite him when they went dove shooting. And while he waited for Wilson to reveal himself, he could only hope that Aurelia would guess there was a good reason he did not accept the challenge.

"You've got to leave the island, Yorke. You don't know that yet, do you, but I can tell you that you have. Dishonoured, by God!" He spat the words out, years of hatred spilling from his mouth like vomit.

"Leave the island?" Yorke repeated guilelessly. "Why?"

"Why? You ask *why*? I can think of three reasons without any effort!"

"What are they?"

"Well, first, you're an adulterer; you've seduced my wife. Then, you've refused a challenge."

"That's two."

"That's enough. Branded a coward and an adulterer — reasons enough, I should have thought."

Ned shook his head. "They would clear half the planters off this island, yourself among them."

"I'm no coward!" Wilson bellowed.

"No, but you're an adulterer!"

"A black wench on a cool afternoon — that makes me an adulterer, does it?" he sneered.

"I'm not your judge, Wilson."

"I tell you what," Wilson said, lowering his voice. "I like you, Yorke, even if you are Royalist. I heard news today that you know nothing about, but I'll help you out. Now, how many men would help a man who has been cuckolding him for months, if not years? Oh, don't deny it; I've known all about it."

Ned saw the eyes narrowing. Wilson had known nothing, but now he was guessing and guessing accurately, except the word was — admittedly only due to Aurelia's scruples — not cuckolding.

"Sell me Kingsnorth, Yorke. I'll give you double what your family paid. Three thousand pounds. The lawyers can draw up the papers this afternoon and we'll sign 'em tonight."

So that was it. Wilson might have been drinking, but the rumbullion had not dulled his cunning.

"Kingsnorth is not for sale."

"Listen, Yorke, sell to me at that price and I'll never breathe a word that you refused a challenge. You can stay on in the island. Buy a smaller plantation. Buy a house. Live the life of a gentleman without all the worry of being

36

a planter. You can still see Aurelia. Be discreet, but you can call."

The man was quick and he was clever. Ned realized that Wilson did not know that a letter from his father had, that morning, warned him that the plantation would be sequestrated as soon as Penn arrived. Wilson was trying to secure Kingsnorth now: buying it so that he did not have to take a chance in the lottery of the sequestration. And he could pay with promissory notes, which would have to be cashed in England, but he knew that long before then Yorke would be a Roundhead prisoner, and no doubt the promissory notes would vanish, so that Wilson would have acquired Kingsnorth quite legally, and at no cost.

"You'll lose it, you know," Wilson said, and his voice was now that of a man who was almost sober. "Orders from Parliament arrived in the *William and Mary*. Orders concerning a certain Edward Yorke, younger son of the Earl of Ilex, lately fled to France and whose estates in Kent and Sussex have been sequestrated by Parliament. And . . ." he said heavily, enjoying what he obviously intended to be the climax, ". . . and whose estate in Barbados is also forfeit. You own nothing, Yorke, neither you nor your father."

"Then why do you want to buy Kingsnorth, Walter, if it does not belong to Edouard?" Aurelia asked, her voice quiet and the question spoken in perfect innocence, as though worried on her husband's behalf.

"Don't bother yourself with such things, m'dear," Wilson said heartily. "I just don't want our friend left penniless. He loses the plantation and the ship, you see. Why, once the governor acts on his orders – which he will do tomorrow, I'm told – Master Edward will be looking for a friendly roof to shelter under. I wish I could offer you hospitality here, but in view of my wife's French blood, you'll understand . . ."

"But Walter," Aurelia persisted, "if the plantation is being confiscated – or is the word sequestrated? – by the order of Parliament, surely if you buy it, they will take it away from *you?*"

"No, no, they won't. Now don't you bother your pretty head." He turned to Yorke. "What about it, then? Three thousand pounds for the plantation. I'll leave you the ship. You can get away in her. Sign the papers today – you go back

37

and get the deeds and we'll ride into Bridgetown together this afternoon."

Ned realized he was nodding his head, not because he was agreeing with the man but because Wilson's mind had worked just as he had expected. But Wilson misunderstood the nodding for agreement and seized Ned's right hand and began shaking it vigorously.

"That's fine, man, and now we're shaking hands on it! Bravo, you've done yourself a good —"

Suddenly Aurelia was tearing their hands apart and, eyes blazing, she was saying to Wilson in a cold, bitter voice: "Not only are you a bully whose only pleasure is whipping his wife, but you are a liar and a thief, and now you plan to be a cheat!"

Ned caught Wilson's swinging fist with both hands and thrust Aurelia to one side with his body. As soon as she was out of range of the man's reach, Ned held Wilson's jerkin and stared into the red-rimmed eyes.

"Whipping?" he whispered, the word choking in his throat.

Wilson's eyes dropped. "Of course not. She's hysterical."

Ned, afraid he would strangle the man as he felt waves of red anger spurting through his body, pushed him away just as Aurelia said calmly, "Yes, whipping me. Every night, when he is sober enough. It's his only pleasure. His black woman whips *him*."

Wilson gave a sudden desperate bellow of pain and collapsed face downward at Ned's feet, the black wooden handle of a knife sticking out from the fleshy part of his right shoulder.

The serving woman, Mary Bullock, was standing behind where he had been. Now she had her arms crossed and a grim look on her face. "I did that orl *wrong*," she said angrily, "'is 'eart, if 'e's got one, is on the uvver side, ain't it?"

By now Wilson was roaring with pain and surprise and Ned knelt beside him. "Keep still. Don't turn over."

He tore away the jerkin and saw the knife blade, narrow and obviously short, had sunk into muscle: the woman would have been hard put to pick another place where the blade would have done so little damage.

"Get some clean cloth and some water," Ned told her. "I can pull it out without harm."

"Not me, sir," the woman said. "You pull it out and I'll stick it back in again! Many's the night my husband and I 'ave 'eard 'im whipping the lady. Why, he's such an 'ard cruel man I've carried that knife since I first come 'ere."

Wilson groaned. "Someone fetch the surgeon! I'm dying while you fools gossip!"

"You're not dying; you're barely scratched," Yorke said quietly. "But seeing the knife gives me an idea. No one knows you came back early . . ."

Aurelia looked down at him, horror-stricken, and Ned slowly winked.

". . . we could do the job properly, bury you at the other end of the estate as soon as it's dark, and sail in the *Griffin* tomorrow."

"No, no, you'd never do that," Wilson gasped. "Listen," he pleaded, "I'll see the governor; I've influence with him and the Assembly. I'm sure I could get the sequestration order overlooked. How about that, Edward?"

Mary, who still had not moved, said firmly: "Either he's dead or my husband and I are quit of this island by sundown." With that she left the room, to return a few moments later holding an even larger knife, and Ned knew she had no fear about using it.

"We have reached an *impasse,* Wilson. You have a knife sticking in your back which I can remove with no trouble to me and very little pain to you. But that leaves us with a wounded Walter Wilson who in an hour will be full of rumbullion and bellowing for vengeance."

"No, no really. It's not painful. If you'll just remove it, I promise I will say nothing as long as you promise not to repeat anything you've heard or said this afternoon."

Ned looked again at the wound. The man was flabby and the blade had gone through an inch of fat before entering the muscle. There was very little bleeding.

He looked at the two women and gave another deliberate wink.

"I'll be honest with you Wilson. If you move, you might cut some vital organ. So you must lie still while we prepare your bed and have everything ready for removing the knife."

"But a surgeon . . . it's a job for a surgeon!"

"Where is the surgeon? Be sensible! McFarlane will be

blind drunk by now, and he lives down by South Point, beyond Christchurch. That's ten miles at least. Twenty miles of riding. He'll be in a sorry state by the time he gets here. However, you choose."

"Very well, you remove it, but for God's sake be careful!"

"I will," Ned said, standing up and gesturing to the two women to follow him out of the room.

He went out through the front door and kept on walking until the three of them were thirty yards from the house, and he saw Mary's husband hurrying to join them. He decided to wait for him, to avoid saying everything twice.

As soon as Ned had described the fracas which had led to Mary sticking the kitchen knife in Wilson's back, the man looked at his wife in amazement and to Ned's surprise seized her and gave her a smacking kiss. "Killed him, did yer, lass? Oh, Mary, I'm so proud!"

"Nay, I got mixed up on which side his 'eart is."

The man's face fell. "Then he's still alive in there?"

Ned interrupted. "Don't worry about him. The position at this moment is simple. If the four of us, you and your wife, Mrs Wilson and myself, don't get off this island tonight, we'll have a hue and cry raised against us."

Aurelia held his arm desperately. "Edouard, I can't leave him – he's my husband!"

"If you *don't* leave 'im," Mary said harshly, "'e'll kill yer with all that whippin' and punchin', quite apart from 'im raisin' a hue and cry. Once he's done that he's got all yer money, this plantation – and Mr Yorke's Kingsnorth. Not bad, for the price of a jab from a kitchen knife. Damnation, Alfred, I wish I'd remembered about the 'eart."

"Is Mrs Bullock correct, Edouard?" Aurelia asked. "About the hue and cry?"

Ned nodded. "The way things are in this island at the moment, I think he could and will rouse out the Provost Marshal, for the reasons Mary has just said. He could have us all swinging from gibbets by the day after tomorrow."

"But –"

"You are not staying," Ned said firmly, "even if I have to kidnap you."

"You won't have to kidnap me, sir," Mary said cheerfully, "and I'd be obliged if Alfred could come."

"But what do we do *now*?" Aurelia asked tearfully.

Ned asked Bullock: "Do you have friends among the other servants – one or two men you can really trust?"

"Yes, sir. Several. Most of them hate Mr Wilson almost as much as we do."

"Very well. In a few moments I shall go in and remove that knife and bandage the wound and put him to bed. I shall then tie him to the bedposts. He'll come to no harm."

He looked at Aurelia, expecting protests, but she was leaning on Mary for support and seemed relieved to find the woman was so calm.

"I want one of your friends to look in on him every hour or so, and give him a drink of water and some food – but not to untie him. The man should wear very old clothes, a mask, and put his hair in a cloth bag, so Mr Wilson will never recognize him.

"Then tomorrow morning at sunrise I want someone to hear Mr Wilson's shouts – he'll be in full cry, you can be sure of that. The alarm can be then raised with the Provost Marshal, but not before sunrise. Can you arrange all that while I'm seeing to the wound?"

Bullock nodded. "I've just the man in mind, sir. And no one will hear Mr Wilson's shouts before sunrise tomorrow. Here, though –" the man grabbed Ned's arm. "Suppose visitors come?"

Ned cursed himself for not thinking of that.

"Tell them Mr Wilson is down in Bridgetown. That he left an hour earlier."

It took an hour to remove the knife, bandage the wound, and get Wilson to bed. With him at last lying in the four-poster, groaning and calling for rumbullion, Bullock arrived with the second knife and held it to a startled Wilson's throat while Ned cut into four lengths the rope that Bullock had brought in from the stables. He tied up Wilson by securing one limb to each of the four posts.

"A solid bed," he commented to Wilson. "But don't struggle too much because you might make the wound bleed. I am not going to gag you, but if you shout your throat will be cut. I have arranged that. And to prove the point, a man will visit you every hour. If you are being quiet he will give you food and drink. If you are being a naughty boy, he will cut your throat. And if you *have* been good, he will raise the alarm on your behalf at sunrise."

"But listen, Yorke," Wilson snarled, "you will be caught: the Provost Marshal will raise a hue and cry. You, Aurelia and those two scoundrels of servants . . . why, think of the scandal!"

"The only scandal will be what you create yourself," Ned said quietly. "Now, are you comfortable?"

Wilson refused to answer and Ned shrugged his shoulders. "Then it remains only to bid you farewell. And as the days and weeks and months, and perhaps years go by, just remember Wilson: all your eggs are in one basket. The moment Cromwell goes, you are finished. And any day I might return secretly to the island and pay you a visit . . ."

Chapter Four

Saxby was standing at the bottom of the double stone staircases which led up to the front door of the house like a scorpion's claw when the two horses came to a stop, lathered and blowing hard after a long gallop. As soon as he recognized Aurelia he ran to help her slide from the horse while Ned jumped down and lifted Bullock's wife to the ground. Bullock was no horseman. Ned had the feeling that his wife Mary sitting behind him, arms round his waist, had kept them from falling off by sheer strength of character.

Aurelia was quietly sobbing and Yorke gestured to one of the servants to lead her into the house. As soon as Saxby had given the reins of the horse to a groom who had come running from the stables, Yorke asked: "How goes the loading of the *Griffin*?"

"All the provisions and water are on board, sir; we're just getting the powder and musket and pistol shot loaded now. That leaves only the sugar – we'll be carrying that until long after dark."

Yorke nodded. "We have to sail earlier than I intended. We need to be clear of here an hour after sunrise."

"You ran into trouble," Saxby said in a comment rather than a question.

Yorke quickly outlined what had happened, making sure that it was far from clear to Saxby who actually stuck the knife in Wilson's back.

"Pity it didn't kill him," Saxby commented, adding seriously as an afterthought: "If we're quitting the island, we could go back and finish him off. It'd be doing a lot of people a good turn, sir."

"Yes, but we'd be known through the Caribbee islands as murderers."

Saxby shrugged his shoulders. "Traitors . . . Royalists . . . bolted apprentices . . . We have six murderers among our indentured servants and twice as many burglars, pickpockets and sheep stealers."

"You're their foreman," Yorke said ironically. "Still, we'll leave Mr Wilson in peace now. If he was dead he could not worry . . ."

"Aye, there's that to it," Saxby said, understanding at once. "As it is, he's never going to be sure now that one of us won't creep up on a dark night and stick a bigger knife on the correct side."

"Anyway, go down to the jetty and make the lads hurry: you can tell them there's an emergency. Don't say any more, though."

With that he walked up the stone staircase into the house, calling for Aurelia. She was in his bedroom being helped by Mary, who was holding up the sheet of polished brass he used as a mirror so that Aurelia could see to tidy her hair. Mary tactfully excused herself, put down the mirror and left the room.

Almost at once, Aurelia buried her head in his arms, weeping uncontrollably. Like most men, Ned had no idea what to do. All he could think of was that he had a great deal of work to finish before sailing at sunrise.

For a minute or two he felt like a kidnapper and was prepared to leave any arguing until later, but at the same time he was embarrassed that Aurelia should be trying to make do with his spartan quarters. His bed was unmade – not that it entailed more than straightening the linen sheet on the leather straps criss-crossing the low wooden frame – but the dressing table had only a comb in addition to the mirror, and on the floor beside it was a pewter basin with his shaving brush, razor and a jug of soapberry juice.

"You do not use a hammaco," Aurelia sobbed inconsequentially.

"No, they're too uncomfortable. You can't turn over."

"That is a bed for a married couple," she murmured.

44

"Yes," Ned said, and she blushed.

Suddenly she stood up, obviously having reached a decision about something.

"Edouard – I must go home: this is madness!"

Ned was startled and felt fear, not knowing how to deal with a woman whose sense of duty was overcoming all logic or reason. Suddenly, and for the first time since he had known her, he lost his temper.

"You can't go back," he said harshly. "He'd kill you. If he didn't strangle you and say it was done by the same person that stabbed him, he would thrash you every day for the rest of his life. Or your life."

He gripped her shoulders, shaking her in an attempt to make the words sink in, and lapsing into French. "He has everything. He has all your money and the plantation is in his name; he'll have Kingsnorth within a month. What does he want you for? He hates you. To begin with, you were simply a source of money: that was why he married you. Now you get in his way."

He continued shaking her as words poured from his mouth. "He never loved you: *that* is what you cannot accept. You think – you have to think, because of your pride – that he married you because you are beautiful and he loved you.

"He married you because when your father fled from France after the Edict of Nantes, he brought a lot of money with him. Your family are wealthy. When he died you inherited a fortune, and Wilson knew it.

"He married you and has used all your money. What have you today? Not a penny piece. Not a ha'porth of love from that man; in fact you have his hatred – because you are still alive and prevent him replacing you with other women at the estate house. But you know better than anyone else what he has done – he keeps women elsewhere.

"But what has *he* got? A great plantation bought with your money and which he would have lost at least a couple of times if the remainder of your money had not saved him from bankruptcy. And soon he'll have this place. Then he'll be by far the biggest landowner on this island, and be a powerful man in the Assembly.

"Yet you want to go back to him."

A sudden thought struck Ned, one that even as he began

speaking he knew was despicable, but his pride, too, was hurt and he was lashing out blindly.

"You don't want to take your chance with me, who loves you and has always loved you from the first day. I have nothing. If my father and brother died tomorrow they could not leave me anything but the memory of the estates in Kent and Sussex; within a day or so Kingsnorth will be gone and my only kingdom will be the deck of the *Griffin*. I have nothing to offer you but myself; if I am killed, you will be alone – as alone as you are now. But I cannot blame you; he may whip you o'nights, but at least he gives you a name: Madame Wilson, the legal wife of the greatest scoundrel I have ever met."

She broke loose from his grip but remained standing in front of him. Her face was white, the skin taut with emotion, she had stopped crying. He saw she was not angry, but whatever deep emotion now gripped her he had never seen before.

"Edouard, you must listen. Do you really think I want to go back to him because you have nothing to offer me – because you have lost everything?"

"What else can I think?" he answered uncomfortably.

"So you think I want to go back because he will soon own both estates, and has my money?"

"Well, he will, won't he?" Ned said lamely.

"Oh, how little you know me. You say you love me – yet you think I can do these things: leave you because you have lost everything, stay with him because he has everything."

"If you loved me, you would sail with us tonight."

"But Edouard – I am only staying now because I know this man: he is hateful, he will raise the hue and cry, he will persuade the island secretary and the governor to send this man Penn and his fleet to hunt you down and hang you. But if I stay, perhaps I can persuade him . . . slowly I can show him he has everything he wants, and that revenge is not necessary."

Suddenly he understood and felt ashamed.

"Darling heart – there's nothing you can achieve for either of us by staying. The governor would never send Penn after us – the fleet will have far more important things to do."

But Aurelia had not finished. "Today he challenged you to

a duel, and you refused, and he said you did not think I was worth risking your life for."

"Skin. He said 'skin', not life."

"Well, whatever it was. Did he speak the truth?"

Ned sank down on the stool, leaving Aurelia standing and looking down at him. It had all seemed comparatively simple when he left home to go to the Wilson estate this morning: he had only to persuade Aurelia to leave the island with him. Now . . .

"He was drunk, so I could not duel with him. One does not fight with a drunken man, either with pistols or swords."

"But in time he would become sober."

"Yes, but I am short of time; I am needed here, to make sure the *Griffin* can sail."

"So he was right."

Startled by both the words and the quiet voice, Ned looked up and realized he was losing a game in which he held all the high cards.

"Would you live – I mean live as a wife – with the man who killed your first husband?" he asked quietly.

"Well, I cannot see –"

"Think about it," Ned asked harshly, looking down at the worn planks of the floor. "Just think about it. Let us suppose we wait for your husband to sober up. We decide on weapons. We duel. We would have time to send for seconds to ensure fair play. And when it is all over, what do you do?"

"Obviously it would depend on –"

"It depends on nothing: I should have killed him. I am, my dear Aurelia, what my fencing master regarded as the finest swordsman he had ever seen; my lessons stopped because he had nothing more to teach me. But supposing we used pistols, eh? You know your husband is a very bad shot. Ask Saxby about me. I am fortunate: I have a quick eye and unusually good balance. Sword or pistol – it makes no difference.

"Would you," he repeated, "live with the man who killed your husband?"

"But . . . but he would have told everyone that you were a coward for refusing his challenge; your name would have

47

been dishonoured. Everyone in the island would have ignored you."

Ned shrugged. "I am leaving the island, but anyway I have never been interested in what the islanders do, say or think. Most of them have the minds, attitudes and drinking habits of peasants."

"That is true," she murmured.

"You still have not answered my question."

"You are trying to trap me!"

"Trap you? How, in God's name?"

"If I say I would never live with the man who killed my husband, you will ask me to live with you because you did not kill him."

Ned jumped to his feet, unable to believe his ears. "I don't steal your money, I don't whip you, I don't come home drunk and punch you, I don't call you a French slut: Aurelia, I just love you. I am not trying to trap you, so right now, this minute, you can choose."

She was sobbing again, twisting a ringlet of hair with one hand, dabbing at her eyes with one of his linen handkerchiefs that had been lying folded on the dressing-table.

"Choose what?"

Ned gave a deep sigh; he seemed to be sinking into a quicksand of emotions, words, decisions, contradictions and, he suspected, misunderstandings.

"Choose what you want to do. Either you return to Wilson, and I'll provide a horse and a groom to escort you, or you stay with me and we sail in the *Griffin*."

"But ... but ... oh, he will kill me; I know he will. Then he will have everything –"

Again Ned sighed. "That settles it. No more talking. We leave Wilson to his mulatto – the one you know about, but there are several more. Now, in that trunk over there are the rest of my clothes. Sort them out and keep only the ones that are worth having. Remember we may have to adapt some for you – it might be more comfortable on board a ship wearing breeches and hose than a skirt and petticoat.

"That other trunk contains cloth. It is good cloth and they use it to make my clothes. Look through that – I imagine we will take it all. And behind that curtain are my boots and shoes. I will take them all."

"Your hats?" she asked, "where are they?"

"I have only that beaver," he said pointing to the one he had been wearing. "I wear a hat only to visit you."

"But the sun! It will kill you with the heat."

"Do not worry; it has already sent me mad."

Her eyes widened in alarm until he said: "That's why I love you. From what you've been saying up to now, only a madman would love you –"

"Edouard," she said, her voice serious.

Ned turned to her, alarmed by the tone.

"There is one other thing. Walter is still my husband."

"I know! But what does that mean to us?"

"While I am still married to another man, you and I cannot share a marriage bed."

"Any bed," he said lightly. "Even a hammaco."

She shook her head. "I made my vows in church before God: they last while he and I live, or the marriage is annulled."

"Start packing those clothes," Ned said, "and we'll discuss it later. There are no beds, marriage or otherwise, in the *Griffin*. I hope you like sleeping in a hammaco."

Chapter Five

The sugar sacks slid down into the blackness of the hold and as soon as there was a shout, the four men hauled on the rope going up to the stay. Saxby, standing by the coaming beside Yorke, gave a satisfied grunt. "That's the lot, sir; fifty-eight tons of sweetness, and the Dutch will give us a penny a pound for it."

Yorke looked along the jetty and could see three or four men approaching, each with a knapsack on his shoulder. "Are these the last?"

"Yes sir, but with your permission I'd like to light a lantern and read out the names, just to make sure."

Yorke laughed and clapped the foreman on the back. "A ship of scoundrels, eh Saxby? A would-be murderess and her two accomplices, for all of whom a hue and cry will soon be raised, a Royalist for whom the Assembly will soon be offering a reward, and thirty-one indentured servants who the Assembly would claim are breaking the terms of their agreement and escaping. You and your assistant and our nine time-expired men are the only ones on the right side of the law. And even you are leaving the island without paying the tax."

"Aye," Saxby said grimly, "but we could stay and seize the ship and the lot of you lawbreakers, and make ourselves rich men on the reward."

"Aye," Yorke said, mimicking the foreman's Lincolnshire accent, "and may the Good Lord and the militia protect you from Mrs Judd and Mrs Bullock!"

"I hear tell that the Spanish still call Sir Francis Drake 'El

Draco', sir; before we've finished they'll be shivering at the thought of 'El Juddo'."

"La Judda," Yorke corrected. "We'll establish her fame as the ruthless woman pirate, along with Mrs Bullock, once she is sure which side a man's heart beats."

Mrs Bullock's mistake over Wilson had, within an hour become a legend in Kingsnorth and "Where is Bullock's heart?" a rallying cry for everyone sailing in the *Griffin* and a source of acute embarrassment for her husband.

Yorke slapped at the mosquitoes which were attacking his face, wrist and hands, delighted at finding a meal at this time of night without having to fly through clouds of tobacco smoke. "Get your lantern and read out those names, Saxby, the offshore breeze should set in any minute."

Saxby hurried aft and a few moments later Yorke saw the series of flashes as he struck steel against flint to kindle some tinder and light the lamp.

Twenty minutes, he decided; in twenty minutes they would be leaving Barbados. In many ways he felt more excited than when he first left England four years ago, bound for the Caribbee islands to take charge of the family plantation. His father and his brother had been wounded only a few months before and the Royalist cause was collapsing in England. It had been the beginning of one great adventure – and the end of an old one. The old one had taught him the bitterness of being on the losing side in two battles and the art of escaping. He was not yet sure what he would learn from the new.

The *Griffin* was to sail by the light of a half moon. Down here in the tropics it was lying on its back like a slice of melon on a plate, instead of standing vertical as in the northern latitudes. It would light the *Griffin*'s way – to where?

In many ways it was a good thing that he had been too busy in the last few hours to think of destinations. Barbados stood out alone in the Atlantic like a sentry box in front of a row of tents extending more or less north and south, the island of La Grenade at the bottom and St Martin at the top, and a dozen islands in between.

He shivered in the darkness although it was hot and the air was loud with the chatter of tree frogs. Until now he had always enjoyed a tropical night: the stars were brighter than he could ever describe in letters to George and even now he could not get used to seeing the Plough so low on the northern horizon, the north star only thirteen or fourteen degrees above the horizon, little more than a hand's span. And the night was never quite dark; one rarely needed a lantern to find one's way.

Now, for the first time, the night seemed to be the edge of the world; very soon he was going to jump over it, like a madman walking along a clifftop. Round him were enemies. Here in Barbados there were the Roundheads, a majority but still biding their time for Penn and Venables to come. They were enemies because he was a Royalist, but chief among them now was Wilson. Stubborn with all the inflexibility of the weak-willed, he hated Ned because of Kingsnorth, and a man always hated the one he intended to wrong. Wilson would say that Ned had stolen his wife – that was how Wilson would see it now: Aurelia was the perfect wife upon whom he had always lavished love and gifts. He would forget the whippings that woke servants and were, Yorke now realized, the only way the wretched man could get any sexual gratification. Yorke had all the normal man's horror of strange sexual habits and the desperate lengths to which they could drive their victims.

Yet they were no excuse for the rest of it, he thought savagely. Any penniless man marrying an heiress was obviously wise to use her money to improve their life together – but Wilson had everything transferred to his name and put in his power before revealing his impotence and vicious habits. Then he could throw Aurelia out of the house at any time, penniless and for that matter naked if he chose to claim the clothes on her back.

Yet Wilson apart, the enemies were not only in Barbados, they were in England, too, and among the men sailing out with Penn and Venables. Enemies . . . in his childhood "enemies" had always meant the French or the Spanish. "Enemies" fought great wars against you, fierce battles like Agincourt and Crecy, or they launched armadas against England. "Enemies" had never, until 1642, meant your own people. He knew of cases, after that date, of a son fighting on the opposite side to his father, of brother fighting brother . . .

Saxby had the lantern alight and was mustering everyone aft so that he could begin reading out the new muster roll of the *Griffin*. What flag should she fly? Damnation, she's English, Yorke said to himself; she is English, built in Rye, and my family were English and living under that flag for many generations before these damned Puritans seized the country.

Yet out here among the Caribbee islands, the enemy was as much Spain as anyone else; in fact more so than anyone else. For the moment the Dutch were still the Dutch, and Cromwell's war against them in Europe was over. Once again the Dutch were traders who bought and sold anything, whose ships appeared among ports and bays of the islands like waterboatmen on a village pond. The French for the moment were friendly, and providing a refuge for the exiled Prince.

But Spain . . . she was the enemy and had been since the first foreigner had dared to sail "across the Line" after Columbus into the Caribbean.

Two hundred years ago under the pressure from the King of Spain, the Pope had proclaimed a bull giving everything beyond a certain longitude west of the Azores to Spain, and since then Spain had tried to ensure that no one crossed the line without her permission. Of course, that meant no one was to sail or trade, let alone settle on any island in the Caribbean Sea or along the coast of the Main, and if they tried and were caught, they suffered the same fate as Sir John Hawkins' men at San Juan de Ulua. If the Spanish mayor did not lock you in his jail for the rest of your life, using you to pound rocks for building fortresses and breakwaters, or dig salt from the salt mines, the Inquisition took you for a non-believer and killed you to save your soul, a price that Protestants begrudged paying.

Well, two centuries had seen some changes. Some, but not enough. Most of the eastern islands were now settled by the English, Dutch or French, but the Spaniards had the rest of the chain – Puerto Rico, Hispaniola and Cuba, and of course all of the northern mainland coast as far as Mexico. For all that, any foreigners caught today by the Spaniards knew that at best he would be sent to the salt mines (from which there was a slight chance of escape) but at worst would be handed over to the priests. Yet it was along the Main that bold smugglers could make fortunes.

The reason was simple enough: the Spaniards kept out

foreign ships and forbade any trading, but could not themselves supply their own people with what they needed – which was almost everything from olive oil and wine to cooking pots and bodkins. So the Dutch, French and British traders smuggled in the goods, landing in deserted bays or (quite often) sailing into some out-of-the-way port after bribing the mayor and customs officer to go away for a few days' hunting.

He saw Saxby put the lantern down on deck, fold up a piece of paper and, after clearing the *Griffin*'s bulwarks in a leap as graceful as an ox escaping from a pen, walk along the jetty to report.

"Forty-six men and women from Kingsnorth ready and anxious to sail sir, plus Mr and Mrs Bullock, and you and – er . . ."

"And Mrs Wilson."

". . . er, yes sir, and Mrs Wilson."

"Very well, get ready to cast off, Saxby, and let's begin our new adventure!"

"Yes, sir. Had you a . . . well, a particular destination in mind?"

"No. I suggest we start off by exploring the northern islands. That will also keep us out of the way of the Roundheads."

Saxby ticked them off one by one. "La Grenade – too mountainous and too easy for the Spanish to attack from the Main, apart from being French. And the French have St Lucia and Martinique, Guadeloupe and Marie Galante. I don't know who has St Bartholomew, but I know it's small and mountainous. That leaves Antigua (last I heard, transported Irishmen and Norwegians were cutting each other's throats), St Christopher, Nevis and Montserrat (don't know anything about 'em), St Martin is divided between the French and the Dutch. The Virgin Islands – too dry for plantations . . ."

"The Royalists are said to be strong in Antigua," Yorke said.

"Ah – and there's plenty of land for plantations."

"But it's too Royalist for our purpose," Yorke said. "Penn and Venables will clear them out; they are bound to go up there."

Saxby rubbed his jaw, the stubble of his whiskers rasping. "I hadn't thought of that. Antigua has three harbours, though. They could take their fleet into any one of them and land."

"Exactly. We want somewhere that won't turn us away, where we can buy land, but which is not so Royalist that it will attract the fleet."

"We'd better discover our own island, sir," Saxby said, obviously completely disheartened.

"We'll get under way," Yorke said, realizing that, standing in the darkness, the apparent hopelessness of their situation was almost overwhelming him too. He did not want to seem unsure of himself in front of his people, and certainly not before Aurelia, who always seemed to sense his moods long before he said a word; almost before she saw him.

He walked down the jetty for the last time, turning to look back at the house, large in the moonlight but seeming gaunt without a light at any window. It had been lonely living there – but only because Aurelia had been five miles away. Five, fifty, five thousand – it had made no difference. Now, because of events more than four thousand miles away, all their lives had changed; had taken a sudden and irrevocable turn, like a file of soldiers wheeling on a battlefield or a squadron of cavalry executing a caracole.

Kingsnorth was lost – but in exchange he had Aurelia. Had her company, anyway, even if she was not yet his wife. He had the ship, too, and a loyal crew; he had cargo that could be turned into capital, and he had his life. The Yorke family, he thought bitterly, have simply gone away; my father and George have said goodbye to Godmersham, Saltwood and Ilex; Edward is this moment making his farewell to Kingsnorth.

There was a movement beside him and a hand crept into his. "We say goodbye to it, Edouard."

"You have never really said hello." He could not keep the bitterness out of his voice, yet did not know what drove him to say it.

He felt her fingers tighten. "Where am I now, Edouard?"

"What do you mean?"

"Am I with Walter, or with you?"

"Well, with me, of course." Again, why had he such a

grudging note in his voice? It was as if a stranger was talking.

"And for how long?"

"For ever, I hope."

"So if I never really said 'hello' to Kingsnorth, do you not think that . . ."

He turned and kissed her; a kiss that left them both dizzy so that they had to clutch at each other on the narrow and rickety jetty.

"Yes," he murmured, "but I'm jealous of every minute we've wasted until now."

As he held her he felt rather than heard a faint drumming, almost a distant rumbling. It was probably an earthquake: the noise would approach and get louder if it was passing nearby but be no more than the rumble of a cartwheel if distant. A few moments later he was sure it was an earthquake (he had often experienced them and they never did any damage here) but then he realized it was approaching too slowly: the drumming seemed to remain constant.

Aurelia noticed his tension. "What is it, *chéri*?"

"There – can you hear it? A faint drumming. Sounds like an earthquake."

"No, it's not an earthquake." After a few moments she said: "The noise of an earthquake comes through the ground. This I can hear through the air. Horsemen galloping on hard ground. Several of –"

"Quick, get on board!" He dragged her after him along the jetty, shouting, "Saxby! Horsemen! Get those muskets and pistols loaded! Take the lantern down below with the women!"

By the time he finished shouting orders he was abreast the ship and helping Aurelia over the bulwark. He heard Saxby shouting instructions in the darkness and the metallic clank of muskets being thrust up the companionway. Someone bellowed for the magazine key and Saxby said the box of Apostles had not yet been stowed.

By now the drumming was loud enough to warn of a band of horsemen galloping along the track running parallel with the beach and about a hundred yards inshore. Galloping horsemen on a night like this could mean only one thing; a party come to arrest him. But there was no breeze so it was pointless to cut the *Griffin*'s lines and hope to drift clear.

Yorke saw Aurelia safely down the companionway and turned to find Saxby hurrying towards him holding two muskets and a pistol in his arms and a couple of bandoliers, each strung with a dozen Apostles, round his neck.

"Musket or pistol, sir?" he asked cheerfully.

"Pistol."

Saxby put down the two muskets and handed Yorke the pistol. "There's the spanning key – and," he grunted, removing a bandolier and passing it over, "the Apostles loaded with pistol ball and the right measure of powder. And," he added, groping in a capacious pocket, "a flask of priming powder."

They could hear individual horses now and the snorting of animals and men that had galloped their fastest for several miles.

"What do we do now, sir?" Saxby asked. "I didn't think they'd be here until long after dawn."

"Wilson must have escaped and raised the alarm. How many horses?"

Saxby listened. "A dozen?"

"That's what I estimated. They'll want me. You stay on board and say you don't know where I am. Let them search the ship. Don't let them touch Mrs Wilson or the Bullocks. I want half a dozen men with muskets and cutlasses to come with me. Call for volunteers."

"Where are you going, sir?"

"Not far: just an insurance."

Saxby called for six men "To go with Mr Edward" and it seemed as if every man present gave an excited yell. Saxby took the six nearest who had muskets and sent them scrambling after Yorke as he hurried towards the landward end of the wooden jetty. The moment he reached the shore he turned to the right, jumping down on to the sandy beach and heading for a stand of palms thirty yards away and close to the track along which the horses were approaching.

Once hidden in the shadow of the palm trees Yorke stopped and looked back at the *Griffin*. She looked smaller than usual, a model on a silver tray, a random breeze pewtering the surface of the sea for a couple of moments and reflecting the moonlight. Her single mast looked too slender for its task; the rigging reminded him of strands of fishing net caught on a post.

The drumming was loud now. "Load your muskets," he said to the six men. "And don't drop your spanning keys!"

He reached down to the bandolier slung diagonally across his shoulder. Twelve small wooden cylinders, looking like peg dolls, hung down from it at intervals. He took the lowest of the cylinders, one of the Apostles, and pulled so that the lower part came away from the upper, which was secured to the bandolier by a strong cord. The lower section contained exactly the right measure of powder for charging the pistol and was slightly narrower than the bore of the barrel. Quickly he tilted it so the powder dropped into the pistol. He took a small wad of flannel and with the pistol's rammer pushed it down on top of the powder, giving it a sharp tap. Then he took a shot from his pocket, put that down the barrel and tapped it home with the rammer, added a wad and then slid the rammer back into its holder under the barrel.

Holding the pistol in his left hand he flicked back the pancover to reveal the priming pan, and using the small flask filled the pan with priming powder, the flask having a small lever fitted into the pourer which released only the correct measure.

After shutting the pancover, he tucked the flask back into his pocket. Priming powder, much finer than the ordinary powder which would propel the shot, was harder to get; anyone with a keg of good priming powder kept it in a safe place.

Now he took the spanning key, which had a socket at one end. This fitted on to a small projection at the side of the pistol – the spindle of the serrated wheel which the main spring would spin against the flint gripped in the doghead and, as the pancover slid back, shower sparks into the pan to set off the priming powder and send a spurt of flame down the touchhole into the breech.

The wheel would only spin if the spring attached to it was tensioned by the spanning key. Pistols with weak springs left spanned, or wound up, for any length of time often failed to spin the wheel fast enough to make sparks. Or, just as bad, the powder in the pan could have been shaken to the side away from the touchhole so that when fired the powder puffed but its flame did not race down to ignite the powder in the barrel. The pistoleer, now faced with a 'flash in the pan', was likely to find his opponent's sword running him through.

A musket was no more reliable, Yorke thought, although if it misfired it made a useful heavy club.

"All charged?"

The men murmured that their wheel-locks were loaded and spanned and ready to fire.

"No one is to fire unless I give a direct order."

The horsemen swung off the track towards the jetty. Yorke guessed that they could see the mast black against the western sky, its shape blotting out some of the lower stars. They slowed down as a cloud drifted across the moon. Yorke glanced up and saw several large cotton balls of cloud drifting over from the east, moving very slowly. Finally the horsemen were forced to stop, the leading rider dismounting and leading his horse, afraid of it stepping into one of the landcrab holes scattered across the foreshore; these were more numerous though slightly smaller than those made by coneys in England. The other horsemen followed in single file behind him.

The horses' harness was clinking now instead of jingling and a voice said: "That's the *Griffin* all right, so he hasn't left."

Another voice, at the end of the file which Yorke recognized as Wilson's, called urgently: "Perhaps we ought to go to the house. If the *Griffin* hasn't sailed, he'll be over there."

"We'll check here first," the first voice growled, and Yorke thought he recognized the provost marshal, a crude bull of a man whose appointment was probably a reward from Cromwell because he had served in the Roundhead Army and could pillage a Royalist home with the best of them. "Dismount everyone, and secure your horses: we'll go out along the jetty on foot."

So the rest of the men were not soldiers: the provost marshal's orders were not intended for men with military training. But what if they tried to board and search the *Griffin* and found Aurelia and the Bullocks? Wilson would certainly try to drag them off – or get his friends to. The pain in his shoulder would be forcing him to lift his tankard lefthanded for some time to come.

Because in the few moments he had to prepare there had been no chance of getting the women off the ship, Yorke had to rely on Saxby's good sense and trust that the plan for his own half dozen men would work. There were eleven men in the provost marshal's party – he had been able to count them in the last of the light before the cloud drifted across the moon. The eleven included Wilson, so only ten men could be armed. If Saxby knew that the last man in the file was Wilson, he would shoot him out of hand.

The men were busy securing their horses' reins to the guardrail on one side of the jetty. They were too far away for Yorke to hear the provost marshal's instructions but as the cloud thinned for a few moments he saw the group move along the jetty towards the *Griffin,* leaving one man with the horses. Wilson? It was likely: a man unable to fire a pistol or wield a sword would best be left minding the horses.

The cloud hid the moon again. "They've stopped, sir," one of the men whispered. "I could hear their boots on the planking."

Realizing the man had acute hearing, Yorke muttered: "Listen carefully and report anything."

He watched the cloud, which at first seemed to have come to a stop, and saw the faint blur of the moon at a thin spot, like a distant lantern seen through threadbare curtains. The cloud was in fact moving slightly to the north-west, and now he could see the group starting to move along the jetty again, hearing the report of marching feet a moment later.

Suddenly, as they drew abreast of the *Griffin*'s stern, the tremendous bellow of Saxby's voice, exaggerated by the silence and the big brass speaking trumpet he was using, ordered: "Halt! Don't move a step forward or back!"

The sudden order hurled out of the darkness from an apparently deserted ship stopped the men as though they had walked into a wall. A minute or two passed before the provost marshal shouted back: "Who is that?"

"Doesn't matter who I am: we have muskets aimed at all your gizzards. Get on your horses and ride back to Bridgetown!"

The provost marshal, voice solemn, intoned: "In the name of the Governor and Assembly of Barbados I order you to lay down your arms and surrender the person of Edward Yorke for whom a proclamation of hue and cry has been ordered and is duly proclaimed again here by me, the provost marshal, by order of the Governor and Assembly!"

"Well done!" Saxby shouted. "Now run home and have a wet; your throat's parched."

The cloud moved away slowly and the moonlight spread from the land along the jetty to the ship and moved on out to sea.

Yorke saw the provost marshal's men were aiming their muskets at the ship. If they fired, Saxby's men would sweep the jetty with pistols and muskets and before the smoke cleared a couple of dozen men with cutlasses would follow. No swordsman could hope to fight off a canecutter armed with his cutlass: weeks spent cutting the springy cane made a cutlass, or machete, an extension of his arm.

Yorke tried to pull his thoughts together: there was an enormous difference between sailing from Barbados in his own ship with his own men to avoid arrest, and sailing out leaving ten men dead on the jetty, including the provost marshal who was the official guardian of law and order on the island. The only man to escape alive would be Wilson . . .

"Keep me covered," he muttered to his musketeers and glided across the sand, crouching low as he emerged from the shadow of the palm trees making for the jetty. Landcrabs scuttled away in their curious sideways gait to disappear down holes; mosquitoes buzzed round his face. The sand was soft, creaking and giving slightly underfoot. He held his pistol canted so that the priming powder covered the touchhole and slid his thumb on to the doghead, ready to cock the piece.

Five yards to the jetty he realised his shoes would sound on the planking. He knelt and pulled them off and then continued moving. Four yards and the jetty met the sloping beach, the piles low this far in. Three yards, two – and then he was stepping up on to the planking, the land to his right, the jetty pointing seaward to his left, the *Griffin* halfway along it. And between him and the *Griffin* eleven horses, all facing the rail on this side of the jetty. Eleven horses and one man standing in the moonlight facing the *Griffin*. He wore dark clothing but a white slash ran diagonally across his back. It was Wilson with his right arm in a sling – to ease the pain of the wound in the heavy muscles above the shoulder blade.

Grains of sand on the planking grated beneath his feet because the cloth of his hose was clogged with sand and if he was not careful he would sound like an old man shuffling. Two paces along the jetty, three, four . . .

He dare not look over his shoulder to see if another cloud was approaching the moon in case his feet snagged a knot in the wood, but any moment the provost marshal or Saxby might start shooting.

Wilson was standing still but the nearest horse to Yorke was restless, probably sensing his approach, and he was afraid Wilson might turn to calm it.

Saxby was hurling abuse at the provost marshal and daring him to move one pace nearer the *Griffin*; the provost marshal seemed to realize his only possible course of action was to make the best of his legal position and possibly overawe the men.

"Hand over Edward Yorke and you can all go free," the provost marshal shouted. "I'll let you go back to the estate without taking names. Just hand over Edward Yorke."

"And my wife," Wilson suddenly shouted, startling Yorke who was within five yards of the man.

"Yes, and Mrs Wilson."

"Don't know an Edward Yorke nor any Mrs Wilson," Saxby shouted back. "Now get off the jetty or you're dead men and the landcrabs'll pick over your bones."

"My wife, get my wife!" Wilson blustered. "Provost marshal, do your duty! Arrest Edward Yorke and free my wife. Remember the hue and cry!"

"Yes, Mr Wilson," the provost marshal called back, his voice full of doubt. "On board there, you have one minute to produce Edward Yorke. After that I am coming on board in the governor's name."

"You try," Saxby said grimly, "and we'll shoot you down in the Prince's name!"

"Half a minute gone!" the provost marshal shouted.

Immediately a flash and bang showed that a pistol had been fired on board the *Griffin* and a shot whined out to sea in ricochet, indicating that the gun had not been aimed at the provost marshal.

"That's just a warning," bellowed an excited Saxby. "Get back to your horses and go away or you're dead men."

Yorke heard men in the group muttering to the provost marshal. Yorke guessed that they were drinking friends of Wilson's who had ridden along to enjoy some sport baiting "that Royalist fellah". Now they were realizing that whoever commanded the *Griffin* was not to be frightened. But the provost marshal, either fearful of the governor's wrath or too proud to retreat, began shouting back.

At that moment Yorke reached Wilson and selected the exact spot in the back of his neck, where his hair fell either side and revealed skin which seemed silvery in the moonlight.

Yorke pressed the muzzle into the neck and pulled back the doghead, cocking the gun . . . Wilson must have felt the metallic click go all the way to his feet: he froze as a familiar voice whispered in his ear: "You should have stayed in bed like a good boy . . . Keep still or this pistol will separate your head from your shoulders . . . Now tell the provost marshal to order his men to put their guns down on the jetty . . . Now!"

Yorke pressed a fraction harder and then felt the man take a deep breath and push his head back a fraction to shout. Realizing that a sudden jerk might cause him to squeeze the trigger, Yorke pulled the pistol back an inch.

"Stevens! Stevens!" Wilson shouted. "Hold on! Tell your men to ground their arms! At once!"

"But sir, they're just about —"

"At once!" Wilson screeched as Yorke once again pressed with the pistol and, careful that Wilson's burly body hid his own from the provost marshal, murmured: "Tell him you are withdrawing all charges; that the hue and cry will be cancelled. Make sure you persuade him. Otherwise no one will notice the extra shot – least of all you!"

"Stevens, Stevens," Wilson almost wailed, "there's been a terrible mistake. I'm asking the governor to cancel the hue and cry; I've no quarrel with Mr Yorke!"

"And now," Yorke said, "tell him to ride back to Bridgetown because you are walking up to the house – you know Mr Yorke must be there and you want to talk to him. And then we'll walk off the jetty . . ."

Wilson followed the instructions, and then muttered: "Do I walk now?"

"Yes, follow me so that you hide me from Stevens. Six of

my musketeers are covering you so don't try to escape, raise an alarm – or attack me from behind."

With that Yorke turned and walked off the jetty with Wilson so anxious to hide him from the provost marshal's eyes that the toes of his shoes kept kicking the backs of Yorke's ankles. Once off the jetty Yorke knew they would both be hard to see against the bushes and clumps of sea grape at the back of the beach, and he swung round towards the palm trees. By the time they reached them, and Wilson found himself staring into the muzzles of six muskets, the provost marshal and his group were mounting their horses.

Yorke listened to an argument. The provost marshal, knowing that he was not now to be put to the test, was full of noisy courage. "Why Mr Wilson did that I don't know – why, in half a minute more I'd have taken the ship!"

"You'd have got us all shot, you puffed up clown," one of the group said bitterly. "You have the mind of a corporal and the legal knowledge of a cockerel. A capon, rather."

"There's no call for that sort of talk, Mr Jeffrey. No call at all. I've got my duties and I hope I know –"

"Do we follow Wilson up to the house?" another of the group asked.

"We do not!" the provost marshal said emphatically. "He said return to Bridgetown, and to Bridgetown we go. Now, someone lead. The devil take the landcrab holes."

The horses clattered along the jetty and on to the sand, reaching the track where they were spurred on, their hooves thudding on the sunbaked mud.

Yorke turned to Wilson and said evenly: "You could disappear at this moment, and no one left in Barbados would ever know what happened to you."

"But you –"

"We could kill you and bury you here and the landcrabs would burrow down to find you. Or we could take you with us when we sail – and drop you over the side when we're about five miles out, so that you could try to swim back –"

"But I can't swim!"

"How unfortunate."

"You'd never *murder* me! Would you?" Wilson watched the shadowy figure standing facing him. The moonlight just penetrating the palm fronds, occasionally bright as a gust moved one a few inches, caught Yorke's face, emphasizing the high cheekbones, the almost beak-like nose, and the eyes which looked like shiny black holes.

Yorke shrugged. "Murder you? I don't have to. You're hated, and any of my men would be only too pleased –"

"I'll do him in, sir," one of the musketeers said eagerly. "Just say the word!" There was a rustle as he drew a sheath knife.

"You see what I mean," Yorke said to Wilson. "You had to ask the Governor to raise a hue and cry against me. I have only to nod my head to raise one against you."

"Think of Aurelia! She would . . ." Wilson suddenly stopped, remembering the scene in his own house a few hours earlier.

No one spoke for two or three minutes. Yorke and his men knew their cruellest weapon against Wilson was silence: a silence which squeezed on him out of the darkness like an invisible garotte, a tiny world of silence surrounding him with an horizon of glinting eyes, a silence which existed despite the wavelets lapping a few yards away, the metallic rattling of tree frogs, the whine of mosquitoes and the occasional impatient snort of his own horse, still tethered to the rail of the jetty.

"What do you want?" Wilson whispered. "Money? I have a thousand pounds. It's yours now. I never really wanted Kingsnorth: Aurelia drove me to it. She loved it and wanted it for herself – you know how selfish the rich are. I promise you I'll speak to the Governor. You'll be able to stay here: don't sail, there's no need. You'll be safe at Kingsnorth: just let me go into Bridgetown . . ."

"Be quiet," Yorke snapped, "you disgust me." He turned and pointed along the beach to the southward. "Start walking. It's five miles before you reach your home. Or maybe," he added sarcastically, "you would sooner go straight to Bridgetown. Come on," he said to his men, and began walking towards the *Griffin,* picking up his shoes on the way. He cut the reins and unstrapped the saddle from Wilson's horse, giving them to one of the men. "Go to the end of the jetty and toss them into the sea." He touched another man on the shoulder. "Lead this beast up to the track, head it northwards towards Mr Alston's plantation, and give it a sharp crack across the rump."

Back on board the *Griffin* an excited Saxby wanted all the details but he groaned when Yorke ended his story by describing how he had set Wilson walking back home along the beach.

"You should've put him away, sir; cut his throat. If you didn't want to dirty your hands, one of the others would've obliged."

"It's not as simple as that."

"I know sir, talking to Mrs Wilson knowing you've had her husband done in," he said, and Yorke was grateful for the man's choice of the word 'talking', "but that man can be the death of us all." Saxby's voice showed the depth of his hatred and fear of Wilson.

Yorke said reassuringly: "We'll be sailing in an hour, just as soon as a breeze picks up, and we'll never see him or the island again."

By now his six men were back on board the *Griffin* and asking Saxby what to do with their muskets and pistols. "Leave them with the others by the mast. Make sure they're not cocked," the master said. "We'll unload and grease them once we're at sea."

Aurelia, cross from being told by Saxby to stay below in Ned's cabin and alarmed by all the shouting, seemed to have given up hope of ever seeing him again and when Ned tried to tease her into relaxing said flatly: "Not until I say goodbye to Barbados. Walter escaped even though you tied him to the bed. He raised the you and cry."

"Hue," he corrected gently. "But it doesn't matter: we're sailing soon."

"Why not now? Why do we wait?"

"For some wind. There's hardly a zephyr at the moment."

She held his arm, as if seeking reassurance. "The wind – it will come before daylight?"

Ned smiled. "We can't command the wind, but it is increasing. In an hour we'll have enough to take us clear of the coast. Be patient, beloved; only one more hour . . ."

Ned was on deck talking to Saxby, the two men watching the clouds as they passed the moon and feeling the wind on their cheeks. Both agreed that it had increased slightly and, with clouds becoming more frequent, there would soon be a sufficient breeze to cast off.

"One thing about going," Saxby commented, "we don't have to rebuild this jetty."

"It's creaking enough with us alongside, even though there's no wind!"

"Aye sir. If we had to be alongside in a stiff breeze, t'wouldn't surprise me if we carried the whole jetty away with us."

"We'd arrive at our destination with our own jetty alongside. Might be useful!"

"Jokin' apart, sir, I wasn't looking forward to drivin' new piles. Enough trouble building this one. But the ship worms have chewed it so bad that most of the piles are three quarters eaten through. That provost marshal was lucky: he moored up his horses at the end where the piles don't get wet so the ship worms haven't been at 'em. If they'd come ten yards nearer the whole thing would've collapsed under 'em."

The first they knew of the shots was a row of red eyes winking at the end of the jetty and a moment later a popping like a dozen corks shooting from bottles of fermenting wine. Then the musket balls hit the *Griffin*'s side, some sounding as though a man was punching the planking, others whining away in ricochet after hitting metal fittings with the loose noise of a blacksmith shaping a horse's shoe.

Both Ned and Saxby instinctively dropped to the deck, below the level of the bulwarks.

"The provost marshal," Ned muttered angrily, sliding over to the pile of muskets and pistols beside the mast. "He ran into Wilson, stopped once he knew we no longer heard the horses' hooves and then doubled back along the beach."

"Yorke," they heard him bellow. "I've warned you of the hue and cry so surrender yourself. You can't sail with no wind. I'll have a hundred men here in half an hour."

Saxby snatched up the speaking trumpet and already Ned could hear the pounding of feet as his own men rushed on deck, eager to get at the muskets and pistols.

"Settle yourselves behind something proof against musket shot," Ned warned them. "This may last a long time. You've two minutes before they'll have reloaded."

"You want a musket, sir?" Saxby asked.

"No. I'll be dodging about. Pity we can't use one of our minions to sweep the jetty."

"Ah," Saxby said regretfully. "A few pounds of langrage would settle the provost marshal's account."

By now the *Griffin*'s men were in position with their muskets and pistols. "Open fire when you've got a target," Saxby called.

"That's the trouble, sir, we can't see no one," a seaman grumbled. "They're hidden in the shadows at the back o' the beach. Now there's more cloud coming up to hide the moon."

Another crash of musketry and the pummelling of the lead balls hitting the *Griffin*'s planking led to one of the *Griffin*'s musketeers shouting: "They're all bunched up behind that clump of sea grape bushes in line with the end of the jetty."

"Fire at 'em, then!" Saxby bellowed. "Come on, let's smell our powder!" He looked up at the sky and nudged Yorke. "Look up there, sir; there's a few gallons of rain in that – we'll have to be sure to keep our powder dry!"

Low on the eastern horizon a broad band of billowing and tumbling dark cloud was approaching, bringing the heavy showers so frequent in the tropics between midnight and three in the morning.

A single musket fired on board the *Griffin,* then a second and third. "They're taking careful aim," Saxby commented.

"Could a shot penetrate our planking?" Ned asked.

"Quick!" Saxby said. "Mrs Wilson – get her out of the cabin and put her forward with Mrs Judd: that transom won't stop shot, leastways, the sternlights won't."

Ned bolted for the companionway, just able to see his way from a single lantern. The cabin was deserted. He worked his way forward, calling her name and hearing her replying from amidships. He shouted back a reassuring phrase which was interrupted by yet another volley from the shore, and heard a shot ricocheting round the cabin he had just left.

What the devil could he do? With no wind, the *Griffin* was sitting alongside the jetty like a crate of pigeons being shot at by a mad sportsman. His own men were firing spasmodically but he knew they were shooting at shadows. He felt hot with anger and embarrassment when he thought how the provost marshal had so successfully tricked him. Stevens was not the sort of man anyone should trust, even to collect a dozen eggs from a market.

As he climbed back up the companionway he heard Saxby calling him urgently and by the time he reached the deck his ears had warned him of what Saxby would have to say. The drumming along the track at the back of the beach told him that dozens of horsemen were galloping up to help Stevens.

While Saxby reported and gave his estimate of the number of extra men – he thought forty or fifty, basing his guess on the length of the column with two men riding abreast – Ned realised it was enough men to rush the ship: the *Griffin* had twenty-five muskets and twenty pistols. If they fired to order and with reasonable accuracy, that would mean a fusilade of forty-five shot. That did not mean forty-five of Stevens' men hit, though: there was no way of avoiding two or three Griffins firing at the same man. Loading took so long that if Stevens led a determined group they would be hit by one fusilade but there would be no time to reload, so the Griffins would then be fighting along the bulwarks with cutlasses.

He saw a figure up in the shrouds. "Who's that?"

"Me, sir, Bullock."

"What on earth are you doing up there?"

"Lookout sir; seems I can see better in the dark than anyone else."

Feeling that events were happening so fast he was almost lost, Ned hurried over to the foreman. "I don't know anything about ships and big guns, Saxby, but couldn't we load the minions on this side so that as they try to board we fire and blow them off the jetty?"

"I thought o' that sir, but it'd take hours because we've never loaded 'em before and some of our people are bound to be hurt by the recoil. Be different if we'd ever exercised at the great guns. Between you and me, sir, the muskits and pistols is more our mark now."

"They'll try to rush us."

"Yes sir, that's what I was going to talk to you about. I've stopped random shooting. All twenty-five musketeers are aft here, aiming over the taffrail and the quarter. They'll all fire at once, which should stop any charge. Then the pistoleers are amidships: if any of Stevens' men get through, the pistoleers will hop on to the jetty and wait until they can shove the muzzles into the mouths of these Roundheads. Then we should start collecting a pile of noheads."

"That black cloud is building up," Ned commented. The dark bulging mass was rising higher and getting nearer.

"Too much rain and no one'll be using wheel-locks or matchlocks: it'll be cutlass and swords, and that'll give us an advantage."

"The devil take it – just look at that cloud!"

It was boiling and swirling over the land, part lit by the moon, part in black shadow. A sudden flash across a quarter of the horizon was followed almost instantaneously by an echoing crash of thunder.

"'Ere they come!" yelled Bullock. "End of the jetty – scores of 'em!"

Saxby put the speaking trumpet to his lips. "Musketeers!" he bellowed. "Make sure your pieces are spanned and cocked . . . Steady now, I'll give the word to fire. Try and pick your target – men on the starboard side look after the left side of the jetty, those to larboard to the right."

Ned watched fascinated and hurriedly snatched up a cutlass which, until yesterday morning, had been in use at Kingsnorth for cutting cane.

The landward end of the jetty was black with men: Ned was reminded of maggots in rotten meat. Then he could hear the thudding of their feet on the planking. Saxby sprang up on to the bulwarks and then down on to the jetty, standing crouched, straining his eyes and trying to estimate the distance. Thin cloud was crossing the moon like gauze curtains flapping in the wind.

Ned saw the speaking trumpet go up to Saxby's mouth.

The thudding of feet, the wavelets hitting the hull and sounding like a mill stream, the chill on his face as the breeze sprang up, pushing the *Griffin* away from the jetty until her mooring lines began to creak . . . he seemed helpless, a spare man clutching a cutlass.

"Stand by!" Saxby yelled. "Now boys – fire!"

All the *Griffin*'s muskets except one fired simultaneously, flame spurting up from twenty-four muzzles. The twenty-fifth fired two or three seconds later and the others in the ship gave the man an ironic cheer.

"Gawd . . . gawd . . . gawd! Just look!" A shocked Bullock perched up in the shrouds was talking to himself and Ned cleared the bulwark to land on the jetty beside Saxby without conscious thought.

"There'll be no work for the pistoleers this time," Saxby said grimly. "Twenty or more cut down. Almost blocking the end of the jetty!" He aimed the speaking trumpet aft. "Come on you dreaming lechers, get those muskets loaded!"

He turned to Ned. "They'll regroup and try again, sir," he said. "Just listen to the moanin' and screamin'. That won't inspire the second group!"

"If they've any sense they'll wait for this cloud and rush us in the dark!"

"If Stevens had any sense he'd have sent the second group along the jetty before our lads have time to reload. It's too late now; I can hear the spanning keys turning."

Ned watched the cloud. A distant curtain hung down from it: driving rain that would last perhaps twenty minutes, buffet houses and shutters with gusty winds, and disappear to the westward, leaving a few gallons caught in the cisterns and refreshing the cane. These night-time tropical showers and not the soil were what made the islands so fertile.

Was Stevens watching that cloud? It was coming up behind him but he must have heard the thunder; it would have been enough to make him look over his shoulder.

Bullock called down: "Men are spreading out along the water's edge both sides of the jetty!"

"Damnation take it," Saxby swore. "They'll be shooting at us from both sides."

"Fifty paces at least: their shooting won't be very accurate."

"Thirty or forty men getting one lucky hit every fusilade will soon whittle us down," Saxby said calmly. "He's spreading 'em out to maintain random fire so we keep our heads down. Then he sends his main force along the jetty to board us!" Saxby spoke with certainty and Ned did not doubt him. Still, heavy rain fell equally on the just and the unjust and soaked their priming powder.

Flashes rippled down the beach to the south and Ned gave Saxby a push: "Quick, back on board!"

He followed with a leap over the bulwark but Stevens' men were firing at the after part of the ship: he could hear the shot thudding into the hull, ricocheting off metal and some, aimed too low, hitting the planking on top of the jetty. A few moments later more red flashes along the beach to the north, followed a moment later by deep popping, warned that the men to the north had fired their fusilade. A cry from the *Griffin*'s taffrail showed that someone had been hit.

Saxby ran aft, warning Ned to watch the end of the jetty. He was back within a couple of minutes to report one man dead and two wounded, the last one, who cried out, unlikely to live.

Ned continued watching the cloud: it had suddenly increased speed and was swirling, torn and twisted by the gusts of wind it was bringing with it. Stevens would send his main group racing down the jetty the moment the cloud blotted out the moon and stars. The cloud was moving like blackberries stirred in cream; the sharp outline of the moon was blurred and, as the whole mass of cloud suddenly began moving seaward and picking up speed, the breeze was chilly on his face.

That sheet of rain, which he could now hear driving down on the trees inland with a venomous hissing, would be on them within a couple of minutes with powerful gusts of wind that would try to tear the *Griffin* from the jetty.

Saxby said quietly: "Any minute now!"

The men along the beach to the south began firing slowly, carefully aimed shots which thudded into the taffrail, which was where they guessed the *Griffin*'s musketeers would be crowded to cover the jetty.

Then that popping that seemed too light, too harmless, to come from muskets began along the northern end of the beach. Suddenly it was almost pitch dark as a particularly thick cloud slid over the moon and almost at once both Ned and Saxby heard the drumming of feet at the far end of the jetty.

Saxby lifted his speaking trumpet. "Ready musketeers – fire!"

It is never quite dark in the tropics and Ned could just

make out the line of the jetty. There was a bulge on top of it halfway between the *Griffin*'s stern and the shore; a bulge which moved towards the ship.

"Pistoleers stand by!" Saxby bellowed.

Then Bullock called a warning as Ned spotted the movement. "The men on the beach are running to the jetty!" he warned Saxby.

"It's cutlasses now, then," Saxby said calmly, "and I'd like to shake your hand, sir: we nearly got away."

Ned felt his hand grasped and returned the squeeze, conscious that the hissing sheet of rain was only a few yards away and the wind was increasing, at first in gusts but quickly steadying into almost gale force. It would last half an hour; these night squalls usually did.

The black bulge was now moving slowly along the jetty, obviously waiting for the men on the beach to catch up and knowing the *Griffin*'s muskets could not be reloaded in time.

"Musketeers, grab cutlasses; pistoleers, make sure you have a cutlass in the other hand!"

The gusts were blowing the *Griffin* away from the jetty, but her mooring lines took the strain and kept her within two or three feet.

"Must be a hundred men on the jetty!" Bullock yelled.

"Funny they're not making a dash for us," Saxby said.

"They're planters and apprentices," Ned said. "They're not used to trotting along a narrow jetty in the dark. And it's wobbling as the *Griffin* moves in the wind. Ah, the rain!"

The raindrops hit like small pebbles just as he realized what he had said. "Saxby!" he yelled, "hoist the mainsail! Get the ship moving! Hurry!"

"But sir, we're still secured!"

"Exactly! Don't cut any mooring ropes, just get the sail drawing!"

Saxby swung round and shouted orders into the speaking trumpet. There were flashes and bangs as the pistoleers fired at the approaching men before running to the halyards and sheet.

The men were five yards from the *Griffin* as the mainsail began crawling up the mast and bellying out: Ned could see a mass of men on the jetty but the sudden thumping of the sail filling startled them so they stopped for a moment. Someone

73

– probably Stevens – bawled an order and the phalanx began moving again. It did not now have the sureness with which it began; many of the men in front seemed to be being pushed by those behind.

Then the mainsail was full and Saxby was giving orders for easing away the mainsheet and the mooring ropes were creaking as the *Griffin* tried to break away from the jetty. Gust after gust hit the ship as Saxby bawled at the men to make fast the mainsheet.

A great creaking began as though the largest door in Christendom was being pushed open on rusty hinges; then through the ship's deck Ned felt the snapping of wood. It seemed more like the kitchen noise of a cook breaking crisp rhubarb but as he swung round to have a better look at the jetty he heard scores of men screaming and as a sudden brief thinning of cloud let a beam of moonlight sweep the shore, he saw that the beach was already a hundred yards away and the jetty tilting like a mill grain platform collapsing in a flood.

Secured alongside the *Griffin* like a raft the jetty was being pulled seaward, but as the ship gathered speed the jetty heeled more and more, and in the distance he heard Saxby's hoarse shouts to the men to grab axes and cut the mooring lines to free the ship.

The men were quick and Ned was thankful Saxby had been very strict about ensuring that there was an axe secured inside the bulwark every ten or twelve feet. The strain on the mooring ropes was enormous; as the axe blades bit into them the strands unwound like suddenly-released springs.

Then he felt the *Griffin* surge forward like a good horse starting a gallop, and Saxby, now standing beside him, said: "I'm glad I mentioned the need for mending the jetty! We owe you our lives."

An embarrassed Ned said: "I led you into this mess. I'm glad that . . . well, anyway, it was a close run affair. And there'll be enough wreckage for those men to hold on to as they paddle back to the shore."

Saxby snorted and said with genuine regret in his voice: "This squall's blowing itself out so they won't drift far. A hundred yards to paddle . . . I'd like to use them for target practise."

Chapter Six

The *Griffin* had run into Falmouth Bay at Antigua, passed the reef which almost closed its circular shape like a lid on a pot, and anchored inside close to a sandy beach. Yorke could see two batteries perched like pelicans' nests, one on a small cay just inside the bay, the other on a cliff opposite, and the guns were all trained on to the ship.

The voyage from Barbados had been good, the Trade winds blowing steadily. With the *Griffin*'s heavy mainsail drawing well they had first sighted Guadeloupe, and then Antigua just north of it. Now, as he waited for a boat to be hoisted out so that he could go over to report to the Governor, Yorke felt nervous. Falmouth looked busy – hardly surprising, because it was the capital. He could see the courthouse in the north-east corner, and other scattered buildings. A few men were walking about – but the men at the batteries were Roundheads: that much was clear from their hats and jerkins.

Still, the brief voyage had done them all good. Saxby knew his seamanship, and he was a good leader of the men. Mrs Judd was very different from the plump and cheerful person who had been the housekeeper and head woman at Kingsnorth: now she was twice as cheerful and if it had been the custom for a ship to have a mistress as well as a master, she would have qualified for the job. She kept the six women busy so that meals were served on time; she found jobs for any man who had managed to evade Saxby's sharp eye. As soon as the flying jib developed a tear she had her women standing by with needles, thread and the four sail palms that were on board, and in spite of Saxby's protest that it was seamen's work, had the tear repaired – and reinforced half a dozen other seams whose stitching to her sharp eye seemed doubtful.

However, she had not understood why the repaired jib, when rehoisted, had not filled with wind like the mainsail and had promptly turned on Saxby, accusing him of being a poor sailor. It had taken him half an hour to persuade her that with a following wind the mainsail took all the breeze, keeping it from the jibs like a shut door stopping a draught, but all the women and many of the men had benefited from Saxby's lesson in seamanship.

Aurelia had been fascinated by it all. At first, soon after dawn and before Barbados had dropped below the horizon astern, still being outlined by a rising sun, she had appeared on deck wearing a pale green dress with a full skirt, the neck cut higher than was fashionable, presumably because there were so many men about. She had walked over to Ned, a wan smile on her face but admitting she had slept well once she had become used to the ship's rolling, but as she spoke she broke off, staring forward, wide-eyed, and Ned had turned hurriedly, suddenly alarmed, to find that she was looking at Mrs Judd and the woman following her.

Mrs Judd had the kind of figure that would immediately remind a miller of upper and nether grindstones: wide shoulders and enormous breasts seemed to move one way when she walked, and a large stomach and generous buttocks moved another, giving the impression that the two sections of her body were only loosely joined at the waist. But what fascinated Aurelia, who knew Mrs Judd from Kingsnorth, was the fact that she was now dressed as a man: black breeches, obviously too tight for her, did their best to contain the lower half of her body, down as far as stockings, which were probably her own; above, a man's jerkin had no chance of enveloping her and her bosoms strained the wooden buttons, one of which had already broken in half.

The woman with her, young and with a good figure, was also dressed in men's clothes and Ned noted appreciatively how the breeches and jerkin displayed advantages in her figure which were usually hidden by the folds of a dress.

More obviously, though, was that both women moved about the *Griffin*'s decks easily, unhampered by skirts and petticoats when a sudden extra roll sent them lurching to leeward, grasping at a rope or reaching for the bulwark.

Mrs Judd, seeing Aurelia in a dress, had greeted her cheerfully and then declared: "If you'll forgive me for saying so, Mrs Wilson, if you wear those clothes you'll catch your heel in the skirt and trip and break a leg. Breeches and hose, and barefoot, is safer, and that's what you need. There's only one thing more comfortable, and modesty forbids that!"

Both the second woman and Aurelia blushed as Mrs Judd gave a great bellow of laughter at her remark, and Ned saw Aurelia watch fascinated as the big woman's breasts bounced up and down, straining the buttons.

"Mr Yorke's brought a good wardrobe, ma'am," Mrs Judd added. "Otherwise, if you want a better fit, I'd be only too glad to make you a pair of breeches."

Aurelia nodded helplessly, for the moment unable to think of an appropriate comment in English, and Mrs Judd, misinterpreting the nod, said breezily as she walked away: "Right, ma'am, you'll have the breeches by noon."

As soon as she was out of earshot an embarrassed Aurelia turned to Ned. "But I cannot wear breeches! How do I tell her?"

"Why bother?" Ned said cheerfully. "They'll suit you well. And she's quite right about them being more practical."

"But all the men . . ."

"My beloved, you must forget masters, mistresses and servants for now; we're all just the crew of the *Griffin*. She's our only home; she may remain so for months. And in the meantime, if in an emergency you are needed to haul on a rope would you sooner be wearing a dress or breeches? And she's quite right about the danger of you catching a heel on your skirt."

"What did Mrs Judd mean," Aurelia asked cautiously, "when she said 'only one thing is more comfortable'?"

"Put modesty to one side and think," Ned said with a grin.

"Oh – she meant *that*?"

Ned nodded. "But I am glad you don't see me like that!" Aurelia said.

The tone of voice startled Ned. This was the woman he

dreamed of marrying, the woman he dreamed of naked in his arms. And here she was . . . "Why?" he asked flatly.

She turned away but was not blushing, so he guessed that whatever the reason it had nothing to do with normal modesty.

"Aurelia," he said, almost pleading, "answer me."

"Ask me again in a few weeks' time," she said in a whisper he barely heard above the hissing of the waves sluicing past the hull.

"Will the answer be different?"

Although when she nodded he felt relief, he could not avoid asking bluntly: "Why, beloved?"

"Mrs Bullock would know . . ."

Then suddenly he realized. "You are still bruised?"

Again she nodded. "It will go."

"It will never happen again!"

She shrugged her shoulders as though indifferent to the past and Ned felt himself swept by a warm wave of love. That shrug – so typically French and so reassuring.

Then she turned to face Ned squarely, as if wanting to use this moment right at the beginning of the voyage, and said: "Ned – do not think too bitterly about him . . ."

"What – when he used to punch you as well? That bruise on your face, the whippings . . ."

"But," she said carefully, "that was all he ever did to me."

There was such a distinct emphasis on "all" that her meaning was unmistakable, but how could it be so? Those negresses, the mulatto he kept in Bridgetown?

"Beloved – it makes no difference to my feelings for you, but remember his mistresses!"

"He did nothing to them: they whipped *him*. He is – how do you say, impotent. That is why we have no children. I suppose," she added bitterly, "that is why I came out here from England with him. He disgusted me but the alternatives were worse. A wife abandoned in a foreign country . . ."

An unusually large following sea lifted the *Griffin* and she rolled violently as she slid down the side of it. Aurelia, unprepared and with nothing to grasp, began staggering towards the ship's side until, a few moments later and before Ned could grab her, she sprawled flat on her face as a heel caught in her dress.

Ned ran to help her up and, finding she was unhurt and only her dignity ruffled, teased her. "Such beautiful ankles . . . such beautiful legs . . . who would want to hide them under breeches!"

"I do," Aurelia said firmly as Ned helped her to her feet. "Mrs Judd gives good advice. May I use some of your wardrobe?"

Ned called Mrs Judd and when she came nodded down towards his cabin, now being used by Aurelia, and winked. "Mrs Wilson would like to experiment with the wardrobe . . ."

The governor was most polite. Yes, he had heard of Mr Yorke's plantation in Barbados; no, he had heard nothing of a fleet due in the West Indies under Vice Admiral Penn and General Venables. Yes, there were estates for sale in Antigua, mostly those abandoned by Royalists and neglected for up to five years – but they could be bought only by permission of the Council of State in London.

Granting this permission, he said, took time (a year or more) and was preceded by a searching examination of the political allegiances of the applicant. He did not say in as many words that Edward Yorke's would not even be sent off to London, but he made it clear that his single clerk was kept busy with other things. He agreed, though, that the *Griffin* could be careened but would offer no guarantees of their safety while doing so. Roving bands of deserted apprentices, he admitted, moved the length and breadth of the island, calling themselves cattle-killers, and took what they wanted, except at some plantations, where the owners had the buildings well defended with loopholes cut in the shutters covering windows.

Yorke's reference to the battery on the cay opposite the anchorage met with no response: the implication was that, like the church and the courthouse, the island looked after its own, and its own had to be supporters of Cromwell.

As soon as Yorke had left the governor's grubby house with Saxby, the master almost exploded. "He doesn't want us staying here, that's certain!"

"I am sure he knows Penn and Venables are on their way and he doesn't want them to find people like us in his waters."

"So what do we do now?"

"Well, with so much barnacle and weed on the bottom we have to careen the *Griffin* as soon as possible, and the bad weather will be here soon. I intend finding a sheltered anchorage and staying there. We'll careen – and wait for Penn and Venables to pass to the westward."

"What's the advantage of that, sir?"

"There are plenty. First, a large British fleet ahead of us will clear the seas of Spanish privateers for a few weeks."

"They'll come back later." Saxby had no doubt about that.

"Yes, but while they're out of the way we can move about safely. Visit other islands."

"Aye, that way we'll be safe from the Dons *and* the bloody Roundheads."

"But Saxby," Yorke warned as they walked along the track to the ship, avoiding the thorns of the wild tamarind and the prickly pear cactus with is fine needle-sharp spines, "wherever we go, whatever estate I manage to buy, we've years of work ahead of us."

"We'd be better off buccaneering," Saxby said bitterly. "There's no call for honest work and honest men these days."

"Buccaneers are no better than pirates," Yorke said.

"No, sir, beggin' yer pardon, they are." Saxby stopped walking and, partly because they were walking over the crest of a hill which gave them a good view of the bay, Yorke stopped too.

"I'd like to say this to you out o' hearing of the others, sir, but buccaneering is something I knows about, and you're wrong."

"Why, were you ever one?" Yorke asked curiously.

"No, sir, but although you didn't know, they've called of a dark night at Kingsnorth to visit me."

"What? Do you mean to say you had – well, pirates – on my property without me knowing?"

"Yes, sir. And I'm glad I did. You'll see you ain't no call to be angry, if you'll just listen to me for a few minutes, sir."

'Very well, but let's sit in the shade of that divi-divi; it's hot here, even though there's a breeze."

They sat but had to move hastily to another tree when they found they had chosen a nest of red ants, several of which had crawled into their clothing before being noticed. Ned and

Saxby slapped themselves vigorously and then sat down again, giving the soil a precautionary stir with their feet.

"Now tell me about the buccaneers."

"Well, sir, will you forget all about pirates."

"That's hard to do in these waters."

"I know, but just think about us. Why we're here. Why we're sitting under the shade of a divi-divi tree."

Yorke shrugged. "Well, we've had to escape from home."

"Ex-ackerly!" Saxby exclaimed, giving his knee a clout which sent up motes of dust which rose in the bright sunlight like tiny insects, "ex-ackerly. Take half a dozen people on board the *Griffin* and trace back why they're there. Just six. You name 'em, sir."

Yorke thought for a minute. "You. Mrs. Judd. Bullock. Me. Mrs Wilson. Yes, and Mrs Bullock, because she married him after she came out to Barbados."

"Very well, start with me. Father labouring on a farm in Lincolnshire, and me working alongside him. Pressgang takes me for a sailor. Suits me – better a life at sea than hoeing rows of 'taters and spreadin' muck.

"But I get tired of it and desert. I settle down on land – not far from where I was born. The war comes and I'm in the King's army. Big battle, I get taken prisoner by the Roundheads, but refuse to serve with them. So I'm a special prisoner now. Royalist and Catholic, they said. *Me* a Papist! Anyway, I'm transported to Barbados in the next ship. So I've had me country taken away from me. I'm no Papist but if Protestant is what the Roundheads are, then I'm no Protestant either 'cos I can't see no sin in laughing and wearin' bright clothes. Not that I want to wear bright clothes; just that I want to be able to if I feel like it."

Yorke nodded but, curious, asked quietly: "You can be absolutely honest now. How did you find life at Kingsnorth, eh?"

Saxby pushed round to face him. "Been the finest time of my life. You've left me alone. No special church services like on many of the plantations. No spyin' to see I'm working and keeping the apprentices at work. Now it's all over, destroyed once again by the Roundheads, and that's the story of one of the six."

"Now tell me about Mrs Judd."

"A fine woman," Saxby said. "I don't know whatever became of Mr Judd, if he ever existed. But she was the housekeeper in the house of some big landowner near Oxford. Banbury, I think it was. Anyway, there was a lot of fighting there, round the house, too. Her master – a Royalist – was away with his troops and she was at the house with the wife and four young children.

"Cromwell's army – well, not his, but under some other Roundhead general – arrived and marched into the house, demanding to know where the master was, and helping themselves to the silver plate. One of the children – the eldest boy, seven I believe he was – tried to stop them and they started beating him. Mrs Judd came out of the kitchen with a meat cleaver and would 'ave taken the soldier's 'ead off, if 'e 'adn't been wearing an 'elmet. So she's sentenced to transportation. We meet in the same ship."

"It's none of my business," Yorke said, "and there's no need to answer. But why have you never married her?"

"To make an honest woman of her? Well, I've asked her enough times but she likes to feel free."

"Free? To do what?"

Saxby gave a dry chuckle. "Well, I'm talking out of turn, I expect, but I thought everyone knew. When we get a new lad as an apprentice, Mrs Judd likes to – well, sort of try his mettle!"

"Good gracious! Well, I suppose that's a good idea. What happens to the ones that don't measure up?"

"The other women 'ave a try."

"Kingsnorth seems to have been something of a brothel!"

"Not really, sir, don't cost a penny, and young men and young women – well, I –"

"Quite, as long as they remember their indentures are lengthened if the women get pregnant."

"They know," Saxby said. "Anyway, who's next?"

"The Bullocks."

"Ah yes. He's a good example. Scottish, as you've guessed from his voice. General Fairfax's army caught him. He refused to change sides, so he's transported. His wife – he met her out here and they married as you know – comes from Gloucester. She was married to a yeoman farmer. The Roundheads took against him, saying he'd no respect for the

Lord's Day. There was some violence and blows were struck. He was killed and she half killed the soldier that did it. They put her in the Bridewell for a year and then transported her. So she hates Puritans like the Devil hates holy water."

"I'm next," Yorke said. "What about me?"

"You'll come into Judge Saxby's summing up, sir 'cos we know the details. There's just Mrs Wilson left out of the six."

"Yes, tell me about her."

"Well, first off, sir, we all hope you'll marry her!"

"There's the matter of her present husband!"

Saxby sniffed, like a schoolmaster dismissing a pupil's excuse. "We won't be going back to Barbados . . ."

"We might, one day," Yorke said mildly, adding: "But anyway, the lady in question considers herself still married."

"Bullock was right," Saxby said firmly.

"About what?"

"Well, it was his wife, too. Said they ought to have left Wilson for dead."

"And his widow regarding me as his murderer?"

Saxby nodded glumly. "There's that to it, I suppose. Anyway, let's consider her. French Protestant, a Huguenot refugee whose parents were chased out by the Papists. Settle down in England, buy some land, treat their people well. The war starts and she has the misfortune to meet that man Wilson, who frightens them all into thinking they'll lose everything to Parliament if she doesn't marry him. If she's his wife, he can protect her . . ."

Yorke had never heard that before. "Was that what happened?"

"So I hear. Mrs Bullock heard it from Mrs Wilson one day – the only time she ever mentioned it, but he'd so knocked her about there was talk of getting the surgeon."

"Go on, then."

"Well, her family really supported the King but Wilson frightened them. And, in a trice, from what I hear, had her married and everything in his name, the parents' land as well."

How little he knew her, Yorke realized. He loved her, he knew every gesture, look, habit – every hair on her head. But he knew almost nothing of how she and her family had been robbed by Wilson. She had never complained – never mentioned it or even hinted at it. Refused to leave the man for – how long? He had been begging her for three years, and she had agreed now only because she had been almost kidnapped by himself and the Bullocks.

"Saxby," he said sternly, "we have wandered a long way from the subject of buccaneers."

"Ah, that's where you're wrong, sir. We've just considered six people who are very typical of hundreds of people among the Caribbee islands at present."

"Typical? In what way?"

"We've all got the same thread running through us, like a bit of cloth. Rebels, sir, that's what we are. Or leastways, we've been *made* rebels, by our own country. None of us can go back. Not even Mrs Wilson, on account of she's a Huguenot.

"Outcasts," Saxby corrected himself, "not rebels. Nor are we alone. What about the Dutch? I'll tell yer, sir. The Spaniards 'ate 'em. Millions and millions of golden dollars they've spent on their army in the Netherlands, and still the Dutch ain't beat. Then there are the maroons, too."

"The what?"

"Cimaroons, I expect you call 'em, sir. They're seamen put ashore on an island because the master doesn't want them, either because they've misbehaved or he's cheating 'em out of their wages. And escaped slaves, too, as well as the apprentices who've been bolting over the years."

Yorke sighed. "What has all this to do with buccaneers, Saxby?"

The foreman looked as though he would have apoplexy. "They *are* the buccaneers, sir."

Yorke sat up sharply. "How can they be?"

"An outcast with a ship – you, sir," Saxby reminded him, "– has to live somehow. He might be lucky to get a crew as you did, but more likely he has to pick up who he can. So he might find some English who escaped after being transported (and risked execution by moving before their term was up), some Dutch who've had their ship captured and sunk by the Spaniards, some French Protestants who came out here to find peace but were followed by the priests, some cimaroons, and a dozen escaped slaves."

"And you dare tell me that such a mixture makes a good crew?"

"Aye, sir. They live well together because they've learned tolerance. But they don't all serve in ships."

"What do they do, then?"

"Well, they go to one of the big Spanish islands like Puerto Rico, or Hispaniola, or Cuba. Very few Spaniards live there now, you know."

This was a new world being revealed to Yorke, and he found it hard to believe. "Very few Spaniards?"

"Yes, sir. You see, they started off many years ago in Puerto Rico, looking for gold. No luck, so they went on to the next island to leeward, Hispaniola. They found some gold but not much and went on to Cuba, where they found a little more. The point is they abandoned one island and went on to another."

"Then they found Mexico . . ."

"Ex-ackerly, sir: gold beyond what any man could ever dream of. And everyone – nearly everyone, anyway – quit Puerto Rico, Hispaniola and Cuba and rushed to Mexico after the gold, leaving all their cattle and asses behind them."

Saxby said that as though he had answered all the riddles that could ever be devised about buccaneers, but Yorke said obstinately: "I still don't see what that has to do with buccaneers."

"Sir," said Saxby, "there are no wolves, snakes, wild dogs or nothing in those islands. There weren't *nothing*. No cows, pigs or sheep, until the Spaniards arrived. But it happens – and you know this is true of Barbados, too – cattle and pigs flourish here. Once the Spaniards came, Puerto Rico, Hispaniola and Cuba became huge farms. No enemies – only men who killed them to eat. Then suddenly most of the men vanish to Mexico and leave these poor beasts in peace, and they breed at a fantastic rate."

"Buccaneers, Saxby . . . the sun's getting high, and we seem to have chosen a divi-divi that's going bald."

"Yes, sir. Supposing you was one of a group, and all you wanted out of life was peace and quiet and *enough to eat*. Where would you go?"

"Cuba, or Hispaniola, and chase those cattle and pigs."

"Ex-ackerly, sir. You'd have meat to eat, fat and hides for

clothes and for trading, and all you'd need would be some powder and shot."

"Which you trade for hides from some passing Dutchman."

Saxby grinned happily. "Now you understand why they've gone westwards, to Hispaniola and Cuba. What's happened mostly is that they've gathered in groups of five or six. They find a nice bay with savannah behind. They build a canoe – they learned that from the few Arawak Indians left, hollowing out the trunk of a mahogany tree – and use it for fishing.

"They tan the hides and store the tallow and lard as best they can, and when they see a ship they row out in their canoe, taking hides and lard, and trade them for powder and shot – and hot waters, too; they're great drinkers.

"But they don't harm no one. They're called 'cattle-killers'. They don't attack the ships – the canoes are too small, and anyway the passing ships supply all they need. The Spanish, though – that's a different question. The Spanish hate them and hunt them down whenever they have cavalry to spare. But Hispaniola and Cuba have long coastlines, Puerto Rico nobody cares much about. Too small and easy for the Spaniards to patrol."

"Yes, I can also see why the Spaniards are so alarmed by them," Yorke said thoughtfully.

"They've no need to be. What good are these islands to the Dons? All they want is gold and silver, and that comes from the Main, not the islands. From Mexico, and down in the South Seas. Anyway, that's the cattle-killers. The buccaneers are a bit different."

Yorke realized that Saxby had a far greater knowledge of the Caribbees than he had given him credit for. Few people still called it the North Sea, to distinguish it from the South Sea, which lay to the south of the Isthmus of Panama, because it led to confusion with the North Sea in Europe, but clearly Saxby had a good working knowledge of its problems, dangers and – possibilities.

It would bear a few nights' consideration before deciding where to buy an estate. They could go ahead and careen the *Griffin* here, and by the time her guns and cargo were restowed, and the ship was ready to sail again, perhaps he

86

would have a clearer idea himself. There must be no mistake: the plantation he bought would have to be the right one.

He turned to Saxby. "How do the buccaneers differ from the cattle-killers, then?"

"The buccaneers go out and *fight* the Spaniards," Saxby said. "They 'ate 'em."

Chapter
Seven

Aurelia ran an affectionate finger up his arm. "You worry so much about where your new plantation shall be that you become *très sérieux*; a 'man of affairs' from the moment you wake until you go to bed. Anyway, you do not intend settling on this horrible island."

"But it is very important," Ned protested. "After all, nearly fifty of us will have to live on whatever plantation I find. Live *from* it, too."

"I begin to hate the idea of staying in one place," she said quietly. "Like the fly – he is safe while he is flying, but the moment he lands on something: bang! A human squashes him or a lizard catches him." Her face was curiously taut, as though the smooth skin had suddenly shrunk so that her cheekbones were bloodless and more pronounced, her mouth a narrow line.

"Do you want us to be like a fly, then? Just sail round in the *Griffin*?" He said it banteringly and was not prepared for her answer.

"Yes. We all want to. All except you, that is."

Startled and shocked, he stood staring at her. It was as though an abbess had suddenly admitted urgent carnal desires. "I suppose you think that selling off sixty tons of sugar is going to keep us in provisions for the rest of our lives? Well, sugar sells for a penny a pound, and there are 2,240 pounds in a ton, so you can see how much we'll get and you can work out how long it will last." He sat down heavily in the chair, still not sure he understood fully what she had just said.

Aurelia smiled at him, then stood up in the new pearl-grey breeches Mrs Judd had just made for her, a perfect match for a russet jerkin which had been the previous day's contribution by Mrs Bullock. She bent down and kissed him. "Edouard," she said, "I wish I would never again hear the word sugar. Anyway, Mrs Judd is going to buy some oxen and boucan them for the voyage."

"What voyage? What are you talking about?"

Aurelia looked at him innocently. "Surely we are not staying long in Antigua? You said you do not like it or its governor."

"Well, yes," Ned said lamely. "But 'voyage' is a large word. We shall simply go over to the other islands – why, some are in sight. Montserrat and Redonda. Nevis and St Christopher are only just to the north, and St Bartholomew and St Martin."

"When do we sail?"

Ned gestured to the *Griffin,* lying hauled over on her side, with men scrubbing at the exposed hull.

"Well, we've done one side, and they'll finish this by tomorrow. But then we have to get all the provisions and cargo back on board and stow them, and the guns, powder and shot."

"I shall be glad to be back on board and anchored away from the shore," Aurelia said. She looked round at the sacks, casks and boxes, and the cannon which had been placed in a half circle, protecting the ship and her gear and crew from an attack from the land. "This is how I think life must be in the army."

"Something like it, but unless we protect the bottom of the ship we will get the ship borers eating the planking."

"I find it hard to believe there are those worms in the water," Aurelia said.

"You'll believe it when you see termites destroying furniture and wooden houses. Termites and white ants. Why did you have the legs of your tables and chairs resting in metal dishes of water?"

"Oh yes, Edouard, do not take me too – how do you say, too literally. It is just that as I sleep at night I can imagine the worms chewing the wood and I think of the ship suddenly falling apart and sinking!"

"Have you ever heard of a ship doing that?"

"Well . . . no." She slapped at mosquitoes on her wrist. "But I think I shall fall apart from the insect bites."

She was silent for a few minutes and then said: "You did not say if you liked me in breeches and jerkin."

"Buccaneers, borers and breeches!" He looked round to make sure no one else was in earshot. "You don't own a dress to compare with those breeches. Why, now I can see you have legs! You have knees and ankles!" Then, with a touch of bitterness in his voice, he added: "I must be grateful for these hints at the real Aurelia."

"The 'real Aurelia' is not just a body . . ."

"No, but –"

His reply was interrupted by Saxby, who came bustling up to report: "They're here!"

"Who are 'they'?"

"General Venables' recruiters. They're marching round the island beating drums and calling for volunteers."

"They're not pressing men?"

"No, sir. From what I've just heard, the governor's refused to allow them to send out pressgangs. They can only call for volunteers."

Suddenly Yorke's opinion of the governor rose. Last week he had seemed an indecisive man, and had not given the impression of understanding Yorke's news of the forthcoming expedition. But now he had emphasized the island's neutrality by limiting the call to volunteers.

"Where is the ship?"

"Round at St John, sir. I'm told they went there because most of the plantations are up that way, along the north coast."

Yorke gestured at the surrounding ring of steep hills. "Nothing for them here."

"Except us, if they could send out pressgangs."

Yorke pointed to the guns. "I doubt if they'd risk those!"

"They could bring their ship round!"

"Yes, but would they, for forty men, risk damage as well? Those guns would be turned on their ship."

"No, I suppose not, sir," Saxby said, realizing for the first time that Mr Yorke had worked all that out when the *Griffin* first arrived in the bay.

"Saxby, this may be our only chance of finding out what Penn and Venables intend doing, and when. Those recruiters – I am sure they spend their evenings drinking and wenching in St John. Supposing you and someone else join them tonight for a few hours. Some free rumbullion should loosen some tongues."

"Aye, I'll take Bullock and we'll hire a couple of mules from that fellow in Falmouth village. A bullock going to town on a mule . . . what if Mrs Bullock wants to come, sir?"

"Let her. She'll add an air of innocence to the proceedings!"

At dawn next morning, as Yorke supervised the group of men climbing down on to the raft they had made from logs, he heard singing in the distance. He paid no attention as he made sure the men had heavy scrapers and scrubbing brushes, and helped haul on the ropes to position the raft near the bow where they could get at the remaining part to be done. The weed stank after a day's exposure to the sun; sweet and rotten.

By the time he was on shore again, where a couple of men had fires lit for Mrs Judd and her women to start cooking breakfast, the singing was nearer and louder.

Mrs Judd eyed Yorke, and said disapprovingly: "That Bullock woman is singing bawdy songs!"

He listened a few moments. "All three of them are."

Aurelia, who was passing and heard his words, said: "Four people are singing."

Both Yorke and Mrs Judd listened carefully and there was indeed a fourth voice, a man's and a good baritone.

"If they think they're going to stagger in here blind drunk and get a meal, they'd better think again," Mrs Judd declared piously. "Into the water with them: a sea bathe will help sober them up *and* get the dust and sweat off them."

Yorke went over to a soapberry bush and wrenched off a handful of fruit. He gave them to Mrs Judd. "You can be in charge of the bath-house!"

"A good scrub won't hurt that Bullock woman. Nor Saxby. Here!" she called to one of the women, "can't you see that pot's boiling over?"

Saxby and Bullock were drunk, but the fifteen-mile mule

ride from St John had begun to sober them up. Mrs Bullock, however, was clutching a bottle as though it was her most valued possession, and had obviously dosed herself frequently on the journey back.

"Refreshin' walk over the hill after we gave the man his mules back," she told Mrs Judd. "An' you stop lookin' at my bottle. Good Holland gin that is."

"Into the water with you," Mrs Judd growled. "An' you can take off that fine dress 'cos you've tore it round the back. Yer bum is stickin' out!"

Mrs Bullock's eyes widened as her free hand explored behind her. "You're right! Must 'ave done it when I slid off that mule. No wonder that bloody mule man was laughing."

Saxby lurched over to Yorke shamefacedly. "Sorry, sir, I'm afraid we overdid it."

"Not if you can remember what happened." He pointed to the sea, lapping quietly at the edge of the almost white sand. "Perhaps a bathe . . ."

"Ah," Saxby said doubtfully. "We're a bit overheated this minute. Perhaps in an hour or two, when . . ."

"Now," Yorke said. "Don't worry about those old wives' tales. You know I've swum every morning for four years at Kingsnorth."

Faced with a direct order, and proof that at least one man had survived daily immersion in the sea, losing all the natural oils from the body, and getting the hair wet, which must be harmful, Saxby lumbered down the beach, unbuttoning his jerkin.

"Perhaps you'd better turn the other way, ma'am," Mrs Judd said to Aurelia, who laughed and said: "I wish I was swimming, too!"

Mrs Judd nodded approvingly. "Me too, and I'd make a splash, though they do say it's bad for you."

Aurelia lowered her voice. "No one ever knew, but every day I swam for half an hour just at dawn. It's a wonderful feeling!"

"Well, you took no harm," Mrs Judd commented. "Maybe I'll start it. What about sharks, though?"

She looked herself over, imagining sharks chewing at her ample body, like dogs attacking a bullock carcase after the butcher had finished with it.

"I never saw one and I never heard of anyone attacked. The men used to wade in with nets to catch fish. They often saw a shark and screamed and ran on shore, but I'm sure they are harmless."

"Tell me, ma'am, can you actually *swim*?"

Aurelia nodded. "Not very well, but enough."

"How far, then?"

"I swam a few hundred yards a day. By then it was getting light and I was afraid someone would see me."

"Is it good exercise?"

"I think so. It always made me feel fresh."

"Reckon it does a lot for the breasts," Mrs Judd said with a frankness that made Aurelia blush, "because I ain't never seen bosoms like yours, beggin' your pardon. Perfect, they are."

At that moment Yorke came back from the beach, having seen that Saxby and the Bullocks were in the water.

"What are perfect, Mrs Judd?"

Aurelia turned away in embarrassment, but Mrs Judd said: "I was talkin' about these eggs I bought in the village."

She pointed at a wooden bucket filled with eggs, and asked: "Who's that fellow they brought back?"

"A deserter from the ship that's arrived to get recruits."

"Why did he desert?"

"I don't know yet; none of them are sober enough yet to talk sense."

After their sea bathe the three men and Mrs Bullock were still drunk; the water was too warm to give them a sharp shock. Instead it made them drowsy, and Yorke told them to sleep in the shade of the bank of sea grape trees separating the band of sand from the land.

Four hours later a shaky Saxby came over to apologize yet again.

"I'm sorry we were so drunk, sir, but we did the job."

"I hardly expected you to spend the night drinking and stay sober," Yorke said to reassure the foreman. "What did you find out?"

"Well, sir, they – the general and the admiral – had plenty of trouble in Barbados. It started in England, when the storeships carrying provisions and artillery were due to be loaded in London and the transports for the men at Spithead. Seems the storeships were so delayed joining them that the troops sailed for the West Indies from Spithead without them. They were all supposed to meet in Barbados but the storeships still haven't arrived."

"So Barbados is having to supply provisions?"

"Much more than that, sir. It's not just food and water but more than half the muskets, pikes and swords for the army. Half the men have no arms."

"How many soldiers are there?"

"We were told fifteen hundred, and Cromwell's commissioners — whoever they are; they include one or two people from Barbados — have to supply another three thousand from the islands."

"Do they expect to be able to do that?" Yorke asked.

"No sir. Not only that, at least a thousand of the men they brought with them from England are the sweepings from the streets and the rubbish from the jails. The jails were cleared of all men except murderers. Taken straight out to the ships they were, without a minute's instruction with pike or musket. And now their pikes and muskets are still in the London ships!"

Yorke thought of men who had spent months, perhaps years, in dark, verminous cells suddenly put on board ships and brought out to the tropics. They would bring cholera and typhus; they would meet yellow fever, agues, blackwater . . .

This was how Cromwell sent a sample of his New Model Army to fight its first foreign war. "Ironsides" he called them, but obviously these were rusty.

"So what is happening in Barbados?"

"Platoons of troops are marching the length and breadth of the island to the beat of drums, calling for volunteers but seizing anyone they can lay their hands on. Ships have gone to Montserrat, St Christopher and here to get men. The smiths in Barbados are working overtime hammering out pikeheads while the carpenters are making staves. The general tried to confiscate all the sporting guns and muskets on the island, but they suddenly vanished, so now he is trying to buy them."

"When is the expedition to sail?"

"Officially it's only waiting for the storeships to arrive, but the tavern talk is that it will wait until the end of next month – before then the winds will be too strong along the south coast of Hispaniola."

Yorke groaned and Saxby nodded. "Yes, sir, any Spanish agent, even if he's deaf, will know that the landing is planned for the end of March, and Santo Domingo is the target."

"Half of Venables' men will have fallen sick by then," Yorke said bitterly. "Anyway, how many have they found here?"

"Four hundred, most of them disgruntled apprentices, and the rest those who have good reason for leaving the island without too much attention – debtors, bolting husbands, men breaking the terms of transportation. The governor will be glad to be rid of them: in fact he's emptied the jail."

"And this man you've recruited . . ."

"John, sir: he's a sturdy fellow and a good seaman. He was the armourer in one of Admiral Penn's ships, and the fact is, sir, we need someone like him. Not many of us really understand those big guns."

"I doubt if we'll ever have to use them."

Saxby glanced up at him. "No, sir, I hope not, but we can't be sure, can we?"

"Did you find out anything about the other islands?"

"Yes, sir, but nothing that helps us. Barbuda, that's the small island just north of here, is no good for our purposes and has very little water. Dominica is still dangerous with Caribs raiding plantations so a man works with a musket in one hand and a hoe in the other. Montserrat can't make up its mind whether to back Cromwell or the Prince and anyway it's mountainous."

"No news of Nevis and St Christopher?"

"I didn't talk about them, though I believe they're the most likely. But –" Saxby broke off, as though nervous of going any further.

"But what? Come on, say what you think."

"I don't like to, sir, because . . ."

"Say it!" Yorke said harshly. "I don't have to agree with you, but I'll certainly listen."

Saxby swallowed and then took a deep breath, as though

he was going to dive to a great depth. "Well, sir, we was talking about being rebels and outcasts . . ."

"Yes, and we agreed."

"Yes, sir. Well, we're going to stay rebels and outcasts while Cromwell and the Roundheads are in power. Apart from you being out of favour, we got to think of the others."

"In what way?"

"The Bullocks for a start. Mr Wilson laid information with the Provost Marshal about you, sir, but we know you would have been arrested anyway when the fleet arrived. But he'll have laid information about the Bullocks, too. He's such a liar, that man Wilson, who knows what he said. Anyway, she did stick a knife in his back, so he has grounds."

"And I stole his wife!"

Saxby shook his head. "No, sir, you rescued her. I know Mrs Judd and her women wish it had been them!"

"We're all together now, for better or for worse," Yorke reminded him. "And you were shuffling your feet because you had something important to say."

Again Saxby took a deep breath, glanced across to where the men were careening the *Griffin* as though to remind himself that he was speaking for them as well, and said: "If it was me, sir, and I know it ain't, I wouldn't buy another plantation hereabouts. Not for 'undreds of miles. The Roundheads will soon control all these islands. Wherever you are, they'll 'unt you down. They'll confiscate a plantation you've paid good money for, and send you back to England as a prisoner of State."

"And you'll all starve," Yorke said.

"And we'll all starve," Saxby said, a hurt note in his voice.

"I was serious," Yorke said, realizing the foreman had thought he was being sarcastic. "But we don't have much choice. We've provisions on board for three months, and we've a cargo of sugar to sell, and I have a small amount of capital. And I have the responsibility of feeding fifty people, seven of them women. We can't live on fish, and without a plantation we can't live on our own produce. So, my dear Saxby, how do we survive?"

"Ever thought o' smuggling to the Main, sir?" he asked, with the same expression Ned had just seen on Aurelia's face.

96

Chapter
Eight

There were only four charts on board the *Griffin,* carefully drawn and coloured by hand, and all four produced by "William Wagstaffe, chartmaker", who had his business at the Sign of the Compasses in Mark Lane, in the City of London.

The first chart covered the English Channel, the second from the Chops of the Channel to the Canary Islands, the next took a voyager across the Atlantic to the islands stretching from St Martin in the north to Trinidad in the south, and the fourth covered the Caribbean sea from the eastern islands to the western tip of Cuba, the Isthmus, and the Spanish Main – the mainland westward from Trinidad.

As Yorke looked at the chart of the Caribbean, he noticed the dedication written in the ornate scroll at the top righthand corner. Unless he had been able to render Parliament some particular service, Mr Wagstaffe was probably no longer in business because he had, as was the custom, always dedicated a chart to an important person, choosing in each case a member of the Royal Family. For the Caribbean the dedication was to "His Royal Highness the Prince Charles" – the man now in exile in France and who would, if the monarchy was ever restored, succeed his dead father as Charles II.

The trouble with Wagstaffe's charts (a fault shared by all the others on sale) was that it made up in curlicues, plunging dolphins and splashing cherubs for what it lacked in physical detail.

Mr Wagstaffe had obviously never sailed among the islands himself; he relied on information from ship-masters. Perhaps one day a master would point out an error which Yorke had spotted long ago – that the island of Grenade was drawn upside-down, but was given the English name of Grenada. Obviously Antigua was wrong because Falmouth Harbour, which was in fact a great bay, was shown on the west side of the island, not the south, and both Montserrat and Redonda, which could be seen from the entrance, were charted in the wrong positions.

If he had spotted these errors despite very little sailing in the Caribbean, Yorke wondered how many more there were?

Smuggling to the Dons . . . it was a good idea and he was angry with himself for not having thought of it. Still, it was difficult to forget all the standards drummed into him as a boy, when he had been taught that smuggling was unlawful. Then, he reminded himself grimly, England had made him an outcast and rated him a rebel, and England was at war with Spain. At least, he assumed she was, though, come to think of it, he did not recall a declaration. Anyway, declarations by either side were of no consequence out here in the West Indies because Spain was perpetually at war with any man or ship, let alone nation, that had the impudence to cross the Line. "No peace beyond the Line" – that was the slogan which was as frequently spoken in French and Dutch as English.

Smuggling goods into towns and villages along the Spanish Main was a crime only in the eyes of Spain. Everyone else, particularly the Dutch, regarded it as a normal way of business. Secrecy was necessary and, one assumed, certain safeguards against the Spanish preference for duplicity. But from what he had heard they paid up readily in dollars or pieces of eight, unless the smuggler wanted to barter, in which case they could offer hides, cochineal and tobacco.

He smoothed out the chart and looked up with pleasure as Aurelia came into the cabin. It was the only cabin in the ship and intended for the master or, if he was on board, the owner. In the case of the *Griffin,* where the owner brought a woman with him, it was now Aurelia's cabin, with himself and Saxby occupying hammacos in the space just forward of it. But it was the only place in the ship that had a smooth table suitable for a chart, and the charts themselves were stowed in a long drawer.

Aurelia looked over his shoulder at the chart.

"Where is Barbados?" she asked.

Yorke pointed to the island. "Kingsnorth is here – and that's Bridgetown."

"And Antigua?"

"Here – and this is the bay we are in, except that the men who drew the chart put it on the wrong side."

"What are these little numbers?"

"The depths of water."

"Where are we going?"

Yorke shrugged his shoulders. "Shut your eyes and put down a finger and we'll go there."

"It is probably as good a way as any," she said, laughing. With that she closed her eyes and touched the chart with her index finger. She opened her eyes and exclaimed: "I missed the islands!"

"Yes, you've just invaded the Spanish Main." He leaned over. "At Coro. It doesn't sound a very interesting place."

"One does not smuggle to interesting places," she said, a practical note in her voice. She examined the chart. "No other towns for miles and miles. What direction is it from here?"

Yorke pointed to the south-west.

"I'm sure the Spanish in Coro want sugar. Now let me think – what else? Cooking pots. No woman and no kitchen ever has enough cooking pots. Knives and forks and spoons – stupid servants are always throwing them away in the water they wash them in. Cloth for clothes – for men and women. Lace for women. Clay pipes for men. Boots and shoes. Saddles for horses. No, they will make their own, because you were saying they have hides. Perhaps they make their own shoes and boots, too. So no boots and saddles. What else? Think, Edouard. What do men need?"

"Women."

She blushed but gave an ironic curtsey. "Apart from them."

"Hope."

"There is plenty of that," she said quietly, "but patience is needed as well."

Ned picked up a slate and noted down the items she had mentioned. "We had reached clay pipes. Ah yes, flints for muskets and pistols."

"So the Spanish can shoot us?"

Now it was Ned's turn to go red. "Are you sure you haven't done any smuggling before?" he asked with mock suspicion.

"It's easy: just think of the things we have to buy from the Dutch. Beaver hats will be no good because a Spaniard walking across the *plaza* in an English-style hat would give himself away. What about kitchen knives, hoes, axes and rakes?"

"Madame, pause for a moment. We can only smuggle to the poor Spaniards – to the rich Spaniards, rather – what we have. At the moment we have only sugar."

"Do not underestimate that sugar *chéri*."

"I am not underestimating it! Why in England sugar is beginning to take the place of honey – at least, among the wealthier – and although the price of rumbullion is not as low as gin, very soon sugar will replace the juniper berry."

"But we are not selling our sugar in England," she pointed out.

"No, we'll be selling to the Spaniards. The Barbados price when selling to the Dutch is a penny a pound."

"That hardly gives us a price to charge the Spaniards!"

"No, but the Barbados price gives us a yardstick. Let's see what we can remember. An anker of brandywine, for example, was 300 pounds of sugar."

"And men's hats with brims were about 150 pounds. Thread – brown thread was about thirty-eight pounds of sugar a pound the last time I bought any. Thread stockings which sold for thirty-six pence in London were forty pounds of sugar a pair."

"The last pair of shoes I bought were sixteen pounds," Ned recalled, "although they offered me the so-called 'new fashion' at twenty-five to thirty."

"Good white linen was seven pounds a yard," Aurelia said.

"And horses – a poor one fetched 2,400 pounds of sugar and a good one 3,000. But the Spaniards are probably well off for horses, and they're difficult to ship: they fall and break legs."

"Walter said that a Dutchman with 100 guilders of commodities made 2,000 pounds of sugar," Aurelia said diffidently.

"Ah – that's what I heard. So we should be able to buy 100 guilders of commodities from them for 2,000 pounds of sugar, and smuggle it into somewhere like Coro and sell it for twice that."

"Why don't the Dutch do that, then?" Aurelia asked.

"Some of them do, but obviously they risk their lives and their ships. The choice for them is simple – a certain profit by safely trading among the British and French islands, or make double the profit at a very high risk trading on the Main. They have the choice, and we do not."

"We can buy a lot of things here in Antigua, or at the other islands," Aurelia said. "Particularly if we pay in cash and keep some of the sugar for the Spanish."

Ned started laughing. "I wish your father could see you now. Dressed in breeches – beautifully made by Mrs Judd and showing off your figure to advantage, of course – and one of my silk jerkins, and drawing up a list of goods as though you are the chief of the smugglers!"

She tapped the position of Coro on the chart. "Perhaps I am. I must say I feel like it, having chosen the destination and the goods we take. After all, *mon chéri*, remember that until now I did not even choose the day's menu . . ."

It was only through these occasional remarks that he was able to piece together a picture of what her life with Wilson had been like. One thing had become all too clear – that to compensate for his impotence he had done his best to humiliate her at every turn. His one mistake had been the Bullocks, who had been outstandingly loyal to Aurelia but had warned her that to help her they would have to appear to side with Wilson. So when Wilson sneered at Aurelia, apparently humiliating her in front of the Bullocks, she knew they secretly supported her. When he would force Mrs Bullock to agree that her mistress was a French slut, both women acted their individual roles but because Aurelia knew of Mrs Bullock's contempt for Wilson, his words had no effect.

"Where were you?" she asked shrewdly, noting his silence.

"I think you can guess."

"That is all over now," she ran her hands through his hair. "It happened to someone else, and she told me about it. And soon I shall forget even what she said."

Ned gestured round the cabin. "But this is no life for you. I want to dress you in fine clothes, have your hair brushed and combed and pinned by your . . ."

She gripped his hands. "You understand nothing, my love. I wait for the day when you can undress me; when you pull out the pins holding up my hair!" With her face crimson she ran from the cabin and Ned, who at least understood that, looked back at the chart. Coro was about six hundred miles to the south. Apart from avoiding some small islands and cays, it seemed easy enough to find.

Chapter Nine

Yorke was standing in the shade of a big kapok tree watching four men playing cards. The Trade wind was brisk, gusting round both sides of the enormous smooth trunk and blowing up the dust caught in the upper roots, which grew out from the cylindrical part of the trunk like the sinews at the back of a horse's hind leg.

The men cursed the gusts, which lifted the cards, even though they were heavy and clumsy, simply squares of thick leaf cut from the signature tree which, as its name indicated, acted as crude parchment, taking the impression of a sharp instrument and drying like stiff leather.

The four men had been carpenters before the Civil War and transportation carried them to exile across the Atlantic Ocean and put them to work at Kingsnorth, where Yorke was only too thankful to have skilled men available.

The four of them, with a couple of masons and half a dozen helpers, had built many of the outbuildings at Kingsnorth. In a peaceful England a good mason could earn half a crown a day, compared with anything between sixpence and a shilling for skilled labourers. In Barbados, transported men counted themselves fortunate to get half of that, although they were fed and housed.

Now, however, the four carpenters, two masons and half a dozen helpers were busy at a completely different task: they were building three boats – canoes, Saxby called them – to be used among the creeks and inlets of the Main. They were longer and beamier than the *Griffin*'s single boat, but they were much more lightly constructed so that they drew less water. Instead of oars they would be propelled by paddles – both Yorke and Saxby knew how cumbersome oars could be in a narrow inlet lined by the stiff tentacles of mangrove roots which grew like tortured rheumatic limbs up and down in the water, one slim branch growing off another at a sharp angle, and the second sprouting a third.

The canoes had to be fast, silent (an advantage paddles had over oars: a man crouched at the side of a boat wielding a paddle did not make the revealing creak of an oar in rowlocks), and capable of carrying a reasonable amount of cargo.

Antigua had mahogany trees, but none of the trunks had been sawn into planks, the planters preferring to buy planks brought in by the Dutch from the East Indies. Fortunately Saxby had stowed a two-handed saw, so he had gone off into the forests on the north side of the bay one day with his assistant Simpson, and found a good tree which had fallen in some storm two or three years ago – long enough for the wood to have seasoned but not long enough for the termites to have destroyed it.

Planking presented no problem: a dozen men with spades soon dug a pit lengthways under the trunk deep enough for the bottom sawyer to work, pusing on his end of the saw towards the top sawyer who was standing astride the tree.

The bottom sawyer had the worst task: the sawdust scattered down into his eyes and the wind did not cool him. Yorke realized he was fortunate to have four carpenters who happily went to work, two working briskly for half an hour and then changing places with the other two.

Saxby then produced a couple of adzes which he had kept stowed away in the *Griffin* for years, thickly coated in tallow to protect them from rusting. Three of the four carpenters had bellowed for joy when they saw the hoe-shaped axes and spent the next hour seeing which of them, standing on a fallen neem tree trunk, could chop the smoothest surface, using the adze as a gardener would hoe but slicing away thin slivers of wood.

With planks cut from the trunk, and some of the crooked boughs (with more cut from other fallen trees) used as frames, each canoe was built, looking in the early stage like a fish skeleton, the backbone formed by the keel and the frames rising like thick ribs at the bow and stern, the frames in between being lighter.

Saxby was in his element. Not a vain man, he found it satisfying nevertheless that he, a seaman turned plantation foreman, could also show carpenters how to build a canoe. The carpenters wanted to name the first one they launched after Aurelia, but she thanked them in a graceful little speech of refusal. She explained later to Yorke that the men had taken her by surprise and she felt superstitiously that if the canoe ever sank, she would die.

When they remembered that all four of them had been lodged in the Bridewell for three months before being taken to the London Dock and put on board a ship for transportation, they had asked Aurelia if she would launch their new vessel for them and name it Bridewell. She agreed, although it was customary, in England at least, for a man to launch a ship, using a bottle of port. When Ned warned her that the canoe was being called after the most notorious prison in London, she laughed and delivered an amusing little speech (cheered all the more because of her French accent, which delighted the men) in which she said they all owed a debt to the Bridewell because, she had been told, the accommodation was so good that only the most discerning guests stayed there while waiting to board ships for foreign destinations.

The second canoe was still being planked up when Bullock arrived back on board the *Griffin* from Falmouth village, obviously bubbling over with important news. He refused to stop to tell his wife and dodged round Mrs Judd's ample and inquisitive body as he looked for Yorke, who was up on the fo'c'sle.

"Sir, they've sailed, more than a week ago!"

Yorke smiled at Bullock's excitement and although he guessed the answer asked, to avoid misunderstandings: "Who have sailed where?"

"The fleet under Admiral Penn, sir, sailed from Barbados!"

"Bound for where?"

"Santo Domingo, sir. They're going to capture the city."

"And when did they sail?"

"Eight days ago from Bridgetown, sir. Their storeships haven't arrived from England but General Venables refused to wait and they are to join him at Hispaniola."

So Venables and Penn had been delayed by their storeships for – three months. From Barbados to Santo Domingo was some 900 miles. It would take the fleet about nine days, which meant that it was likely they would be attacking Santo Domingo tomorrow.

"Where has this news come from?"

"Oh, it's common knowledge, sir. General Venables sent a local sloop to deliver messages to Antigua, Montserrat and St Christopher saying that more men are still needed and they should be sent on to Santo Domingo. The governor here sent out a crier with the news but the only volunteer is a man lodged in the jail a couple of days ago because he killed his wife with a machete."

"He could be making a mistake," Yorke said soberly. "The gallows might be preferable to what Santo Domingo has to offer that expedition."

Saxby had arrived to hear the last of Bullock's report and Yorke's comment, and he agreed. "No storeships, which means no artillery or horses and no provisions and water beyond what the fleet carries, which won't last long. Not enough men and only half those armed until the storeships arrive. And once on shore, cholera and yellow fever will kill 'em off faster than the Dons because they're not used to the heat."

Although he knew Saxby was probably right, his judgement was coloured by his hatred of Cromwell and the Parliamentary forces, and Yorke could not forget they were Englishmen and but for the Civil War they might be fighting alongside the *Griffin*'s men against these same Spaniards.

"There won't be any Spanish privateers near," Saxby said cheerfully. "They'll either be making for Santo Domingo to see what pickings there are or, if they don't know the condition of the English expedition, they'll bolt home to the Main."

Yorke thanked Bullock and gestured to Saxby to walk aft with him, where they could talk undisturbed.

"How long before the last two canoes are ready?"

"The second will be finished within a couple of days and,

judging from the first one, will need to be in the water for three or four days for the wood to swell so that she takes up properly. Another week beyond that to build the third one."

When Yorke nodded, Saxby said: "Perhaps we could make do with two, sir."

"No – from what I've been thinking about smuggling, we must aim at unloading the goods as quickly as possible. The longer we spend in Spanish waters the longer we give them to decide to cheat or trap us."

"But they want the goods and they know if there's any cheating we won't come back, sir," Saxby protested.

"We are not the only smugglers. They could take all our goods, sink our ship, kill the men and put the women in bordellos, and who will know? A Dutch sloop could arrive the very next day, find there's no business because the Dons have just robbed us, and sail without any hint that there's been trouble."

Saxby was silent for two or three minutes. "You think it could be like that, sir?"

Yorke nodded. "The Spaniards simply want our goods. They'll pay if they have to, but don't forget that we are the enemy and because we don't share their religion we have no souls."

"No peace beyond the Line?" Saxby muttered.

"Yes, but remember that two men pointing loaded muskets at each other might just as well be unarmed."

"True – but supposing a third man comes along . . ."

"In that case, Saxby, we must make sure he is a friend of ours."

"But how do we do that?"

"How many boats would you, a Spanish harbour master, expect the *Griffin* to carry?"

"One normally, but two if she's smuggling, sir."

"But we shall have four, Saxby."

"If they see we have four, they'll be all the more prepared."

"Ah yes," Yorke said vaguely, "if they *see* them all."

"When shall we be sailing for the Main, sir?"

"You say the third boat should be ready in two weeks. By then General Venables will have attacked Santo Domingo and the word should have reached most places along the

Main, so the Dons there will assume they are safe . . . If we sneak in to a remote port a few days later . . ."

Choosing a destination by Aurelia shutting her eyes and touching the chart with her finger was, Saxby had explained with masterly tact, a very romantic way of doing it, providing her hand stayed well up to windward – at the eastern, or Atlantic end of the Main. But choosing somewhere like Coro, more than 600 miles into the Caribbean, and thus 600 miles to leeward, meant they were wasting 600 miles of the Main.

Saxby had asked Aurelia's permission to use the cabin and with her and Yorke watching, he had unfolded the chart and described to the *Griffin*'s owner, who made no claims to seamanship beyond knowing how to sail the *Griffin,* that their life was now governed by a single phrase, "keeping to windward".

With the Trade wind blowing generally from east to west, from the Atlantic across the Caribbean towards Mexico, and with it being so easy to run with the wind astern and so difficult to fight in the opposite direction, beating to windward, they must begrudge every yard lost to leeward.

"Look at it like this, ma'am," he said to Aurelia. "Think of it as the side of a hill. This bit here –" he pointed to the line of islands running north and south and almost touching the coast of the Spanish Main at Trinidad "– is the top of a hill. All this –" he moved his hand westward, towards Panama and Mexico "– is going downhill. The farther we get downhill, the harder the climb to get back up again."

Aurelia nodded, glancing at Ned as if to reassure him that she was interested. "Yes, Mr Saxby, I understand. Is there not a special phrase for it, when you are at the top of the hill?"

"Yes, ma'am, that's 'having the weather gage'."

"So we should begin with the 'having of the weather gage'."

Ned smiled and said: "It is easier to say we should 'have the weather gage'."

"Very well, we have this gage, and then . . .?"

"Well, ma'am, we don't know what prices we'll get, nor what sort of reception we'll find, so my idea would be to call at a small place first, right up here –" he pointed to a town marked on the chart as Carúpano, a town on the south side of a bay. "You see, we'll be approaching from the north, at right-angles to the coast. These islands, Los Testigos, are about forty miles off the coast, but we can find Carúpano because of the mountains." He pointed at the chart. "Here is Carúpano, but look, these peaks are high. La Carona is inland and one side of the town; San Jose is the other, and both are about the same height. Then Puerto Santo, not very high, and a headland, Punta del Taquien, are just west and will tell us if we've gone too far."

"Why choose this particular town?" Aurelia asked.

"Well, it is a nice big bay. There's a headland at one end of the bay and a small island at the other. Carúpano itself lies in a valley between two streams – something else that will help us to identify it. But don't forget, the canoes may be landing in darkness."

"Supposing we find Spanish ships there?" Ned asked.

"We turn and come out again. But I don't anticipate any. Fishing boats perhaps, but nothing else. And no other port for –" he measured two spread fingers against the latitude scale "– fifty miles either side. So from there we can gradually work our way westward – there's a thousand miles before we get to Panama!"

Aurelia nodded and then turned to Ned, looking puzzled. "*Chéri,* there is something I do not understand. I understand very well when Mr Saxby explains 'the weather gage' and I understand the wind blowing always to the west, and the trouble it is to make a ship go against the wind . . ."

"Yes, my love," Ned said encouragingly when she stopped, her brow wrinkled as though she felt she should know the answer but did not, and was embarrassed to ask the question.

"Well, as we go along the coast and selling our cargo, the Spanish pay us in gold, or perhaps exchange hides and tobacco . . . that is correct?"

Ned nodded and waited for her to continue.

"So eventually we reach, say, here –" she pointed to where the Main curved round and dipped south to Panama "– and we have sold all our cargo, and in its place we have gold, or silver, or hides, or tobacco . . ."

"Or a mixture of them all, ma'am," Saxby said helpfully.

"Yes . . ." she said it doubtfully, so that it sounded like "Ya . . . a . . . s". "But we cannot go back to Barbados or Antigua or any of these islands for more goods, because Cromwell's men will seize you, and we can't sail to England for the same reason. All we have is money. So where do we go next."

Saxby and Yorke stared at each other in dismay.

"I'm damned if I know, beloved." He kissed her full on the lips. "Don't blush; Saxby and I are the ones who are blushing."

Chapter Ten

Yorke had been pleasantly surprised to find that so few of his crew were seasick. The first voyage from Barbados to Antigua had revealed two men so sick that they were incapacitated, but his main concern, Aurelia, was completely immune along with Mrs Judd and Mrs Bullock. All three women displayed the determination in their characters in different ways, he noted, and it was as if they were too determined to be ill. Anyway, whatever the reason, Mrs Judd and Mrs Bullock kept their women busy in the *Griffin*'s galley so that the crew had regular meals.

They had sailed from Antigua and called at Montserrat, taking the risk that orders might have reached its governor to detain the ship, to supplement their selection of cargo, and then began the long voyage south towards the Main, keeping just distant enough from all the islands so that they could see them but were too far to the west to be spotted.

Slowly the latitude noted on Saxby's slate decreased. Sixteen degrees north, and that was Guadeloupe on the eastern horizon, with the mountainous box of Dominica to the south, followed by Martinique; fourteen degrees cut right through St Lucia, and then came St Vincent (with Barbados a hundred miles or so beyond); twelve degrees just scraped the southernmost tip of La Grenade, and then just ahead of the *Griffin* was the Spanish Main, with the island of Trinidad tucked in so close it was almost touching.

La Grenade was just dropping below the horizon astern when he and Saxby sat aft on one of the guns to have a final discussion about the simple but disturbing question asked by Aurelia. "Fact is," Saxby said, "we don't seem to 'ave much choice. It's like having one keg of rumbullion: when you drink that up, you go thirsty."

"Not quite," Ned pointed out. "More like the tavern keeper selling his last keg of rumbullion in mugsful. At the end of it he has an empty keg – but he has the money he charged for the drink."

"True . . . true . . . But what good is money? I never thought I'd live to hear myself ask that, but a man adrift in a boat could starve and die of thirst while sitting on five hundredweight of gold bullion."

"He'd be dying in style," Ned commented and waited while Saxby excused himself and bellowed an order to trim the mainsail better. The *Griffin* was sailing much faster with a clean bottom, but as Saxby had said within an hour or two of them leaving Kingsnorth, she was designed as a floating box that would carry the most cargo for the least taxes and dues, which were calculated on her various dimensions.

Once Saxby was sitting on the gun again, Ned said: "I think the Dutch merchants have two prices for their goods. Those who only trade among the islands have a comparatively low one because they take few risks, while those smuggling to the Main charge the Dons a high price because of the danger they run of being caught by *guardas costas* or betrayed by their 'customers'."

"That makes sense," Saxby said, "but I think they'll charge the high price in Puerto Rico, Hispaniola and Cuba too, because it's just as dangerous up there."

"Yes, by 'the islands' I meant these islands." He turned and gestured astern.

"So what you're thinking, sir, is that once we've got our money from the Dons we sail north again, find some Dutchmen, and buy more goods at the low price, and go south again to the Main and sell it."

"It seemed a better idea when I thought of it," Ned admitted. "Now you put it into words it doesn't sound so good."

"It's the margin of profit, sir, as you well know. Can we make enough profit buying from the Dutch at the low price and selling to the Dons at the high price? That profit has to feed us, keep the ship in good repair, and pay for the next consignment from the Dutch."

"If only we knew the difference between the high and the low price . . ."

"I don't reckon it'll be enough for us to live on, sir," Saxby said bluntly. "And I'll tell yer fer why. Like you say, the Dutch traders have got two alternatives, but I think it ain't just danger. Trading among the islands is selling a few pots and yards of cloth here an' a few pots and yards of cloth there, visiting p'raps six islands and three dozen anchorages. On the Main (no further to sail really, coming direct from 'Olland) they can probably sell a whole cargo in one town, unload in a night, collect their money or goods and sail straight back to 'Olland. There's a risk, for sure, but against that is the speed."

"So we are back with Mrs Wilson's question."

"That's right, sir."

"Wait a moment. What about that Dutch island just off the Main, five or six hundred miles along the coast. Curaçao, that's it. I wonder what they use it for."

"You mean, if we could buy goods there?"

"Yes."

Saxby shook his head. "They might have goods, but they wouldn't sell to us, and even if they did the price would be outrageous. After all, the goods have been shipped there from 'Olland in the first place, and Curaçao isn't above fifty miles from the Main. Dutch smugglers may stock up there, though I can't see there being too much of a profit even for them. Curaçao must be full o' middlemen, quarrelling with each other as they buy from the ships coming from 'Olland, and sell to them smuggling to the Main. That's assuming the ships from 'Olland don't go to the Main and do the actual smuggling – and the more I think about it the less I think they do: they'd be big; too much draught to creep into narrow and shallow bays and inlets on a dark night."

"Then we're wasting our time. We just sell the goods we have, and then hope something turns up."

"Like piracy," Saxby said.

"Seriously, would you be prepared to take up piracy?" Ned was startled at Saxby's matter-of-fact voice.

"Of course, sir. We all would – the crew, I mean, and the

women. Mrs Judd, for sure. Can't speak for Mrs Wilson, o' course, but I reckon she'll feel the same way as the rest of us."

"Which is?"

"That with every man's hand turned against us in our own country, we've got to make a living as best we can."

Yorke stood up and walked back and forth across the deck half a dozen times while Saxby took the new clay pipe he had been holding and began filling it with tobacco.

Piracy! Only three months – four, rather – had passed since the *William and Mary* had arrived in Bridgetown with a letter from his father warning him that the Kent estates were lost to the Roundheads at last and that Kingsnorth would be sequestrated. Four months since the same letter warned him that Parliament was also intending to have him arrested as soon as a fleet arrived under the command of Admiral Penn.

Yet within hours of reading the letter he had collected Aurelia, loaded his people on board the *Griffin,* and sailed. Fled, to be exact. Then only a few days ago he had accepted the fact that the only way for them to make a living was to smuggle to the Main. Now a closer examination of the word "smuggling" showed that it would eventually be spelled "piracy", although admittedly against an enemy of Britain.

There was only one person he wanted to talk with at this stage, and that was Aurelia. Other men might laugh and say he ran to the petticoats the moment he faced a problem, but apart from the fact that she now regularly wore breeches, Aurelia so far had proved shrewder than any of them.

He found her swinging in the hammock which they had rigged for her in the cabin after she complained that at sea sleeping in a bunk was like being a pebble shaken in a box.

She looked up at him and smiled impishly. "You and Saxby talk a lot but decide little, eh?"

Ned sat on the edge of the bunk and tried to look innocent. "What on earth could make you think that?"

"You talk together for an hour, and then I hear you walk back and forth, back and forth across the deck, like a dog on a rope. You forget it is just here –" she pointed to the deckhead above her hammaco. "Men with a contented mind do not walk thus."

"Why should I not have a contented mind? I have you with me, the ship, a good crew . . ."

"*Mon chéri,* unless you can eat me, or sell me, we both know we all have a limited time together . . . That was what you were discussing with Saxby."

"Yes," Ned admitted. "He and I have dodged the subject for a few days. I suppose each of us hoped the other would think of something."

"But neither of you did."

Ned shook his head ruefully. "No, not really."

"There is only one answer," she said calmly, much as she might announce they would have to eat white meat for dinner because there was no red meat left, and was apologizing that they were reduced to servants' fare.

"I know," he said. "At least," he qualified it warily, "we thought only of one. What had you in mind?"

"*Parbleu!* Piracy, my darling. If only you had a commission or letter of marque from the governor of Antigua, or someone like that, you could call it buccaneering and not feel guilty, but because you do not have such a letter you cannot legally be a privateer. So be a pirate. You had no other choice from the moment you sailed from Kingsnorth!"

"Did you realize that *then,* or are you saying it now just to tease me – or make me angry?"

"No, I realized it. I thought I might be wrong because perhaps there were things I did not understand about ships, but I was fairly sure."

Ned stared at her with admiration, love and awe tumbling over each other. "You knew that, yet you still came?"

"You mean, that I came, knowing that I might end up a pirate's mistress?"

"Well – yes. Although so far," he could not resist adding, " 'a pirate's housekeeper' might be a more accurate description."

"Come and kiss your housekeeper."

He stood up and walked over to her, having to brace himself and hold the hammaco against the ship's roll. As he bent his head she whispered mischievously: "Do all pirates have housekeepers?"

He kissed her and then said with mock ferocity: "No, they have mistresses!"

"They are the successful ones who can afford to dress them in ropes of pearls and gold bracelets!"

"As soon as I can afford it, I will dress *you* in ropes of pearls and gold bracelets. And nothing else!"

She blushed and looked away. "So you have an added incentive to be successful!"

The chart drawn and coloured by William Wagstaffe, chart-maker, gave very little detail of the coast of the Spanish Main: from Trinidad at the eastern end it showed a few islands lying offshore and belonging to Spain, then came Bonaire, Curaçao and Aruba, claimed by Holland, and then a huge gulf which turned into the Lake of Maracaibo. Saxby had been wise in choosing Carúpano as their first port of call. The islands of Los Testigos were a scattering of rocks and islands, some 800 feet high, forty miles short of the coast. Once the *Griffin* had passed Los Testigos, she had forty miles to run to reach the mainland, steering for the twin peaks inland of Carúpano.

Yorke examined the chart once again. Yes, if they managed to sell, say, a quarter of their cargo at Carúpano, then another seventy-five miles westward was Puerto la Cruz, with Barcelona five or ten miles beyond. All far enough from Cumaná, likely as not, to be free of *guardas costas*.

There was a knock at the door and Ned looked at Aurelia, who was lying back in her hammock embroidering. She shook her head: she was not expecting anyone.

The door swung open in answer to Ned's call and Saxby came in, squinting as he came out of the bright sunshine.

"They're the Los Testigos islands all right, sir," he reported, "and the visibility's clear enough that we'll pick up those peaks on the horizon afore its dark."

"No sails in sight?"

"Nothing, sir. Our guns are ready to be loaded and run out, but I'm not too sure about our gunners . . ."

"Well, we've done our best with them – you have and Burton has, rather. I wonder how many ships come up to this coast with their guns manned by sugarcane cutters, coopers, boilerhousemen, carpenters, muledrivers and masons?"

"For our sakes, let's hope all of them! Still, they've improved with pistols and muskets. A couple of hours a day at drill was worth it. Still, I wish we had more handguns – twenty pistols and twenty-five muskets for a ship, a launch and three canoes . . ."

"Don't put much faith in pistols: accidentally leave these wheel-locks spanned overnight and next morning the mainspring is so strained it won't spin the wheel fast enough to make the flint give a spark."

"Aye," Saxby agreed, "but if the men don't start off with them wound, they'll lose the spanning key, so the wheel won't make a spark anyway. And matchlocks are no good for this sort of work: the match goes out, or it pours with rain, or spray comes on board. . . ."

"Which is why they're better off relying on their cutlasses," Ned said. "They've used them long enough cutting cane that the blade is all of a piece with their arm. And with a cane cutlass, if you miss the first time you can strike again and again. With a pistol you can miss only once."

Aurelia looked up from her embroidery. "You sound as if you intend to conquer the Main, not bargain with the Spaniards."

Saxby grinned and said: "We've nothing to lose by not trusting 'em, ma'am. When you're supping with the Devil y'know, you take a long spoon. And we're almost in sight of the supper table at Carúpano."

No one paid the *Griffin* the slightest attention as she sailed into the Bahia Carúpano with the last of the daylight. Saxby anchored her a mile to the eastward of the town.

Aurelia, who had found the mountains of first Antigua and then Montserrat a welcome change from the flatness of Barbados, was delighted with this stretch of the Main, where long sandy beaches alternated with sharp cliffs, rounded hills beyond and tall mountains in the distance.

She stood with Ned after the *Griffin* had anchored and the men furled the mainsail neatly, but careful to leave the gaskets so that they could be thrown off in a hurry if they had to escape.

She stood close to him and held his arm, and whispered: "You are not going with the canoes, are you?"

It was a statement or a plea rather than a question.

"I must, dearest. No one speaks Spanish. I have a few words, and some French. I'll probably end up with Latin," he said, hoping to make a joke of it.

"I speak Spanish," Aurelia said. "I will come with you. I shall be the translator."

"No you won't!" Ned said firmly. "You will stay on board here with Saxby."

"But you need someone to speak Spanish. The whole thing is absurd if you go to bargain and cannot speak to them."

"We'll manage."

"All right *mon chéri,* as you wish."

Ned had been expecting a long argument and was thankful that she accepted that going on the preliminary of a smuggling expedition was work for men.

"If we manage to sell them a quantity of goods and they agree we unload in daylight, then you can come ashore to have a walk and look round."

"Thank you, *chéri.*"

"But you'll have to dress in men's clothes and wear a big hat."

"I'll grow a moustache, too," she said teasingly. "No, I will stay on board like the dutiful housekeeper."

Lights were appearing among the houses which formed the small town of Carúpano, far enough away to seem like fireflies. The wind had dropped with the sun and at this low latitude, only ten degrees north of the Equator, the darkness came suddenly.

Aurelia stood back as she saw Saxby coming up to Ned.

"Lanterns, sir: use them ordinary, or keep them hidden?"

"Ordinary – the Dons have no idea who we are: we might be a ship from Spain for all they know, though I imagine they assume we're Dutchmen."

Saxby said: "I'll get the first of the canoes hoisted out, then?"

Yorke waited a few moments. This first visit to a Spanish port was not how they had imagined it. They had sailed into an open bay at dusk and anchored as though their visit was usual. He and Saxby had originally thought of them creeping in like thieves in the night. No doubt as they worked their way westward, near the bigger ports, it would come to that, but here in Carúpano – what would make the best first impression, the *Griffin*'s regular boat or a canoe?

"I'll go in with the boat to meet the mayor, or whoever it is, and we'll have one canoe lying out a hundred yards or so with the pistols and muskets in case of trouble."

"Very well, sir: the boats' crews, then. Who will command the canoe?"

"What about John Burton?"

"I was going to suggest him, sir," Saxby said. "He's done wonders training our men – and the lady," he added, nodding towards Aurelia, "– with the small arms. He's about our best seaman, and he'll understand what he's supposed to be doing."

"So Burton it is. And a dozen men?"

"Five paddles a side means ten men, and if you need help from pistols and muskets, I'd like to see another ten men . . ."

"Twenty! We'll have hardly anyone left in the *Griffin!*"

"We need only a dozen or so – after all, we have Mrs Judd and Mrs Bullock!"

Ned laughed and said: "Very well, let Burton pick his men. He knows them all by now and he'll know who are the best shots with the coolest heads."

"Yes, sir, and I'll choose your crew myself. Six oars, bowman, boatkeeper if you need one. Eight should do it."

When Yorke nodded, Saxby said carefully: "I'd suggest that you go in without a light. Or, rather, you use a lantern with a screen across the front. It might be a good idea to arrive suddenly out of the darkness at the jetty and ask for the mayor. If they watch a boat and lantern coming in, you might find a crowd of rascals and vagabonds waiting for you."

"You're right. But have Burton and the canoe waiting as far away as possible, where he can hear me shout, but so no one on the jetty knows he's there. Tell him to watch out for local people fishing in small boats."

Yorke had a brief conversation with Burton while his oarsmen were climbing over the rope ladder and down into the boat. Burton was quite confident; he had chosen his men with care and had all the pistols loaded and in a skip which he was going to keep beside him. He would only wind up the wheel-lock mechanisms at the last moment.

"Five of us have spanning keys," he told Yorke, "just in case something happens to me, and of course the musketeers each have their own key."

"But the musket mechanisms are protected against spray or some clumsy work with a paddle?"

"Yes, sir: Mrs Judd and her women have made some cloth covers to go over the breeches."

"And Mr Saxby has given you your instructions?"

"Yes, sir. It's such a dark night that only people to seaward of us would see the canoe, just a dark patch against the lights of the town. I can't see fishermen noticing us, but even if they did they won't leave their lines!"

"And when we return, we'll hold up the lantern."

"Very well, sir."

Yorke went to the bulwarks, where Saxby assured him the boat was ready. He was disappointed that Aurelia was not there, but she might be superstitious about brief farewells, or embarrassed at kissing him in front of the men.

He scrambled down the ladder, stepped cautiously across the thwarts, careful not to tread on the oarsmen's feet, and took the tiller.

"Cast off aft . . . cast off forward . . ."

The six oarsmen rowed steadily and Yorke reflected that considering that they had been plantation workers until a few weeks ago, they had made the change to being seamen with gratifying ease.

There were few lights at the eastern end of the town, and like most of the others dim, as though they were rush candles showing through open windows. It was a hot night, becoming sultry, so few people would have the shutters closed. The cluster of lights indicated the centre of the town and then became fewer to the west. The town *plaza,* church and *alcaldia* would be there, and it was unlikely that the mayor, the *alcalde,* lived far from the town hall.

Now the lights were showing up the buildings and Yorke was surprised to find they were nearer in than he thought. The jetty, which he had seen in the last of the light, was simply a stone-faced structure running parallel with the shore. With a north wind the seas would smash any vessel alongside it. Still, tonight the highest wave must be a foot or less.

The oars creaked in the rowlocks and Yorke turned to look aft. There was no sign of the canoe. The *Bridewell* had been painted black and by now Burton's men would be paddling well to seaward of him. Suddenly he realized he could not see the outline of the *Griffin* and for a moment almost froze with a sudden loneliness. Would he be able to find her again? Then he recalled that waving the lantern in her direction would bring a response from Saxby.

He was beginning to realize the vast difference between a plantation owner who also owned a small ship capable of an occasional voyage to another island and, in an emergency, a voyage to England, and a buccaneer. He found himself using the word in preference to "pirate": if there had been a Royalist governor on one of the islands, he would have been able to get a commission, so that the *Griffin* became a legal privateer.

A sudden curse in Spanish, a black shape passing down the starboard side, and he realized he had missed by a few feet a rowing boat with a pair of Spanish fishermen sitting in it, tending their rods and lines.

"Bowman! Keep a sharper lookout!"

The bowman made neither excuse nor reply and Yorke guessed the fellow was as startled by the encounter as the fishermen.

Equally suddenly the jetty was almost alongside and three feet above them, with four more fishermen on top scrambling and cursing as they hauled their fishing lines clear of the boat.

The men on the larboard side just had time to lift their oars out of the way before the boat was alongside and he was thankful to see the bowman jumping on top of the jetty with a rope, followed by the boatkeeper, who leapt up from his seat just forward of Yorke. There was no doubt a series of correct orders to give at moments like these but Yorke contented himself with the knowledge that even if he gave them the boatmen would not understand them.

There were stone bollards along the top of the jetty and the bowman and the boatkeeper secured the painter and sternfast to them while Yorke scrambled up followed by the oarsmen.

By now the four fishermen, calmed down after their shouts of "Caramba", had walked up to watch, muttering to themselves and, Yorke suspected, realizing that the visitors were smugglers. Certainly they showed no fear.

Yorke walked over to them and asked a question which almost exhausted his entire Spanish vocabulary: *"Donde alcalde?"*

The four shadowy figures seemed to go into a conference with each other, repeating Yorke's words (precisely it seemed to him) but without comprehension. They appeared to try different emphases, as though tasting them. *"Donde* alcalde? Don*de* alc*alde?* . . ."

Suddenly Aurelia said in what Yorke guessed must be perfect Spanish: "Will you please take us to the mayor?"

The men, as surprised as Yorke, exclaimed: *"Una doña!"* and then, their natural politeness overcoming their surprise, bowed to her and said: "Yes, *señora,* please come with us!"

In the darkness they could not distinguish Aurelia: she stood among the oarsmen and Yorke knew she would be wearing breeches. The boatkeeper passed up the shaded lantern but Yorke decided that its light would only emphasize the weakness of his force, so he told them to keep it ready in the boat.

Already the fishermen were striding along the jetty, followed by the oarsmen, and Yorke had to hurry to catch up.

How had Aurelia joined the boat? She must have taken the bowman's place. No wonder they had nearly rammed that rowing boat and the jetty. As he strode along, he stumbled now and again because the surface of the jetty was uneven, and they had been at sea long enough that for a few hours walking on shore gave them the impression of climbing up a gentle hill that moved slightly. He thought of ordering her back into the boat – but would she be any safer there, with the bowman and the boatkeeper? He cursed as he realized there was only the boatkeeper: Aurelia had been the bowman, so only one person now guarded the boat instead of two. Or should he keep her with him, where he could watch her and where at least the six oarsmen could help protect her?

He had an uneasy feeling that her command of Spanish was their best weapon, and she would insist on coming on shore at each of the many towns and villages they had yet to visit.

The group ahead of him swung into what was obviously the town *plaza*. There was a small and shadowy building forming the landward side, and a large church opposite which had a door open and through which he could see some votive candles burning. There were houses on the other two sides and the fishermen were heading towards the centre house on the west side, one with a lantern on a hook beside the door.

Before Yorke could stop them, the fishermen were hammering at the door, shouting cheerfully a word which he could distinguish very clearly and understand at once. *"Contrabandistas, señor! Contrabandistas!"*

But it was immediately obvious that the fishermen were not raising an alarm; they were (too loudly for Yorke's liking) simply announcing visitors, and if the tone of their voices and general manner were any guide, not unwelcome ones either.

The door flung open and a stream of Spanish came from a small, paunchy man lit from behind by a candelabra in the room and from the front by the lantern hooked on the door frame.

Aurelia, broad-brimmed hat pulled well down over her face, stepped forward and spoke quickly. The man – Yorke guessed he must be the mayor – stood dumbfounded, his hands held out as if in supplication. Aurelia seemed to wait for him to answer and when he said nothing started speaking again.

By now the mayor was recovering from his surprise: his hands dropped to his sides, and almost immediately the right hand rose to tidy his hair and then both gave his moustache a twirl. As soon as Aurelia stopped speaking, he gave a deep bow, waved away the fishermen, and gestured for her to come into the house. She looked over her shoulder and Ned stepped forward.

She took his hand and pulled him through the door so that by the time the mayor was back inside the room she was ready to introduce Yorke.

The mayor assumed Yorke spoke Spanish and launched into a long speech which, from the number of times the hands gestured towards Aurelia, was in her praise. Once he had stopped, she said: "He welcomes us. He is surprised to meet a lady in such circumstances. I am of great beauty, he says, which shows what good eyesight he has since my face is almost completely hidden by this hat."

"It's the breeches," Ned said facetiously. "Spanish mayors delight in them – on women smugglers!"

Aurelia stood to attention as though she was an obedient member of the crew. "What do you want me to tell him about our business?"

"Tell him we have for sale sugar, an assortment of pots and pans, cutlery, farming implements. If he wants details, you know the items."

She launched into a long description, pausing every now and again as the mayor asked a question. Finally the man made a brief comment.

"He is interested in all the items, particularly those for the kitchen. They are very short of them here. He says the wives have been complaining."

"When was the last ship here?"

"Nearly a year ago: he mentioned it arrived on his wife's saint's day."

"Ask him when they want to come and inspect the goods. Not more than twenty of them on board at a time and we will collect them with our boats."

As soon as Aurelia translated that, the mayor started a furious speech, lifting his hands towards Heaven and clenching both fists as though he was thumping a table. Aurelia waited until he paused for breath and at once began talking to Ned, making it impossible for the mayor to resume.

"He will not agree to that. He says that if you take twenty of Carúpano's leading citizens on board, what is to stop you sailing off and ransoming them?"

The idea seemed so ludicrous to Ned that he laughed and was promptly reproved by Aurelia. "It is not funny," she said firmly. "The mayor is very concerned, and I think he has a right to be."

"Yes, yes, my love, I was laughing only because obviously *I* have a lot to learn about smugglers. Tell him I will land twenty of my people as hostages while his people are on board."

Aurelia translated, listened to the reply and said: "He says thirty because his twenty are important people and thus more valuable."

Yorke shrugged his shoulders with elaborate unconcern. "Twenty-five, and if he's not careful I'll include Mrs Judd."

Stifling a smile, Aurelia translated and the mayor nodded. "Do they want to come on board now or in daylight?"

The mayor suggested eight o'clock next morning, and then added casually that it would be more convenient if the ship came alongside the jetty: it would save so much rowing, because at least sixty people would want to buy.

When Aurelia told him that, Ned shook his head firmly. "Buyers can put their mark on the items they choose, and they will pay when the boats land them at the jetty. If the buyer isn't there to pay for his goods, they're taken back to the ship."

"Oh Ned," Aurelia said, "that is being *too* distrustful!"

"He wanted the ship alongside the jetty so his soldiers could seize it, my love, so don't be misled by his innocent expression."

Aurelia paused for a moment, absorbing Ned's words. "You're right," she said, "I missed the inflexion, but that is what he had in mind."

"Tell him the boats will put twenty-five of my men on the jetty as hostages at five o'clock in the morning and take the first twenty buyers out at a quarter past five."

"We agreed on eight o'clock," she reminded him.

"That was before he suggested the ship came alongside the jetty. The less time he has to think of more plots the better, so tell him the new time."

The mayor grumbled but eventually agreed, and finally Ned said: "Tell him that to avoid misunderstandings over who buys what, and the price, he should send out a man who will mark the names and prices on the goods."

When Aurelia translated the mayor asked suspiciously why one of Yorke's own clerks could not do it.

"To avoid any cheating. If the mayor's man makes the marks, all the Spanish buyers will accept them."

Again Aurelia translated, and then reported the mayor's answer. "He wants one of your clerks to do it – no, listen Edouard, I am sure the reason is that he knows his own people will not trust *his* clerk."

"Well, the buyer and Bullock can mark them together. Ask him if there is anything else."

Aurelia did so and told Ned the brief reply. "He says he assumes you will look after him."

"Look after him?"

"A bribe," Aurelia said patiently. "He wants payment for the risk he is running. After all, if the Spanish government heard about this, he would go to prison."

"How much?"

Aurelia asked and said: "He leaves it to you."

"Sugar?"

"He says it depends how much."

"Fifteen hundred pounds."

"He says that is not enough."

"That's the price of a poor horse in Barbados. Tell him I'll go no higher and we favoured him by visiting Carúpano first. Most ships won't bother with it."

That was a shot in the dark but as Aurelia translated Ned saw that it hit. The Dutch smugglers, he realized, obviously worked the ports much farther to the west, nearer to Curaçao, and rarely came as far to windward as Carúpano. If Ned walked out now and sailed, everyone in the town would guess that the mayor had been too greedy and, on the mayor's own word, the wives were grumbling over shortages.

Aurelia said: "He agrees only because his people are so short of goods. He will sacrifice himself. But he wants the sugar landed tonight, before business starts."

Yorke nodded: that was reasonable enough. The essential thing about a bribe was that it should be paid in secret.

"Very well. One last thing, though; tell him that payment for goods must be made in specie."

"Specie? Oh, you mean gold or silver coins?"

Ned nodded and she translated. The mayor began another long harangue, saying it was usual to trade some hides.

"No hides. No trading. Hides smell. And we'd take all night to decide on prices."

The mayor knew he was beaten and with a deep bow to Aurelia and a peremptory nod to Ned, indicated that he had to visit the town's businessmen to prepare them for their early start.

The bargain hunters of Carúpano may have had to leave their beds a good deal earlier than usual, but they were well dressed, with silk hose, ostrich plumes or bright feathers in their hats, and doublets covered with more lace than had been the fashion in England for fifty years or more.

Ned had expected the first twenty men to arrive in old clothes, protesting their poverty, and while they looked over the samples displayed on deck, commented about it to Saxby.

"Mrs Wilson," the master said succinctly. "They heard from the mayor about the lady who speaks Spanish. I'll bet each of them was torn between wearing old clothes to plead poverty, or wearing his best clothes to impress Mrs Wilson!"

"Well, we gain because we'll get higher prices!"

"Aye, but as soon as we get down to putting a price on whatever they've chosen, I'd be glad, sir, if you'd leave it to me and Mrs Wilson."

Ned looked startled. "Why, don't you think . . ."

"No, sir, and nor does Mrs Wilson."

"So you've been talking it over, then?"

"Aye, and Mrs Judd and Mrs Bullock too, and," Saxby said with a grin, "it was agreed you was a very nice gentleman but if we weren't careful, the Dons would – well, buy too cheaply."

"All right, you'll be the manager." He saw Aurelia and waved to her. "Saxby's been telling me what a good business couple you two make, so tell the Dons that Saxby's the captain. Then they'll know that his word is final; they won't come appealing to me."

"I shall be glad when they start business: starting before the sun is up . . . Brrr, I am so *cold!*"

There was a call in Spanish, and she and Saxby walked forward, to where a group of Spaniards were busy inspecting the goods under the watchful eye of seamen, with Mrs Judd walking among them. The enormous woman's effect on the Spaniards varied: some eyed her with longing, obviously speculating; others seemed nervous, as though unsure what could happen in a ship where women seemed to play an important role, and thinking it wiser to equate bulk with authority.

Ned went down to the cabin and swung himself up into Aurelia's hammaco. The thin feather mattress and silk sheet still held the impression of her body and although he intended to spend the time thinking over the *Griffin's* next move, he dozed off. He was woken by an excited Aurelia to find it was noon, the sun streaming bright through the skylight.

"*Chéri!* You sleep while Mr Saxby and I make such bargains! All our men are back on board, the money is collected – boxes of pieces of eight! – and Mr Saxby is looking for you because he is anxious to sail!"

Ned swung himself out of the hammock, shaking his head to wake properly, embarrassed to have the owner found sleeping when the ship was at anchor in an enemy port and with a score of the enemy on board at any one time.

"Are the goods landed?" he asked anxiously.

"Yes, just as you arranged. The buyers and Mr Bullock marked the items – Mr Saxby and I arranged the price – and after the buyers were taken back to the jetty the canoes took over the goods. Burton and Bullock handed over the goods and took the money."

Yorke nodded, annoyed with himself for having spent the whole of the time in Aurelia's hammock.

"Oh yes,' Aurelia added, "Mr Saxby decided the *Griffin*'s boat should be the treasury, so armed seamen sat in it while Burton handed down the money. And Edouard . . ."

Ned looked up: he recognized the way she said: "And Edouard . . ." It was always the preliminary to bad news or an unwelcome decision. "And Aurelia . . .?"

"The Dons thought we were Dutch and took great delight in telling us of a great defeat of the English."

Ned was not surprised: he guessed the news that Aurelia was going to give him. It was an expedition which could not hope to have succeeded. Untrained men not accustomed to the climate and without artillery, and half their small arms in the storeships which could still be in the London docks for all the good they were doing, would have been better employed cutting sugarcane than fighting well-trained Spaniards.

"You don't seem sad, Edouard – you do not ask what happened!"

"I don't need to. Penn and Venables attacked Santo Domingo and were driven off. Now they are trying to beat their way back to Barbados against the Trade winds."

"You are only partly right. According to the word

reaching Cumaná, the main port nearest here, they landed twenty or thirty miles past Santo Domingo, tried to march back to the city and their their camp was struck by cholera and thousands died. The fleet then sailed westward."

"West? *West!* Oh, perhaps they'll try to get back to England through the windward passage between Hispaniola and Cuba."

"The Spanish feared an attack on Hamaica."

"Hamaica?" he repeated, puzzled until he realized she was pronouncing the J of Jamaica in the Spanish way. "Why, Jamaica's a small island."

He took the Wagstaffe chart from the drawer. "Yes, here it is: west of Hispaniola and south of Cuba. What's the use of such a place? The Spanish from Hispaniola or Cuba can easily recapture it. Hmm . . . so that's all Cromwell gets for his great expedition! I'm glad I'm not Penn or Venables reporting that they picked one lemon when the Lord Protector sent them to get a whole apple orchard!"

"Apples do not grow in the islands," Aurelia said.

"Oh, madame, do not be so literal!"

"I am French. We are logical."

"Lovable, too, most of the time. But let me remind you that limes, lemons, oranges, bananas, tobacco and sugar did not grow here until the Spanish first planted them. There were no cattle, horses, hogs, asses or mules – until the Spanish brought them. Nor palm trees."

"Is that really true? No bananas? No sugar? No cows and sheep?"

"Quite true. No dogs either, nor poultry."

"Why did you not tell me before?"

Ned gave a short laugh. "Madame Wilson, you have forgotten that in three years' acquaintanceship in Barbados we were never alone, and your husband disliked any conversation of which he was not the centre."

She nodded in agreement. "Well, now you have a long time in which to catch up with my education."

"Are you ready for your first lesson?"

She looked startled but said yes.

"I love you."

She looked coquettishly at the back of her hands. "I learned that lesson long ago."

"How long?" he asked, suddenly curious.

"Oh – I don't know!"

"Try and remember – I want to know!"

"You will become unbearable!"

"Stop being French and so logical!"

"I think you fell in love with me when you first saw me. There, are you satisfied?"

He was, but he was hurt that she did not ask him a similar question.

"Edouard, you look so like a dog who has had his bone taken away. You want to ask when I fell in love with you."

Ned shrugged his shoulders. "Of course not. It is of no importance."

She laughed delightedly. "I love you when you sulk. But I do not need to think about it."

"Why? You do not care?"

"I know. I can tell you the exact date!"

"Stop teasing. I was serious."

"So was I. It was the seventeenth day of March, 1649."

Bewildered, he thought back. "How do you know that?"

"It was the day we first met," she said matter-of-factly, not asking for any confirmation. "But *chéri,* Mr Saxby is waiting for orders."

Chapter
Eleven

The Peninsula de Araya is a long finger of land running parallel to the coast, with occasional cliffs and headlands joined by beaches. Three small islets lying just offshore are low and bare, the centre one being white and the highest. The peninsula forms a banana-shaped gulf on its inland side and the port of Cumaná on the mainland makes the other side of the entrance.

Afterwards Ned and Saxby blamed themselves for not passing ten miles offshore, but they were anxious not to miss the little port of Barcelona, their next destination about twenty-five miles past the western tip of the peninsula and the entrance of the gulf.

They were not sure later whether the *guarda costa* had been lying in wait for them, hidden by the western end of the peninsula, or whether she had simply left Cumaná to look for the *Griffin,* no doubt warned by a messenger sent by the mayor of Carúpano who, with his bribe of sugar by now well hidden away, was anxious to show the captain-general of the appropriately named province of Sucre what a zealous fellow he was.

The *guarda costa* was a cutter smaller than the *Griffin* but mounting fourteen guns, five each side plus bow and sternchasers. She had a narrow beam, sweeping sheer and was built for speed: her role was to guard the coast against foreign smugglers and pirates, and her captain knew his job.

The moment Saxby saw the *guarda costa* coming out from behind the point he turned the *Griffin* up to the north, but it took time, and while Burton got his men to the guns the bulky ship had sagged down towards the *guarda costa,* which came alongside to fire her starboard broadside, stretched across the *Griffin*'s bow, and then ranged along the larboard side to fire her second broadside. She then began dropping astern, obviously reloading both broadsides.

While this was going on Aurelia, Mrs Judd and the other women were pulling the wounded away from the *Griffin*'s guns, which had yet to fire. Burton was bellowing orders, trying to get the men to work fast without making mistakes.

Saxby was standing by the two men at the huge tiller while Ned went to join Burton, who paused long enough to say: "Another couple of broadsides like that sir, an' we're done for. Our guns are so small we might as well be throwing bricks at him."

Ned went aft again to tell Saxby.

"Aye, sir, I didn't say nowt at the beginning, but Burton's right."

Mrs Judd hurried up. "Four dead, eleven wounded." With that report she hurried forward again.

Ned looked at Saxby. "A third of our people. Once Burton gets our guns firing we might . . ."

Saxby shook his head and looked astern as the *guarda costa* tacked across the *Griffin*'s wake, three hundred yards astern, and began bearing away slightly to come up alongside again.

"There's only one chance, sir. Order everyone below except me and the helmsmen!"

Yorke stood still, trying to work out what Saxby intended.

"Hurry, sir, for the love o' God; it's our only chance. Trust me!"

Yorke shouted the order. Burton called back, beginning an argument, but Saxby's bellow cut him short. Aurelia and Mrs Judd protested at leaving the wounded on deck but an enraged roar from Saxby silenced them. Within a couple of minutes the *Griffin*'s decks were empty of men: the guns stood loaded, slowmatch burned, but only Saxby, the two men at the tiller and Ned were on deck.

The *guarda costa* sliced up a bow wave that glittered in the sunshine like scattering diamonds and Ned watched her, knowing that this must be how a rabbit watched an approaching stoat. Whatever Saxby intended, he knew this was no time to interrupt him with questions, but sailing along like this with not a man at the guns seemed the same as surrendering.

Was that what Saxby intended doing? Now, the stocky figure was peering over the taffrail, watching the *guarda costa* and calling an occasional order to the men at the tiller, but he was planning some sort of trick, not surrender.

That was the only advantage of fighting the Spaniards. Against the French or Dutch one could, if completely outnumbered, surrender and know that as a prisoner one would be treated reasonably well. As a prisoner of the Spanish, the choices were the salt mines or the stone quarries for the rest of one's life, or being handed over to the Inquisition. Three alternatives to which an honourable death in battle was preferable. Which made him wonder what Saxby intended doing.

The *guarda costa* was approaching fast and he could see heads watching over the starboard side and the stubby black fingers of the guns poking out of the ports. The red and gold flag of Spain streamed out, and for a moment he wished the *Griffin* was flying her colours. Perhaps it was better that a ship and her crew without a country fought – if this was called fighting – without colours.

Fifty yards . . . forty . . . thirty . . . He could picture the Spanish gunners poised with their linstocks, ready to dab the glowing end of the slowmatch into the touchhole. Twenty yards . . . now the *guards costa*'s jibboom was level with them as they stood at the taffrail . . .

Suddenly Saxby darted to the tiller, yelling at the two men, and heaving against it with his shoulder. He screamed at Yorke to duck down.

The *Griffin* turned with what seemed to Yorke to be a curious mixture of maddening slowness and awful majesty right across the path of the *guarda costa,* whose jibboom and bowsprit came over the *Griffin*'s afterdeck like an enormous lance.

There was a scattering of guns firing, but Ned realized they were probably set off by gunners careless with their linstocks as they tried to avoid being flung down by the impact. Then he heard a curious crackling, like a tree collapsing under a woodman's axe, and he turned right aft to see the *guarda costa*'s bowsprit sliding off the *Griffin* as her mast slowly toppled over: falling sideways as though it had all the time in the world, with shrouds parting under the strain and sounding like horse whips and the great sail splitting diagonally and then flapping like a big tent collapsing.

Saxby's roar of triumph overriding the cheers of the two helmsmen brought Yorke back to the present: the *guarda costa* was lying dead in the water, her sails now fallen over her like a shroud, her mast in two pieces like a broken twig of greenwood, the stump still sticking up vertically from the deck but the rest in the water, an end held to the stump by rigging, halyards and sail.

More important she was being left astern while the *Griffin* slowly turned westward to run before the wind, her mainsail beginning to slam as Yorke ran to ease the sheet.

Saxby shouted: "On deck everyone! Come on, Mrs Judd, get back to your wounded!" Just as Burton led a rush up the companionway, he paused to look round for the *guarda costa* and was nearly knocked down in the crush of men and women doing the same thing.

Because of the height of the taffrail and the fact that the companionway they were using was so far forward, the *guarda costa* was out of sight for them. Burton ran to the larboard side and peered out of a port – and let out a cheer. Within a few moments the whole crew were surging aft, cheering Yorke, who promptly pointed to Saxby. "He did it; I had my eyes shut!"

Saxby was unimpressed by the cheering. "Get the wounded below and sew those dead men up in hammacos with a shot at their feet. All of you ought to be weeping, not cheering. Not a bloody gun fired by you – and the Dons hit us with two broadsides. Tinkers and tailors, that's what you are! Canecutters and sons of whores! I'd put you all back in the Bridewell if I had my way!"

As soon as he paused for breath Mrs Judd's penetrating voice came across the deck. "Any more of that Saxby, an' you sleep on your own!"

The threat was more than enough to silence the master, who bustled forward, calling for his assistant Simpson to come with him to inspect the damage.

Suddenly he was shouting again. "Carpenters, where are

those bloody carpenters? Quick, get below and sound the well, we might have taken a shot 'twixt wind and water and be sinking!"

"I've sounded," one of the carpenters said in an offended voice. "Just like you said after we've been shot at. Straightaway I sounded the well. You said –"

"What did you find, you whoreson?" screamed Saxby, thoroughly exasperated.

"None," the man said crossly, and Mrs Judd, bending over one of the wounded, lifted her head to deliver an ultimatum.

"One more paddywhack like that Saxby and your hammaco'll be as busy as a monk's cell for the rest of this voyage."

Grumbling to himself Saxby began to walk round the *Griffin*'s decks, noting shot-torn bulwarks, a dismounted gun, a deck scored deep by a roundshot that by chance came through the bulwark one side, gouged its way across the deck planks without hitting guns or fittings, and smashed its way out through the bulwark the other side.

Ned looked round for Aurelia, realizing guiltily that he had given her no thought from the moment Saxby had ordered everyone below. Now he saw her with Mrs Judd and the other women, bandaging the wounded while seamen waited to carry them below.

The only man on board with nothing to do, it seemed, was the *Griffin*'s owner. He walked aft and leaned against the taffrail, looking astern at the dismasted *guarda costa,* whose hull was now almost out of sight behind the swell waves pushed up by the Trade winds. Then he looked at the distant pearl-grey rippling mountains of the Spanish Main. He thought of Saxby's first angry words when the men began cheering them. The man was right: every one of them, Ned himself included but leaving aside Saxby and Burton, were a sorry crowd of canecutters who had no business at sea until they had learned a great deal more.

While the *Griffin* steered westward towards Curaçao she skirted a chain of islands which, lying more than a hundred miles off the Main and parallel with the shore, stretched for five hundred miles. Saxby was careful to note down the names as they came in sight. Most of them were uninhabited cays, some great rocks and others patches of coral and sand. His slate already recorded Isla la Orchila, Cayo Grande, Cayo Sale and Islas de Aves when he warned the lookout to watch for Bonaire. This, the first of the three islands used by the Dutch, was the one they would see before Curaçao, and by the time Bonaire was in sight decisions had to be taken.

The cabin appeared even smaller than usual. Aurelia swung in her hammaco, Ned sat crossways in the bunk, while Saxby and Burton sat on the cabin sole, their backs resting against the bulkhead.

None was cheerful; an hour earlier they and everyone on board the *Griffin* had attended the funerals of the four men killed by the *guarda costa*'s broadsides. Finding that in the rush to leave Barbados no one had remembered a prayerbook, Saxby had spoken as much of the funeral service as he could remember, and the hammacos with their now rigid contents had been slid over the side by tilting a plank.

Mrs Judd's report on the fourteen wounded had been more hopeful: only one was in any danger; the other thirteen had been cut by flying splinters and five of them would be able to work next day with bandages protecting the wounds.

Yorke had earlier visited the men in their hammacos and at first found them shamefaced at having been wounded while the *Griffin* had not fired a shot in reply. They explained that by the time they had lifted out the half-portlids, primed the guns (they had been left loaded) and run them out, the *guarda costa* was alongside and firing. It would not happen again, they assured him; once their cuts were healed they were going to practise and practise so that even a seagull would not pass unscathed. Burton, as armourer and gunner, and the man responsible for the training so far, was equally shamefaced and obviously, it seemed to Yorke, took the entire blame for the fact that they had been caught unawares.

"It's happened and we've learned our lesson," Yorke said, but Burton was not to be consoled.

"I should have advised you and Mr Saxby that the ship's company must be at general quarters when we're sailing past a headland like that. It's an obvious place for a trap. The fact is," he admitted like a small boy owning up to scrumping a neighbour's apples (Yorke was amused to find how easily the old Kentish word came to mind), "everything went so easily at Carúpano that I thought the Dons were glad to see us . . . They bought all they wanted and didn't haggle too much."

"It was that mayor, I'll be bound," Saxby growled. "Always beware of greedy people who smile: they're really only showing their teeth. He sent a warning to them at Cumaná."

Aurelia coughed delicately – far too delicately for Ned not to look up inquiringly. "I was thinking," she said gently, "that we know what happened and why, and we sold about a tenth of our goods at Carúpano for a good price. We are sailing westward, I know, but where are we *really* going? What are we going to do until we learn a great deal more about smuggling or buccaneering, or piracy – the name hardly matters? We cannot sail on and on . . . We lose the, *comment dit-on,* the weather page."

"Gage. Yes, you are quite right and you've put it fairly," Ned said. "It was no one's fault – certainly not yours, Burton, and but for you, Saxby, that damned *guarda costa* would have kept on circling us like a dog worrying sheep until she'd sunk us. If anyone's to blame, it's me – I own the ship and I started off on something about which I knew nothing . . ."

"I suggested smuggling," Aurelia said.

"And I proposed piracy," Saxby added.

"And I agreed to both," Ned said, "and no doubt if someone else had suggested barratry I'd have agreed to that too, though I'm not quite sure what it means."

"The master or crew stealing from the cargo," Saxby said.

"Hmm, it's not as bad as it sounds. Anyway," Ned said firmly, "from this moment any blame rests on me and no one else."

"No one answered my question," Aurelia observed.

Ned looked at Saxby. "Do you have any ideas?"

"None, sir. We could call at Curaçao and see if the Dutch will buy any of our goods."

"True, but once we have sold our goods we are back with Mrs Wilson's question of two days ago: then what do we do? Although we didn't answer the question then, we seem to have had it answered for us now."

Saxby looked puzzled. "I suppose so, sir, but . . . well,

what was the answer?" He shook his head like a bull confused by a small barking dog which would not be still for long enough to provide a target.

Ned looked at Aurelia. He found that more frequently he was turning to her not so much for advice as for comments and criticisms that showed a different point of view. Her womanliness and her Frenchness seemed to provide a calm logic that the rest of them lacked. Perhaps it was simply that she was a woman; the French logic was, in his experience, a cloak Frenchmen draped over themselves when they indulged in what anyone else would call sneering.

"We are not at war with the Dutch," she said. "Why should we not call at Curaçao and see what we can learn from them?"

"The mynheers don't give away owt for nowt!"

Aurelia's eyebrows raised at Saxby's comment and he gave a rumbling laugh.

"Owt for nowt?" she repeated.

Ned said, "Comes from 'aught for naught', but they pronounce it differently in the north of England. What he's really saying is they do not give away anything for nothing; they need something in return."

"They are good tradesmen!"

Burton said diffidently: "Perhaps it would help if we went in to buy something. We have spare money now!"

"Water is what we want," Saxby said. "Water and salt meat."

"The Dutch will be selling salt fish," Ned said. "They buy salt from the Spaniards, take it back to Holland, salt down the herrings they catch in the North Sea, and bring them back and sell it to the Dons."

"Fresh herrings," Saxby said wistfully. "Fried in a nice batter. This fish out here – no guts to it!"

"That is true, Edouard," Aurelia said, as though Ned was disputing it.

"Yes. The reason is simple. The colder the water the tastier the fish. All the fish you French catch in the Mediterranean is so tasteless you have to hide it in a strong sauce. Out here in the tropics it is much worse – most of the fish are utterly tasteless, and no one bothers with a sauce."

There is much about food that is beyond my understand-

138

ing," Aurelia said. "White meat and red meat, for instance. In England and out here, white meat is considered fit only for the servants, and red meat is for their masters. Why? I like poultry. A slice of turkey or a slice of beef – *pour moi* the white meat!"

"Me, too," said Saxby. "That's one of the reasons I prefer to eat with the servants."

"Ha – tongue seasoned with herbs, a kid 'with a pudden in its belly', a fricassee of pork, sucking pig, a loin of veal stuffed with limes, oranges and lemons," Ned said. "You'd exchange all that for a scrawny fowl?"

"Curaçao," Aurelia said. "Will we be able to buy water there?"

Saxby shook his head doubtfully. "From what I've heard, it's all flat and sandy, covered with divi-divi trees and goats, and it rarely rains."

"That's why the Spaniards don't bother with it, I suppose," Burton commented. "But there's no need for us to know they're short of water until after we've arrived. We can have a good look . . ."

Yorke nodded. "Very well, we'll go to Curaçao, but I don't expect the Dutch to reveal any of their secrets to us." He thought for a few moments, and then added: "I'm not sure there *are* any secrets. I think we went into Carúpano in the normal way. The Spaniards seemed to know what to do, especially the mayor. Had we been Dutch I don't think he would have betrayed us. Somehow he guessed we were English."

"Or French – from my accent," Aurelia said.

"Possibly, but it does not matter. The Dutch probably have the smuggling monopoly – or perhaps they will take goods in exchange, instead of insisting on money, as we did. The traders in Carúpano might have had warehouses full of hides."

Ned tapped the bunkboard with his fingers. "Yes, that's what we have to learn about smuggling: when to take cash and when to take goods in exchange."

Aurelia gave her hammaco a violent push. "You men!" she exclaimed crossly. "You should leave all this to Mrs Judd, Mrs Bullock and myself. You keep on talking about learning about smuggling, but you forget that even if you were the most skilful of smugglers on the Main, you have only one cargo to smuggle and nowhere else to buy more goods. Let me put it into simple language that a man can understand. You have an anker of brandy and you own a tavern, as I've told you before. You sell the brandy mug by mug, and put the money in your pocket. Soon the anker is empty of brandy but your pocket is full of money. What do you do then?"

She gave the hammaco another angry push. "You cannot buy more brandy because there is none to buy. You can use the money in your pocket to buy so much food, but after a month you have eaten it and you have no more money.

"Now, *mes gars,* what do you do? If you were in England you would end up in the debtors' prison. The Marshalsea, *non*? Well, you are in the Caribbee Sea, not the Marshalsea, but the problem is the same."

Saxby chuckled and said: "That was an old joke – a man pretending he was a seaman was said to have cruised the Marshalsea."

"Mr Saxby," Aurelia said sternly, "Mrs Judd, Mrs Bullock, myself and the other three women are determined to stay out of the Marshalsea or any Spanish, Dutch or French equivalent, so will you apply yourself to the problem."

"My apologies, ma'am, I ramble on, and certainly we do –"

"Mr Saxby!"

"Curaçao, ma'am!" the master said hastily. "To see what we can find out."

"I agree," Burton said hurriedly, alarmed at his first sight of Mrs Wilson being both French and determined.

"Me, too," said Ned. "So we are all agreed."

"Oh no!" Aurelia said. "You are thinking of Curaçao as a confessional! You go in, explain your problem, the Dutch priest tells you to say six prayers and pay a fine, and off you go. But *where* do you go? To the Marshalsea! There is nothing, nothing, *nothing* that the Dutch can tell you that will avoid that."

She sat up in the hammaco her legs out over the side and glared at Ned. She pointed a finger at him as though it was a pistol, her aim, Ned noticed, constant despite the rolling of the ship making the hammaco swing.

"You have the ecstasy of the bankrupt or the repentant sinner!"

"The what?" asked a startled Ned.

"Oh, I have seen it so often. The sinner goes to confession, gets forgiven, and walks down the road with a smile on his face and his heart full of fine intentions. The bankrupt is freed by a friend's charity, walks away from the debtors' jail with a smile on his face, the slam of the door music in his heart, which is equally full of fine intentions. The fine intentions disappear with the setting sun . . ."

Ned wondered how often she had forgiven Wilson for some vileness, heard him express "fine intentions" and seen them vanish at sunset. "Which are we, sinners or bankrupts?" he asked ironically.

"You have the sheepish look of both," she said, relenting slightly, "but you are bankrupts. You are bankrupt of ideas. If you had any ideas, you would be sinners – and that is something we would welcome!"

Ned looked at the other two men and shrugged his shoulders. "Apart from piracy, when we have improved our gunnery and shiphandling, I have no ideas."

"Nor me," said Saxby. "We need to drink some ale with these Dutchmen and see what we can learn."

Burton nodded, obviously relieved that Mrs Wilson was raising no objection.

Saxby and Burton were just leaving the cabin when an excited yell of "Sail ho!" came from aloft and the master pushed Burton aside as he pounded up the companionway, bellowing up at the masthead lookout: "Where away?"

Yorke arrived on deck to find Saxby staring over the larboard bow and then telling the lookout to shout down a description because the ship was not in sight yet from the deck.

Fifteen minutes later, most of which Burton had spent up the mast, it was established that the ship now coming into sight was a sloop perhaps half the size of the *Griffin* and probably making for Curaçao from the Main.

Saxby was taking no risks this time: the guns were loaded, the arms chests containing the muskets and pistols brought up from below, and Burton watched carefully as they were loaded and made sure each man had a spanning key to wind up the mainspring.

The strange sail was obviously behaving warily, careful to get across the *Griffin*'s bow so that she could not be cut off from Curaçao. Then she dropped her jib and partly brailed her mainsail, obviously waiting for the *Griffin* to come up to her, but ready in an instant to hoist her jib and let fall the mainsail and escape should the *Griffin* prove to be an enemy.

"We'll stay on this course," Saxby announced. "She's scared of us but curious. There's something about the shape of the hull that makes me think she was built in England. And that being so, I reckon she'll be thinking the same about us."

"Or could have been captured by the Spanish," Yorke said.

"Mebbe, but yon ship has paint on it. You don't see paint on a Don – leastways, not a little sloop like that, nor even a bigger one like this."

Chapter Twelve

The two ships, sails furled, drifted westward half a mile from each other, slowly turning like a pair of ospreys playing in the air currents over a headland. The boat from the *Pearl* was streamed by her painter from the *Griffin*'s stern and the five men and one woman who had rowed across in her were sitting or standing round on the *Griffin*'s low poop talking to Yorke, Saxby, Aurelia and Burton. Mrs Judd and Mrs Bullock made sure they stayed within earshot by busying themselves with various mugs of rumbullion and limejuice, though no one seemed to be very thirsty.

Yorke had stood back and let Saxby greet the visitors, while Burton had a dozen men below with muskets and pistols, waiting for his shout, but very ostentatiously no one was near the *Griffin*'s great guns. There was no hint that they were loaded.

The visitors were English and had accepted Saxby as the master, Burton as the mate, Simpson as another mate, and obviously did not know what to make of Yorke and Aurelia, whom Saxby had simply introduced as "Mr Yorke" and "Mrs Wilson".

When the four men and women had been introduced by their leader, Yorke was struck by the idea that the woman's role on board the *Pearl* might bear comparison with Aurelia's in the *Griffin*: she was English and, at a guess, came from somewhere no farther east than Hampshire and no farther west than Dorset. Like the leader who introduced her, she spoke clearly; meeting her in an English town one would assume she was the lady of the manor. Black-haired with deep brown eyes, she had wide sensuous lips that smiled easily, a tiny nose, a slim body that could become plump and a way of moving that missed being graceful because she moved too quickly. She was dressed in what could in London become a striking new fashion, Ned thought: her skirt had been slit vertically front and back and the edge of each half had been sewn together to make two tubes. It meant she could swing her legs over bulwarks and thwarts, or scramble up a rope ladder (as she had done before the Griffins realized she was a woman). On her, the divided skirt looked thoroughly womanly. What Ned found disconcerting was the upper part of her body: she wore a man's jerkin made of fine cloth, and there was nothing beneath it except herself, and she had the most prominent nipples that Ned had ever seen.

He was covertly looking at them when the leader repeated a question and Ned turned with a polite: "I beg your pardon?"

"I didn't hear your name when the master introduced us. My name's Whetstone."

"Yorke. Edward Yorke."

The man's eyes lowered a moment, as though searching his memory. "I knew a George Yorke once. About your age."

Were the waters of the Spanish Main a place to exchange confidences? Ned decided to wait.

"I've heard of a Thomas Whetstone, too."

The men laughed and the woman smiled, saying: "The scapegrace nephew of Oliver Cromwell, Lord Protector, regicide, warrior – and so on."

Whetstone, who Yorke now realized was Sir Thomas Whetstone, one of London's more notorious gamblers before the Revolution, smiled and, holding the woman's arm, said formally: "Miss Diana Gilbert-Manners, whom I have to introduce as my mistress because my wife is still alive in England and quite devoted to her uncle-by-marriage."

Aurelia had heard the introduction and Ned said: "Mrs Wilson – Aurelia – is French. Or rather was born in France. She sailed with us from Barbados."

At once he could have bitten his tongue: Whetstone nodded and said: "Now I place you! The Kingsnorth plantation. Your father is Ilex. Two estates in Kent. Your brother George is the heir."

"Thomas, be tactful," Diana said. She had a deep, rich voice compared with Aurelia's lighter and more musical tones, and she turned to Ned. "In these days, Mr Yorke, it's wiser to consider politics more carefully than armorial bearings. Mrs Wilson is obviously that wretched man Wilson's wife. He's a Parliamentarian. Are you?"

The question was direct but not threatening; obviously she wanted to get politics to one side so they could talk freely. Whetstone made no secret that he was Cromwell's nephew and Ned now remembered having heard that he left England because of debts but could not recall if that was before or after the Revolution. Anyway, it was more relevant now that, inexperienced as the Griffins were, the *Pearl* was too small to harm her.

"No, I'm not," Ned said quietly, and decided to tell them a little more so that Whetstone could be forced to reveal more about himself. "In fact my father refused to compound and he and my brother have gone to France, and an expedition sent out here under Admiral Penn and General Venables was supposed to sequestrate Kingsnorth and arrest me. So I left Barbados with those of my people who wanted to come."

"And Mrs Wilson?" Diana Gilbert-Manners obviously wanted to make no mistakes. "Pardon my bluntness, but we live in strange times."

Whetstone gave a dry laugh, gesturing at his mistress's skirt and Aurelia's breeches.

Aurelia answered while Ned was still thinking what to say.

"I loved Edouard from the time I met him, three years ago. I hated my husband from a few hours after the wedding ceremony."

The other woman nodded. "I understand. Some men become brutes when marriage vows make them masters. That is why I have Thomas under control!"

Whetstone looked impishly at Aurelia. "Mrs Wilson will not make the same mistake again!"

Aurelia shook her head. "I have not made the mistake, but I am still married . . ."

Whetstone's jaw dropped and Diana Gilbert-Manners

looked startled. "My dear," she said, dropping her voice, "do you mean that you and Mr Yorke – er, don't . . . er, aren't . . .?"

"No. Not until I can obtain a divorce."

"Or your husband dies," Whetstone said grimly. "I respect your scruples, but you wreck two lives, you know; your own and Yorke's."

Aurelia turned away. "Please," she said. "It is hard enough now . . ."

"Of course, of course," Whetstone said. "None of our business, but remember, dear lady, the Caribbee is not England; here we are our own lawmakers, judges – and executioners. Life can be cut very short. Hurricanes, the Dons, the gallows, the rack, rocks, drunken brawls: few men die of old age out here beyond the Line, madam. Seize happiness when it smiles at you, that's my motto."

Diana Gilbert-Manners had the glowing mixture of health and happiness that showed she both agreed with and benefited from Whetstone's philosophy. Whetstone, Ned realized as he watched the man talking, was a handsome man. A thick and roughly-trimmed square black beard and flowing moustaches certainly obscured his face but his mouth was generous, his brown eyes deepset with wrinkles at the corners which revealed a good sense of humour, and long black curly hair that was so neatly dressed that Ned guessed it was his mistress's pleasure to comb it.

He wore a loose jerkin but instead of breeches and hose he wore the short frock, or circular apron, which had been popular with seamen half a century ago. His legs were bare from the knees down, heavily tanned like his arms and face. And that, Ned realized, was what was so fascinating about Whetstone's mistress: unlike the white women of gentle birth who lived in the tropics, she was deeply tanned: her face, neck and shoulders. And, because he could not see any white line starting, Ned suspected the rest of her body too; certainly her breasts.

Aurelia was beginning a slight tan; the sun reflecting up from the sea came under the brim of her hat, and despite Ned's suggestion that she let the sun tan her face naturally, she had all the upper-class attitude towards tan: only servants were tanned because they worked in the fields.

However, as Whetstone had just said, out here the old rules did not apply, but it was going to take Aurelia a long time to accept that. It was a pity that Diana Gilbert-Manners and Whetstone would not be around to help start her re-education.

Whetstone coughed, a well-modulated cough that indicated that what he was about to say came outside the boundary of normal polite conversation but that he knew it and Ned was not obliged to answer.

"I get the impression, Yorke, that you ran the plantation and that this man Saxby —" he nodded at the master, who was over on the other side of the deck talking with the rest of Whetstone's party "— is the master of the ship, and you have few experienced crew."

Ned nodded but said mildly: "Does it show as clearly as that?"

"No, not really, providing you are simply trading between Barbados and Curaçao."

"What makes you think we are not?" Ned asked out of curiosity.

"You have been in collision within the last few days —" he turned and pointed to the starboard quarter "— and that gouge across your deck was caused by roundshot which came through one bulwark and went out of the other. And I've seen four men with bandages."

"That shows we have been in action, but surely not that we are inexperienced?"

"There are other shot holes, but I note your guns have not been fired because the paint inside the bulwark is not scorched. That means that some ship — a Spanish *guarda costa*? — fired a few broadsides and then collided with you, presumably because you made a mistake that she did not anticipate."

"Thomas! Apologize at once!" Diana Gilbert-Manners was angry with him now.

"No, ma'am," Ned said, "there's no need. He's quite correct except for the last part: Saxby ran across the *guarda costa*'s bow, so she lost her jibboom and bowsprit and that brought her mast down."

"So thanks to Saxby you lived to tell the story," Whetstone commented grimly. "But what were you doing so close to the Main? The Dons normally stay within sight of the coast."

Ned told him of their smuggling visit to Carúpano and the *guarda costa*'s trap off Cumaná.

"Yes, that's an old trick," Whetstone commented. "The mayor makes a profit both ways. They don't do it to the Dutch, who seem to have the smuggling monopoly along the Main, and the Dons need their regular calls so they can dispose of their hides and coffee and tobacco. And salt, of course: salt mined by all their prisoners. Don't get captured off the Main; it's terrible working in those salt mines. Not salt pans, where they let in sea water and wait for the sun to evaporate the water and leave the salt behind, but deep mines. Like coal mines. The deposit of centuries."

"You sound as if you are speaking from experience!"

Diana Gilbert-Manners' hand gripped his arm as Whetstone said quietly: "I am. I'm one of the few who ever escaped alive."

"We never take Spanish prisoners," Diana Gilbert-Manners said, in the sort of tone she might have used to say that they never drank Spanish red wine.

"What are you doing now, then?" Aurelia asked.

"Buccaneering. The Spaniards call it piracy," Whetstone said with a mirthless laugh.

"This is privateering, then? You have the commission, or letter of marque?" Aurelia asked.

"One could call it 'privateering' out of politeness, dear lady, but I do not have a letter of marque – who is there to issue one to a Royalist nephew of the Lord Protector? More to the point, to whom would I show it? Who would bother or dare to ask?"

"I wish to ask you a question, Sir Thomas, but do not feel obliged to answer. But first I must ask Edouard's permission. Forgive me for a moment." She whispered for several moments to Ned, who nodded several times. "*Alors,* you know already we are not very experienced smugglers, and our next attempt could be our last. When your ship came in sight, we were all debating – well, what the future held for us."

Whetstone held his mug upside-down so that Mrs Judd could see it. She bustled over with a jug and poured rumbullion until Whetstone told her to stop, and when he said he would like limejuice with it she bellowed for Mrs Bullock, who hurried over with another jug.

"'Ow about you, dearie?" Mrs Judd asked Diana. "You ain't drinking."

"Thank you, no; I leave it to the men."

"Very wise. Once they get a skinful you can make 'em do anything!"

Whetstone gave a bellow of laughter and Diana said cheerfully: "I learned that lesson at my mother's knee!"

As soon as the two women had moved away, Whetstone said: "When did you leave Barbados?"

"About a week before Penn and Venables arrived."

"Where did you go?"

"We had a look at Antigua and then Montserrat."

"Why?"

"In case I could buy a plantation. It was a silly idea, but my father's letter telling me he and my brother were going to France and warning me to get away was a shock."

"Bad place, Antigua," Sir Thomas said, shaking his head. "Wrong type of men go there. Like all the rubbish that drifts into one corner of a harbour. Then what did you do?"

"Well, we decided to try smuggling. We had the sugar loaded at Kingsnorth, and some trade goods I bought in Antigua. We went into Carúpano, told them we'd trade only for cash and did good business."

Whetstone nodded. "That's why the mayor betrayed you. His people were left with goods they normally exchange, and he guessed you were English and new to the game. But after you've sold all your sugar and trade goods, what then?"

"That's what we are trying to decide," Ned said. He was cautious enough not to say that with the ship full of money but empty of goods, they had no idea when Diana looked at Whetstone and gave a jolly laugh that made her breasts vibrate in a way that made Ned suddenly thankful, for his own peace of mind, that Aurelia's jerkin was less revealing.

"Oh Thomas, all this is a familiar story, eh?" she exclaimed.

Whetstone nodded ruefully and explained. "I left England with the *Pearl* and Diana. My debtors were proving very insistent. Diana had money which she was quite prepared to spend on my welfare but she adopted quite a callous attitude towards the fate of the debtors."

"What he means," Diana said, "is that I paid for all provisions and trade goods for the *Pearl* and the wages of her crew for three months –"

"Why three months?" Aurelia asked.

"You'll see in a moment," Diana said. "Then, having a pretty shrewd idea from Thomas what his Uncle Oliver was planning, we embarked my family at Portland and took them to France with their most treasured possessions. Now you continue, Thomas."

"Well, I signed on men that I selected very carefully. I wasn't concerned if he was an escaped murderer, a lawyer, a counting house clerk or a pickpocket – they all have much in common, of course – but I was very careful with seamen. I made it clear we were bound for the West Indies and they'd be paid for three months. After that, I told 'em, we'd all be earning our own pay, and it would make them rich men or see them launched over the side sewn up in a hammaco. I was careful signing on seamen because I didn't want any sea lawyers arguing at the end of the three months."

"Did you have any?" Ned asked.

"One."

"Tell them, Thomas."

Whetstone looked embarrassed. "We were somewhere south of Barbados when this fellow starts grumbling. We had not yet begun buccaneering but we'd met a couple of buccaneering ships and had good news from them. Well, this man really starts causing trouble and came towards me one day with a knife screaming he was going to kill me. I must say I believed him, and so did the rest of the crew."

"Thomas, finish the story!" Diana said.

"There's not much more to it. Before he could get to me a couple of men had grabbed him and slung him over the side."

"Did you have any more trouble with him?" Ned asked.

Whetstone shook his head. "We didn't stop."

Diana saw the shocked look on Aurelia's face. "You must understand, my dear, that one bad man can infect the crew. Our men knew that and threw him over the side. Remember, out here you face yellow fever, the Spanish and mutiny. All can kill you, if you let them. We have stayed alive because Thomas has a loyal crew – and is a successful buccaneer."

Whetstone tapped Ned's arm. "Believe me, success is the best protection!"

Aurelia asked the question just as Ned was trying to phrase the sentence. "What is buccaneering really? Is that an indiscreet question?"

"Buccaneering . . . well, earlier you mentioned a letter of marque and I don't have one, so what we're doing I suppose is piracy. It's legal if you have a letter (sometimes it is called a commission), and illegal if not. But that's not important: just remember that if the Dons or yellow fever catch you, they kill you, whether you have a commission or not. Anyway, let's call it buccaneering.

"Buccaneering really means some English governor or other gives you this commission to make war on the country's enemies – I nearly said 'the King's enemies' – at your own expense and using your own ship. We're at war with Spain, so a buccaneer, or privateer, can capture Spanish ships and cargoes and bring them into an English port where the Admiralty court considers it all and condemns the Spaniard as a prize to the buccaneer."

"So then you sell the ship and cargo?" Ned asked.

Whetstone gave a bitter laugh.

"In the old days, the court charged various fees, the judge had to be paid, and the King had a percentage, and you had what was left: you sold ship and cargo, ransomed the crew (or let them free) and that was that."

"What is different now?" Aurelia asked.

"Madame," Whetstone said heavily, "your friend and I share two things in common. We have superb tastes in the women we love, and we are Royalists. Pray tell me what English Admiralty court today will listen to us, and legally condemn our captures as prizes? Can you imagine those Roundheads in Barbados? Or Antigua? Or Surinam? That is why I have no commission, or letter of marque. That's why what I do is called piracy. And why Diana said we act as our own judge out here . . . When we've fought a Spanish ship and captured her, we hardly need an English Admiralty court judge to charge us a fee and tell us she is Spanish and our prize . . ."

"So what do you do?"

"Capture the Dons' ships, sell their cargoes to the Dutch (who smuggle them to the Main and sell 'em back to the Dons), and often we sell the ships to the Dutch too, if they are not too badly damaged."

"So you were on your way to Curaçao when we came in sight," Ned said.

Whetstone glanced at Diana, his eyes asking a question. She thought for a few moments and then nodded.

"No, we weren't going to Curaçao. Or rather, we were calling in for water and to pay some bills and collect money owing to us. Then we were going to make a long passage."

Both Ned and Aurelia stood closer to each other: there seemed no doubt to either of them that what Whetstone was going to say would greatly affect their lives.

"Before I tell you where we were going, I must give you some news. It reached Curaçao last week and there is no doubt about it: a Dutch ship saw some of it and shipped three deserters who told them the rest.

"Penn and Venables did not capture Hispaniola; in fact they never reached the capital. They landed in the wrong place and marched towards Santo Domingo. The Spaniards chased 'em off and they went back to where they landed and camped. It rained and rained for days – and the storeships with their tents and supplies still had not arrived from England. Within two weeks, five thousand were dead from cholera.

"The gallant admiral and the gallant general knew that the Lord Protector would find it hard to believe they could be so stupid; he would suspect treason. So, knowing that the island of Jamaica had once been taken by a single privateer, they decided to capture it with their fleet.

"It is a small island south of Cuba and west of Hispaniola. Anyway, off they went, and since they outnumbered the Spanish by about fifty to one, they captured it. So Jamaica is now English."

Aurelia murmured: "All those poor men dead from cholera . . ."

"My uncle emptied the jails of England to supply the men for that army," Whetstone said bitterly. "I don't know which is worse – to rot in England from jail fever, where your only crime was to be in the Royalist army, or to die of cholera in the pouring rain in a field in Hispaniola."

"Your voyage?" Ned prompted.

"Ah yes. Seeking new pastures, really. We have raided the smaller towns along the Main and ransomed the leading citizens so often that the government in Spain has sent out a dozen or more *guarda costas* – you've already met one.

"But if we use Jamaica (or the Caymans, some tiny islands not far away) we have hundreds of miles of the Cuban coast to raid, quite apart from Hispaniola and Puerto Rico. Places that have heard only gossip about privateers!"

Whetstone's eyes were lighting up as he thought about it and his arm had gone round Diana's shoulders. "Ransom and still more ransom! Ten thousand pieces of eight for archbishops, five thousand for bishops, and for mayors and tradesmen, according to the size of their business. Why, for a couple of years we won't have to fire a broadside at another ship! Just improve our musketry and buy some more pistols, and another grindstone for sharpening swords and pikes – remind me when we get to Curaçao," he said to Diana.

"But Jamaica . . ." Ned said cautiously. "The new governor and the garrison will be entirely Roundhead! You won't dare enter the place!"

Whetstone gave Diana a squeeze. "He's learning fast, this son of the Earl of Ilex. No, Yorke, my dear fellow, if Sir Thomas Whetstone sails the *Pearl* into whatever the main port of Jamaica is called, he'll end up hanging from a gibbet and I dare not think what would happen to Diana. But if John Brown and his wife Mary, joint owners of the *John and Mary* sloop, registered in the port of London, sail in with a cargo of goods like flour, sugar, rumbullion and sweet potatoes, well, I'm sure they'll be very welcome." He grinned at Aurelia. "Why, the new military governor of Jamaica, or whoever is in charge, might even give them a commission so they could take up privateering!"

"You are very brave," Aurelia said to Diana. "Or you love him very much."

"I love him, I suppose," Diana said, jabbing Whetstone in the ribs with a finger, "but more to the point I have confidence in him. I think it will work."

"It had better," Whetstone said. "She thought of it!"

"We haven't much left here along the Main," Diana said soberly. "The Spaniards are even leaving the towns on the coast and building new ones fifteen or twenty miles inland. You whisper the name *La Perla* along this coast and everyone loads his possessions into leather panniers, slings them across his horses' backs, and gallops into the distance."

"There is nothing along the Main for us, then?" Aurelia asked.

"No, nothing," Whetstone said bluntly. "The Dutch have a monopoly of the smuggling."

Diana said: "Why don't you come to Jamaica with us? Change your names, carve a new name on the ship – no, you've no need to do that; no one in Jamaica will know the *Griffin*."

"Yes," Aurelia said, "we would like to do that, wouldn't we Edouard?"

Chapter
Thirteen

As the island of Curaçao dropped below the horizon astern and the *Griffin* followed the *Pearl* on to a north-westerly course at the beginning of a long voyage to Jamaica, Ned felt thankful that he would be having no more dealings with the Dutch. He found them close and secretive; their manner towards strangers reminded him of the time at the Godmersham estate when as a boy he had accidentally come across half a dozen poachers setting a trap for deer: they were sullen, frightened and yet, to a young boy, menacing – until he found they had expected him to shoot at them with his sporting gun, which was loaded with bird shot.

Whetstone had no liking for them either, but he grinned and slapped their backs and was cheerful with them because for the past few years he had had to rely on them and, he admitted, although they drove a hard bargain they could generally be forced to keep their word, because more than most they looked to tomorrow, so today's bargain was kept because it could lead to bigger bargains in the future.

Both Saxby and Whetstone had complained that they were putting a great deal of faith in Mr Wagstaffe's skill as a chartmaker: they had found that Curaçao was nearly thirty miles further south than marked on the chart. Had Wagstaffe placed Jamaica correctly?

Ned had been startled, listening to Whetstone and Saxby discussing the navigation: to him it seemed a black art, something that should be approached with suitable awe, but they were speculating whether Jamaica, like Curaçao, had been placed too far south, or too far east or west, and Whetstone had finally rolled up his own copy with the comment that if they sailed past it they would soon know because they would reach Cuba about one hundred miles to the north, whereas if they allowed too much for the west-going current they would find the end of Hispaniola.

"Never trust charts myself," Whetstone declared. "This fellow Wagstaffe never sailed these waters; he relies on information from the masters of merchant vessels. I could tell him a few things about the Main coast, seven hundred miles of it, but I never would: I don't think even the Dons have a proper chart of it – I've never found one in all the Spanish ships we've captured. They seem to rely on copies of Wagstaffe. Most of them looked like copies of copies of what someone remembered when he sobered up!"

Once Whetstone had gone back to his ship Ned tried to force himself to think of her by her new name, *Peleus,* and Whetstone by his new name of Whetheread. The *Pearl*'s carpenter, so Whetstone said, was pleased with the choice because it left him the first two letters unchanged but it was even more fortunate that one of Ned's men, hearing of the *Pearl*'s carpenter's task, had mentioned to Saxby that if Sir Thomas needed any changes in the certificate of registry, he could perhaps be of assistance. Saxby had brought the man to Ned to discover that Edward Hart, formerly employed on the Kingsnorth plantation as a labourer, owed his transportation to his skill at forgery landing him in the Bridewell.

"All I need is a sharp knife to scrape a layer off the parchment," he explained, "that way the *Pearl* vanishes, and the names of the original owners. Then I need a quill and some soot to make fresh ink. The new name for the ship is good," he added. "Means I have the first two letters to give me the style, and the new name having an extra letter means I can make a good job fraying the parchment. If the carpenter has a nice piece of shagreen, I can get the parchment really smooth and I guarantee no one'd ever spot the change."

"If he hasn't," Yorke said, "it won't take long to catch a shark and skin it. It's time we had some shagreen at work," he told Saxby. "I keep getting splinters in my hand from the woodwork. A good rub with shagreen and then a few coats of boiled linseed oil . . ."

"Aye aye, sir," said Saxby, wondering where Mr Yorke had picked up that information and guessing, without any particular regret, that it would not be long before his own role in the ship would be that of the mate, not master.

These last three months had seen a big change in Mr Yorke. Had it come from inside or had it been forced upon him? Saxby was far from sure, nor was he very certain what caused it. Back at Kingsnorth Mr Yorke was always quiet, going his own way, not mixing with his neighbours. No one could blame him for that; they were a hard-drinking and vicious gambling crowd and, from what Saxby heard, once they had the rumbullion inside them and the dice were rolling, likely as not the night would end up in a fight and, once a month, sometimes more frequently, a duel. So Mr Yorke spent his evenings in his own home. He had more books than anyone Saxby had ever heard tell of; he read so much Mrs Wilson worried about his eyesight.

As an employer, no man could wish for a better: he had come out to Barbados four years ago to take over the Kingsnorth plantation from a scoundrel who had ingratiated himself with the old earl, Mr Yorke's father, and he had spent exactly one month apparently doing nothing. In fact he had been listening and looking. The scoundrel – Saxby even now would not think of the man's name, let alone speak it – had tried to poison Mr Yorke's mind about most of the people employed on the plantation. Meanwhile Mr Yorke had met Saxby, an under-foreman at an estate in St Philip's parish, at the other end of the island.

Then one day he rode over, offered Saxby the job of running Kingsnorth, paid off Saxby's employer, paid off the scoundrel and told him that if he was still on the island in a month's time the provost marshal would be after him with a warrant for massive peculation, and that was that: Kingsnorth was, one could say, under new management!

Yet Mr Yorke had made no bones about his own personal position: Saxby could remember their detailed talk almost word for word. Mr Yorke had said he knew nothing about farming in the tropics, but he felt something was badly wrong with the crops grown at Kingsnorth and most of the other plantations.

"The soil is so rich here that if you throw down a splinter

of wood today, you'll have a tree tomorrow. Yet this plantation loses money – and I'm making allowances for the peculation that's been going on."

Saxby was proud of the next sentence spoken to him. "Saxby," Mr Yorke had said, "I don't know what we should be growing but I have an idea you do, so speak up and let's start planting!"

That was when Kingsnorth had changed to sugar. They had to build the *ingenio*. Saxby recalled that he had even had to explain to Mr Yorke that that was the word for the sugar mill, with a boiling house, filling room, cisterns, stillhouse and so on. He had stood by his word that Saxby should plan the best as he would get it.

All of which made it more of a tragedy that by the time it was all built and working overtime, and the crops were growing well, they had to make a bolt for it in the *Griffin*. Four hundred acres under sugarcane, a hundred of pasture, another hundred left as woodland and forming a windbreak to the eastward, five acres of ginger, fifty of cotton, and fifty growing provisions for the plantation . . .

Several other plantation owners used to call after the first year to inspect the plantation; several had made Saxby tempting offers to go and work for them, but there was no money or promise that could tempt him away from Mr Yorke. He was the master, yes; but it was not like that. More as though Mr Yorke was the senior partner.

Saxby could remember the day he mentioned Mrs Judd to him. He had waited for the right moment and then started off, oh ever so tactfully, to find Mr Yorke smiling and saying it was high time Saxby fell into the arms of a good woman! So Mrs Judd had moved in, and without either she or Saxby realizing it was happening, Mr Yorke had employed more women about the place. Certainly the plantation house needed a few servants to keep it tidy and make sure Mr Yorke ate proper meals – and Mrs Judd ruled over them like an empress.

It was Mrs Judd who first said that Mr Yorke was a lonely man who walked alone. When Saxby had laughed at her and said it was like calling a black man black, she had rounded on him. Some men were lonely, she said, because they did not like people or because people did not like them or because there were no folk to keep them company. Some men walked alone because they did not need other people to lean on; they could decide which way to walk and what decisions to make without discussing it with everyone. Mr Yorke was lonely because there were no people to keep him company, but he walked alone because he could decide for himself.

How right she was! For example, the morning Mr Yorke received the warning letter from his father – he had collected Mrs Wilson, closed down Kingsnorth and sailed, all within how many hours? Twelve or so. And he had not abandoned anyone who wanted to come with him, even paying off those scallawag new indentured servants who stayed behind, reckoning they could claim to be the same as time-expired and ask for the lump sum. Little did they realize that the ships now regularly coming in with all these negroes from the Guinea coast would soon put an end to white labour out here. For £20 a man, a plantation owner could buy a young slave and have him for the rest of his life, eating simple food and working a lot better in the heat than some scoundrel dragged out of the Bridewell or sent out here by Cromwell, prisoners of war who knew nothing but how to hate and sulk and dodge work. For £15 the plantation owner could buy a negro woman and start breeding from her, like a horse or an ox. In a dozen years he would have half his investment back; in thirteen, providing both the children were boys, he would get the whole.

Saxby found himself grinning. That scoundrel Wilson was always going on about what a great man this Oliver Cromwell was, and how the New Model Army had swept the Royalist troops from the battlefields. The prisoners transported were always badly treated, jeered at, severely punished for the slightest thing – the Bullocks were a good example. But it had been Cromwell – Parliament anyway – that had finally lost Wilson his wife and, at the same time, from what the Bullocks said, turned that bully into a very frightened man.

So Mr Yorke (the Yorke family, rather, because of course Kingsnorth belonged to the family, not to Mr Yorke alone) had lost a plantation and gained – well, not exactly a wife but a remarkable woman: he would rate her as a Mrs Judd of the aristocracy. If only Mrs Bullock had known which side a man's heart was on, Mr Yorke would be married to Mrs Wilson by now.

Still, this Miss Gilbert, or whatever her name was, might cause that to end up happily. She was not married to Sir Thomas and they made no bones about it: he had left a wife in England, but Saxby did not get the impression that Miss Gilbert had ever been married. What a woman! Another Mrs Judd! And perhaps Mrs Wilson might one day follow her example.

Mrs Wilson, though, had a quick brain. She was not a great talker – the fact that she was French might make her shy – but when she did say something it usually brought them up all standing. Mr Yorke listened to her, but in the last few days Saxby had the idea that she was making him talk more, explain his ideas, drawing him out. Giving him more confidence, in fact. The trouble was that once Mr Yorke knew how Kingsnorth should be run, he had gained plenty of confidence. Now at sea he was starting all over again.

It was lucky the man he chose to be the manager of Kingsnorth had served in the Royal Navy; even luckier that he had deserted! It had meant that the *Griffin* was used to fetch and take from the other islands, so that Saxby had been able to train a dozen men as occasional seamen.

Mr Yorke, though, was in the same position as the day he first arrived in Kingsnorth from England, knowing nothing about running a plantation in the tropics. Now he had his men (and women!) on board the *Griffin* and though luckily he knew the rudiments of seamanship, he was having to learn smuggling, buccaneering, piracy, how to fight sea battles . . . And Saxby remembered how he had been scared for Martha Judd's safety when that *guarda costa* came out from behind that headland. Mr Yorke must have felt the same for Mrs Wilson – and it was just as bad for the Bullocks.

So they had all had their share of good and bad luck! Mr Yorke had lost Kingsnorth and gained Mrs Wilson: Saxby had lost an interesting job at Kingsnorth but gained command of the *Griffin* and finally got a hitch on Martha, who sometimes hinted she would fly the coop; and the Bullocks reckoned they had made a good exchange.

Martha in those breeches! And then Mrs Wilson, and very becoming too. Women being women, it would be interesting to see if Martha and Mrs Bullock and Mrs Wilson rigged themselves out in the same sort of split dress as Miss Gilbert, or whatever her name was, or whether she would copy their breeches. As long as they undressed before they went to bed he doubted if their men would mind much.

Jamaica. It was a stroke of luck when they sighted the *Pearl*'s sail on the horizon. The *Peleus,* he corrected himself. This Sir Thomas Whetstone seemed to know most of the answers. Mr Yorke said he was a Royalist, even though he was Cromwell's nephew. Well, from all accounts Cromwell was a country gentleman before he took to treason and killed the King, so it made as much sense as anything did these days.

To have been buccaneering along the Main for three years – he could see why the Dons would like to get the garotte round Sir Thomas's throat. And they did catch him once and sentenced him to a lifetime in the saltmines, but they thought he was just another English seaman; they did not realize – until he had escaped and found the *Pearl* and rowed out to her in a stolen canoe – that they had "Don Tomás" in their hands!

Saxby looked astern in time to see the western tip of Aruba drop below the horizon. He picked up the slate and noted the course, then went below to check the time by the watch, which was kept in a drawer, well wrapped up. The sun was setting and he called to the lamp trimmer. It would soon be time to close with the *Peleus*. Sir Thomas had suggested they sail side by side, each with a lantern at the bow and the stern.

Five hundred miles. If the weather stayed reasonable it should take them less than five days. The *Peleus* was smaller but she was faster than the *Griffin,* which was still laden with three quarters of her original sugar cargo and trade goods. "Watch your heading," he said to the men at the tiller.

Down in the cabin, Aurelia sat sideways on the bunk and combed her hair while Ned swung in the hammaco. The wind had freshened during the night and with the sea on her starboard quarter the *Griffin* was rolling more than she had done since she left Antigua.

"I shall cut my hair short," Aurelia announced. "It is too

much trouble. And the salt air and the spray makes it so sticky. And we do not have enough water for me to wash it daily."

Ned did not answer, curious to see how many more reasons she could find to wield the scissors. "And anyway I am tired of this fashion. And Diana's hair looked much nicer, cut short. So practical. She can tuck it into a cap in bad weather. And it makes it easier for her to disguise herself as a man."

"She has other more obvious things she needs to disguise," Ned commented.

"Yes, aren't they splendid," Aurelia said with a frankness that startled him. "She has a canvas screen on deck so that she can sleep in the sun."

"That's all she wears?"

"Behind the screen – yes. I like the tan. It is such a change from all the white faces I see. Do you like it?" she asked innocently.

"It suits her," Ned said warily. "It means she doesn't get sunburnt accidentally. That can be very painful."

"I tan just as easily," Aurelia said casually, holding up an arm. "I wish I had a tan like that; it is so irritating to cover myself against the sun to stop sunburn."

"We'll put up a screen for you. Then you can become tanned all over."

"Is it good for you, though? Doesn't the sun dry up all the natural oils so the noxious night vapours can penetrate the body?"

"Diana seemed well enough."

Aurelia nodded. "She said she had been as brown as that for three years, so I suppose it is all right."

"Try it," Ned said. "You can always stop and go back to being pink and white."

"You sound as though you do not like me pink and white."

"It's not a question of 'not liking'," Ned said warily. "I'd like you any colour except perhaps purple with orange stripes, but for this sort of life being tanned means you don't get accidentally burned."

" 'This sort of life'." Aurelia took up the phrase and repeated it slowly. "*Mon chéri,* we must be careful not to be the log floating down the river, just drifting where the current takes us."

"Do you think that's what is happening now?"

"I am asking *you* the question."

Ned came over and sat beside her on the bunk. He took away the hair brush and held her hand. "It was happening, yes. But I think it has stopped now."

"What stopped it? Why are we suddenly controlling our – *comment dit-on*, our destiny?"

"I think meeting Whetstone stopped us just drifting. Probably prevented us making some dangerous mistakes."

"So you agree with his plan to try Jamaica?"

"Yes – don't you?" he asked, suddenly alarmed that she might have changed her mind.

"Why should we have any more luck in Jamaica than along the Main?"

"You can't compare the two. We learned an important lesson from Whetstone –"

"What was that?" she interrupted.

"That because of the Dutch, English ships cannot make a living smuggling along the Main, and that piracy along this coast is finished: like shooting on land which has been poached over for centuries. No game left; the birds have either flown or been killed."

"Why will Jamaica be any better?"

"Jamaica itself won't, but we can use it as a base to attack hundreds of miles of the Cuba and Hispaniola coast."

"So you are quite content to be a pirate for the rest of your life, like Thomas, with Diana following him like – like a faithful dog?"

Ned felt that suddenly, quite unexpectedly, and quite unprovoked, Aurelia had brought their relationship to a crisis. It was a strange time to do it because she could not leave the expedition. Yet in the last few hours his ideas, attitudes, hopes and fears had been slowly settling in his mind; he had found, for example, that he no longer worried about next week or next month. In contrast, at Kingsnorth one planted seed today to harvest in many weeks' time; there could be no spontaneous activity in conducting a plantation.

This life in the *Griffin*, though, where the next dawn was sure to bring more surprises, needed sudden decisions. It tumbled dangers on them like tiles sliding off a roof and next week was of no more concern than last and happiness was now, not tomorrow. It was the life he wanted. For the past four years at Kingsnorth he had lived a premeditated life of planning and waiting, planting and then harvesting, never doing anything in the morning that had an effect in the afternoon.

In the last few weeks he had changed; he would never return to the old Ned, yet it was the old Ned that Aurelia knew and, he presumed, had loved and agreed to accompany on that confused last day at Kingsnorth.

Now, with the *Griffin* rolling her way to Jamaica, the hammaco swinging, the sea swirling past only inches from their backs as they sat in the bunk, the sunbeams dancing across the cabin as they came through the skylight which let them through one moment and reflected them the next as the ship moved . . . was this the time to tell her?

Well, they would be in Jamaica in three or four days.

"Yes," he said tentatively. "We have no choice, and that's no fault of ours. I am beginning to enjoy the life. If we could get a proper commission in Jamaica and become buccaneers, that would be better, but if not it does not matter. Whatever you call it, we're fighting the Dons."

"Robbing them!"

"Yes, we're robbing them, and they'll garotte us if they catch us."

"What will become of me?"

"What will become of Diana?"

"I am not Diana!"

"I am not Whetstone, but all of us have been forced into this life by Cromwell. The Lord Protector's world is not ours."

"So you look forward to the life of a robber, a kidnapper, a pirate . . .?"

He turned and looked her straight in the eyes. "I have two choices. I can return to England a prisoner of State, and probably spend the rest of my life locked in a cell alone and rotting of jail fever, or I can be a buccaneer and fight the Spanish as best I can, and relieve them of enough money so that my people can eat."

"And me? What about me?"

"If I'm a prisoner of State jailed for the rest of my life, you will never see me again; if I am a buccaneer you can be with me all the time, like Diana and Thomas. Yesterday, when they were on board, I thought you envied them the life they had led, and wanted it for us. Now . . . now you sound as if you wish you were back in Barbados."

"Whetstone has cast a spell over you! Diana has bewitched you: you have lewd thoughts about her!"

"I'm sure Thomas has lewd thoughts about you, my dear. Provoking lewd thoughts in men is the sincerest flattery a woman can expect. No woman cares to admit it, of course."

"Do I provoke lewd thoughts in you?" she asked, looking up at him coquettishly.

"Of course!"

"Just because of Diana?"

"No! From the first time I saw you!"

"You said nothing . . ."

"You'd have slapped my face if I had. 'Mrs Wilson, send the servants away and take your clothes off . . .' Can you imagine it?"

"I can now, but not then."

"Aurelia, what is all this about?"

She inspected a handful of her hair.

"I wanted to be sure that buccaneering was the life you wanted, not just the life you had been forced into by the arrival of those horrible men, Penn and Venables."

"Very well, are you satisfied now?"

"Yes. I think you will make a good buccaneer."

"And you?" he asked anxiously. "What about you?"

She turned away slightly, as if embarrassed. "It was something Diana told me. She said that in the eyes of God she and Thomas were married, even if not in the eyes of the church, because they knew that tomorrow either of them could be dead. I said that in the eyes of the church I was still married to Wilson."

"What did she say?"

"She said happiness did not wait on priests; that too many women hesitated and were left mourning dead lovers for the rest of their lives and regretting withheld favours."

"That is why she lives with Whetstone," Ned said, "even though they can't marry. Sensible woman. She realizes there's no one out here to judge and sneer, and even if there was she would not care."

Aurelia nodded. "This is not easy to say. Edouard . . ."

Suddenly Ned felt chilled: now Aurelia was going to end a relationship before it had begun; she would probably ask to be put on board the *Peleus*. She –

". . . and you are not helping me say it. But would you –" she began speaking in French "– prefer us to live like Thomas and Diana?"

"Prefer?" Ned exploded happily. "Dearest, for the rest of our lives, even if you make it seem you changed your mind because I have only a week or two to live!"

Soon after daybreak on the fifth day Burton was the first to sight a bluish-grey cloud on the horizon fine on the larboard bow, and after examining it for several minutes with the *Griffin*'s battered telescope Saxby reported that what seemed no bigger than the shadow of a pearl was Jamaica.

"What we can see," he told an excited Aurelia, "is the eastern end of the mountains that are the island's backbone."

Burton was just aiming a musket in the direction of the *Peleus* to attract her attention when in the *Griffin* they saw a small puff of smoke and heard a desultory pop.

"Fire as a reply!" Saxby called to Burton. "Sir Thomas will guess we've sighted it and were just about to signal him."

The master then turned to Yorke and, acknowledging the new name that appeared on the *Griffin*'s certificate of registry as her owner, formally reported: "Mr Kent, sir, Jamaica's in sight ahead, distant about fifty miles."

Ned smiled and said: "Thank you, Mr Saxby. Now I say 'Carry on', don't I?"

"That's it, sir. But, beggin' your pardon but including Mrs Wilson, I 'ave to deliver a message from the ship's company h'at this time, the moment we first see Jamaica."

Curious, Ned looked round for Aurelia who came over and stood beside him, and he held her hand, nodding and saying: "Well, 'Carry on, Saxby!'"

"The ship's company of the *Griffin,* sir and madam, that's to say all of us who came with you from Kingsnorth and Mr and Mrs Bullock, want to take the h'opportunity h'of –" he broke off in confusion, the seriousness of the occasion, with all the ship's company watching, thrusting too many aitches across his path.

"H'I mean to say, with a new land ahead of us, we want to give you both our best wishes for your new life."

Ned looked round at all his men and the five women standing near Mrs Judd. "Thank you, and Mrs Wilson and I return those wishes. But I don't want to underestimate the risks. You must realize, without my telling you, that we don't know what we are going to find. You know you are the regular ship's company of the *Griffin,* not former indentured labour or people transported. Mr Saxby will be signing you on as regular members of the crew, just in case anyone wants to examine all our books. I am Mr Kent, the owner; we sailed from Portland and picked up our present cargo in Barbados. If anyone asks more questions – but I doubt if they will – make up a likely story!"

He waited a few moments and then said: "I am not sure what we shall do after we get to Jamaica. I think buccaneering will be our only choice. Buccaneering if we can get a commission from the governor, or whoever is in command; piracy if not.

"However, when you volunteered to come with me at Kingsnorth you thought (as I did) that smuggling would keep us in food. So if buccaneering is not to anyone's liking they can leave at Jamaica, and I will pay them their wages."

From the mumbling and throat clearing, Ned realized that few if any of them had contemplated leaving; on the contrary, if Mrs Judd and Mrs Bullock were good representatives, they were looking forward to whatever came along.

Chapter
Fourteen

The entrance to the enormous harbour was narrow. To starboard was a long, low sandspit running east and west with a small town built on it; ahead to the north-east was the great bulk of the island, ridge upon folded ridge of mountains fading into the distance like swell waves, their lower slopes a rich green; to larboard, westward, the land seemed swampy.

Whetstone was sailing the *Peleus* as though he had been in a dozen times before, bearing away round a cay, bearing up to round a coral reef lurking just below the water, yellowish-green, like some enormous flat-topped vegetable growing up from the sea bed.

Ned could see that two men perched high in the *Peleus*'s shrouds were waving down from time to time, warning Whetstone of underwater obstacles ahead. Whetstone was easy to recognize: Ned had never seen a bear except in the Vauxhall bear garden, but he imagined that was how a freed one walked. And near him – naturally so, as though she was one of the ship's officers – Diana stood wearing a wide plaited straw hat like a cone.

"Diana with that hat," Aurelia said, "she looks like – *comment dit-on, une toupie.*"

"A peg top! Yes, but wait: perhaps Thomas will fetch out a whip of string and start her spinning!"

"It's a very practical hat."

"Plaited from palm fronds. I'm sure Burton will make one for you."

She pointed in surprise as, rounding the end of the long, sandy peninsula, they could suddenly see the size of the almost enclosed bay. "Why, it is big enough for ten fleets!"

The *Peleus* turned to starboard and began tacking to the eastward, further into the anchorage.

"Not many ships, sir," Saxby said. "Two frigates, four storeships, and those local canoes. Fishermen's dugouts from the look of them."

Both the *Peleus* and the *Griffin* were flying English colours and Saxby pointed to a building on the sandy peninsula, which now cut them off from the sea.

"Flag flying over there, sir. Reckon it's the army headquarters."

Ned slowly continued his inspection of the whole anchorage and finally commented: "Penn and Venables had an easy job here!"

"How so, sir?"

"There's not one fort anywhere. Just a battery on the end of the sandspit covering the entrance. I saw three guns."

Saxby stared round the anchorage. "Aye, that's right. Penn must have sailed in just like us! Now, will it be all right to anchor near those two frigates?"

"Anchor near the *Peleus*: Sir Thomas is less likely to make a mistake than us."

An hour later, with the ships anchored within hail of each other, a boat left one of the frigates, went over to the house on the sandspit flying a flag and, having picked up an army officer, rowed towards the two newly-arrived ships. Long before they were within earshot, Whetstone shouted across: "Ned – I'm coming over with my ship's papers so we can deal with these clodhoppers together. You agree, eh?"

"Safety in numbers," Ned yelled. "Bring Diana – she can dazzle the soldiers while Aurelia distracts the sailors!"

Whetstone's hearty bellow of laughter echoed across the water and they saw Diana take off her hat and wave it. The *Peleus*'s boat was swung out and they watched as half a dozen seamen scrambled down into it. Then Ned saw a flash of bright colour, and then Whetstone followed down the ladder.

"Look! Oh Ned, why did you not tell me?" Aurelia exclaimed. "Diana is in a dress with her hair so elegant!"

"Well, it can't be all that elegant – she doesn't have a woman on board! Anyway, go below and put on a dress if you wish – I'll send reinforcements. Mrs Judd, Mrs Bullock!" he shouted. "Emergency! Combs and brushes!"

Sir Thomas Whetstone, in his role as Thomas Whetheread, wore dark grey breeches above light grey hose, a mustard-coloured jerkin, and a black felt hat with a flat brim topping the bearded face. Diana's dress was also a sober grey – the flash of colours which Aurelia had spotted were her petticoats, now mostly hidden by the dress, which would have satisfied even the strictest Puritan minister. The dress would, Ned thought to himself, but there was no disguising that the woman wearing it was beautifully built and knew it.

"Where's Aurelia?" she demanded. "Thomas forgot to shout over that we ought to wear dresses. I hope she has something suitably drab. Colours, bare hair and bare arms are the original sin to these people, though Thomas demands more!" She glared at the approaching boat. "Just look at them. Hats look like black flower pots. Luckily Thomas bought one last year from a Dutchman. Well, I'll go down and see Aurelia."

The frigate's boat came alongside the rope ladder and the *Griffin*'s men took her painter and sternfast. The first man on board saluted Whetstone, who was standing beside the break in the bulwark where the ladder was rigged.

"John Hulls, sir, lieutenant of the *Urgent,* Commonwealth frigate, over yonder."

Whetstone bowed, as though vastly impressed at meeting a naval officer. "Thomas Whetheread, sir, owner and master under God of the *Peleus,* lying over there."

The lieutenant turned and introduced himself to Ned, who with suitable nervousness said he was Edward Kent, the owner of the *Griffin,* but the master was Mr Saxby, whom he presented.

"Ah," the lieutenant said briskly, making way for the army officer struggling up the ladder, "having both owners and masters together makes it so much easier."

Finally the army officer lumbered on board and was promptly introduced by the *Urgent*'s lieutenant as Major Slinger, of the 22nd Foot.

Whetstone raised his eyebrows and said to Ned: "Shall we go down to your cabin so that these gentlemen can inspect our papers?"

Ned looked suitably embarrassed. "Give me a moment, gentlemen: our respective wives are – er," he hurriedly changed what he was going to say, in view of Major Slinger's lugubrious features, "making themselves tidy in anticipation of your visit."

He hurried below and knocked on the door. Aurelia told him to come in. She looked beautiful, and that, Ned realized, was all there was to it. Dress her in old sacks, black serge or grey poplin and she would still be beautiful, just as nothing could make Diana look like a nun.

"Well?" Diana demanded with mock severity. "Are we suitably attired?"

"You both look like Royalists' doxies rather than Roundheads' spouses, but that's Nature's doing. I'm bringing down a couple of officers, so please look demure!"

Major Slinger, the first to be introduced because of his seniority, both in rank and age, was clearly having trouble with his Puritan beliefs as his bulging eyes swung from Diana to Aurelia and back.

Diana, with the expression of a mother superior of a strict Protestant order, curtseyed and was suitably shy when the gallant major wanted to kiss her hand. Instead of lifting her hand to his lips he bowed deeply and, because Diana was not expecting it, looked as though he was going to bite her fingers.

Aurelia, now knowing what to expect, carried it off without speaking a word, but Lieutenant Hulls was determined to show that the navy knew what to do.

"Y'sarvant, ma'am," he said, kissing Diana's hand and then doing the same to Aurelia, but obviously unable to choose between the two of them. Major Slinger did not hesitate: within a moment he had Diana trapped in a corner and was commiserating with her for having such a heartless husband who made her accompany him on such a long voyage from England.

Diana, seeing that Thomas could hear the major's words, simpered: "Yes, Major, and how understanding of you to realize it. So many thousands of miles – or is it leagues? I always mix them up. And such huge seas. Why, I swear that one went over the mast. And the sharks and whales and dolphins following us all the time, just waiting to eat us up!"

"Dolphins are not dangerous, ma'am," Lieutenant Hulls volunteered reassuringly. "Sharks, yes, but not dolphins."

"These were," Major Slinger declared in a parade ground voice. "Why, the lady saw their teeth, didn't ye, ma'am?"

"Oh indeed! A thousand teeth in every mouth, and a dozen mouths always snapping. The noise of all those mouths snapping shut – why even Thomas admitted it reminded him of war drums on the Benin coast!"

"Slaving, eh?" Hulls said. "Wretchedly unhealthy place, I'm told."

"Lost half my crew from sickness," Whetstone confessed, although he had never transported a slave in his life nor been near West Africa. "You know the rhyme –
    'Beware and take care of the Bight of Benin,
    There's one comes out for five that go in.' "

The lieutenant shivered. "As bad as that? It's bad enough here. The dead at Hispaniola . . ."

"Hispaniola?" Whetstone said innocently. "What happened, the Dons hit by the plague?"

The lieutenant glanced at Major Slinger who, having heard the question turned his back and continued an animated conversation with Diana.

"The fleet tried to land at Santo Domingo."

"Whose fleet – are the French out here?"

"No, ours." Hulls said miserably. "We were supposed to capture Hispaniola but thousands died of sickness, and we came on and captured this island instead."

Whetstone looked as shocked as a bishop hearing a bawdy joke. "The Lord Protector won't be satisfied with that!"

"No . . . well, Admiral Penn and General Venables have gone to England to report and have taken the fleet."

"You seem to have little left to defend Jamaica. Aren't you worried that the Spaniards will attack?"

"Yes. There are just the two frigates, and the four storeships, which arrived late with our artillery and horses."

Slinger finally tore himself away from Diana and came over to Ned and Whetstone. "Yes, well, the lieutenant has told you. We have more than two thousand starving soldiers here."

"Starving? With all the fruit on the trees?" Whetstone said.

"Yes, starving," Slinger barked. "They're not animals, you know; you expect them to climb trees like monkeys and pull down fruit?"

Whetstone shrugged his shoulders and Slinger continued: "I must see your manifests. I shall requisition any food you are carrying, apart from your crew's provisions."

"You won't," Ned said calmly, surprised to hear his own voice but finding the decision easy to make. "You can buy it at a fair price, but you're not requisitioning anything."

"Oh yes, I am! I'm the deputy military governor here, and what I say must be done."

Ned shook his head and continued: "I am a peace-loving man and I have only two things to say. First, the *Griffin* and *Peleus* can be sailing out of here in about three minutes with you and the lieutenant still on board. Second, if the frigates chase us, we simply drop you both over the side for them to pick up. So, Major, you can read the manifests and give us your prices in writing and signed by you, or we'll cut our anchor cable now."

"You'll regret this, Mr Kent! You sound like a Royalist to me! Well, we've cleared them out of Barbados, and we don't propose letting them wriggle in here!"

"What did you do in Barbados, then?"

"Ha, root and branch, root and branch. We sequestrated their estates and sent 'em back to England as prisoners of State. All of them. Well, except one scoundrel that escaped before we arrived. Younger son of the Earl of Ilex, I'm told. Still, he couldn't take his plantation!" He laughed at the thought of it. "So his precious plantation was sold to a loyal Parliamentarian."

Ned nodded in agreement. "Quite right; it's the only way to treat them. As you said, root and branch!"

"Yes – now, your manifests, please."

Saxby stepped forward with a handful of papers.

"Sugar . . . trade goods . . . Where's the cargo you brought out from England?" Slinger asked.

"Just piece goods, Major; we bought the sugar in Antigua

173

and Montserrat. Fetches a good price in England, you know!"

"Not a bit of good to us. Well, a few tons. But we need flour. Now, not next year. How about you?" he asked Whetstone.

"In ballast, I'm afraid. I was going on to the Moskito Coast for logwood. Might pick up some fustic, cochineal and indigo if the Spaniards want to trade."

Major Slinger now looked a worried man; Diana walked across the cabin without him noticing.

"Flour, we must have it!"

"Why don't you send your storeships across to the Main?" Ned asked. "The Dons have it; they'll sell it at a price!"

"But we're at war with them – we've just captured this island from them!" Slinger expostulated.

"Major, you're a soldier; I'm a businessman," Whetstone said confidentially. "Let me assure you that a ship visiting a small Spanish port discreetly can get all the flour she wants. Of course it'll be maize flour, not wheat, but it eats well. No Don can resist a profit."

"But I can't send the storeships," Slinger wailed. "They are due to sail for England in three days, escorted by the frigates. I have written orders from the general, and the captains have written orders from the admiral."

"Oh dear, oh dear," Yorke said sympathetically. "So all you have are the fishermen's dugouts. Well, at least you have some fish."

"No, not even fish!" Slinger said lugubriously. "All the fishermen have bolted into the mountains."

"I thought these islands had enormous herds of beeves and hogs," Whetstone said. "At least you have plenty of meat!"

"No, no, no," Slinger moaned. "The foolish soldiers sent out to catch cattle used muskets and all the livestock has bolted. Most of it was wild anyway."

"How did the Spanish catch it before you came?" Ned asked.

"They had specially trained negroes using horses who ran them down with lances."

"Won't they work for you?"

Slinger shook his head. "They bolted when they saw us coming. They released all the domestic animals and drove

174

them up into the mountains. They're all somewhere over on the north side of the island."

"Well, you need to prepare land for growing your own food," Whetstone said briskly. "No fighting for your soldiers now, so they can change from swords to shovels. Your blacksmiths can beat out ploughshares, eh!"

But Slinger did not laugh. "I should not talk of this, I suppose, but the lieutenant knows of it and will not gossip. The fact is that most of the officers will not encourage their men to prepare the soil. We've even offered them land for themselves if they will settle here and produce crops. But they refuse."

"Why?" Yorke asked incredulously. "I'm told that in Barbados land costs £20 an acre!"

"The officers are soldiers. They hate the tropics. So many died in Hispaniola from cholera, black vomit, malaria . . . Even here we lose a hundred men a week. All they want to do is to get back to England; to them, clearing and planting land might lead the Lord Protector to decide to keep Jamaica, and leave them out here as the garrison."

Ned, thinking of Kingsnorth, now owned by Wilson, gave a cynical laugh which irritated Slinger. "What is funny, Mr Kent? Do you find the death of more than half an expedition humorous?"

"No," Ned said shortly, "what's funny is the stupidity of soldiers who would sooner starve than dig. Sailors see things differently: if they fall in the sea, they swim to avoid drowning."

"Sugar," Whetstone said suddenly. "Are you going to buy the *Griffin*'s sugar?"

"I suppose so," Slinger said.

Whetstone told him the price and added: "In view of your earlier remarks about requisitioning, perhaps the lieutenant would allow you to use his boat to fetch the money first. Then we can begin unloading – at the wharf in front of your headquarters, do you suggest?"

"This is all *most* irregular!" Slinger protested.

"Yes," Yorke agreed. "We are the first merchant ships to call, I imagine."

"Well, yes," Slinger admitted.

"Do you have the money?" Whetstone demanded.

"Yes. I need the governor's approval, of course."

"You will not have trouble getting that. Listen carefully. How much will you pay for flour?"

"How do I know! I'm not a merchant. I only know the price of sugar because those drunken planters in Barbados talked of nothing else."

"Very well, talk to the governor and decide what you will offer – for grain and for flour."

"But I don't understand. To whom do we make an offer?"

"To Mr Kent and to me. And if we accept it, as soon as you've unloaded the sugar we will sail and get you grain or flour. It'll take about two weeks."

"Can you guarantee it?"

Whetstone looked him straight in the eye. "I guarantee it."

"How many tons?"

Whetstone turned to Yorke, who said: "I can load 400 tons."

"So you can have 600 tons, Major, providing your price is right."

"Where will you get it?"

"How much of the sugar and grain money will find its way into your pocket and the governor's?"

"What an outrageous question!"

"Quite. We are going to enemy territory; that's all you need to know, particularly when thinking of a price. Now, supposing you fetch the purchase money for the sugar, and we'll be preparing to bring the *Griffin* alongside the jetty."

At dawn next day the *Griffin* and the *Peleus* weighed anchor and ran down the harbour, past the jetty where two companies of soldiers had made short work of unloading the sugar, and with the *Peleus* leading they rounded the sandspit and headed out into the open sea.

Aurelia, back in breeches, stood beside Ned watching the peninsula foreshorten and then lengthen again as the *Griffin* turned south-east and they saw it from seaward.

"Are we pirates or buccaneers?" she asked mischievously.

"Madam, you saw the gallant major deliver the commission signed by the governor. We are buccaneers!"

"But we have no *boucan*!"

"No, once again we'll have to make do with salt beef, but

Thomas says that when we get back we'll go on to the Cayman islands and catch turtles, and then up to Cuba, where there are so many beeves that a fleet could supply itself with *boucan*."

"Ned," Aurelia asked, almost plaintively, "when we do get fresh meat, may I cook my own steak? All that smoke, and the meat gets so dry over the boucan."

"When did you learn about boucaning?"

"Oh, he tried it several times." The faint emphasis on the "he" told Ned yet again that he had nothing to be jealous about, but he found that at night even in the cramped bunk while holding her naked in his arms, he would be jealous of her past, when Wilson had held her. He had reminded himself that the man was impotent, and that she had never loved him, and that no lover had less to be jealous of than himself, but it was no good. Finally he admitted to himself that even if she had had a pet puppy, he would have been jealous of it. Love and jealousy seemed to be two sides of the same coin.

Oddly enough last night, after they had left the jetty with the *Griffin* and anchored out in the harbour, clear of the swarms of mosquitoes and sandflies, she had shown that she too could be jealous. Her long hair loose and making a soft shawl over his shoulders, her breasts melting into him and a leg flung over his thigh so that he did not know when his body ended and hers began, she had asked him about the first woman he had ever loved.

Ned had told her her name, described the colour of her hair and eyes, and how deeply they had loved each other and sworn eternal devotion. By this time Aurelia was lying beside him on one elbow, the moonlight through the skylight showing her eyes narrowed and her breasts taut, the nipples stiff with anger.

"This woman – this Rosemary, why did you not marry her, if you were both so *épris*?"

"Oh yes, we were enamoured; that is exactly the word!"

"So now you betray her with me! And you betray me with her! *Mon Dieu,* have you no shame?"

"No," he admitted. "I betrayed you both without a moment's thought . . ."

"Oh! You beast!" Aurelia tried to scramble out of the

bunk but because she was on the inside she had to pull herself across Ned's body, and the moment she was above him he pulled her down, struggling, her hair falling across his face and, tickling his nose, making him sneeze.

The absurdity of the situation started him laughing and this made a furious Aurelia pummel him in her efforts to get free. Finally Ned managed to stop laughing and hold her still long enough to say: "Beloved, we were both four years old at the time!"

To begin with she would not believe him. "How do I know this?"

"You don't, my dearest, but I told you her name. Diana will know her; ask her who she married, who she is now."

"Who is she?" Aurelia asked suspiciously, as if half expecting to meet her on board another privateer.

"The Countess of Rolles. And probably with her husband in exile in France, or wherever the Prince is living."

"You make me foolish," she said crossly, rolling to her side of the bunk and turning her back on him.

"No," he said, clasping her body close to him, "that's the first time a woman has ever been jealous of my past. You don't know how flattered I am."

With the sun rising and Ned feeling the effects of a night spent making love instead of sleeping, Aurelia said: "Where are we going for this corn?"

"Thomas reckons we should find enough at Riohacha, about 450 miles and the nearest part of the Main."

"Will they want goods or money?"

"Thomas thinks they would have preferred sugar, but we wanted to make sure the English governor of Jamaica was an honest man; that's why we made him buy the sugar."

"Do you think he is honest?"

"Probably, anyway he produced the gold. He hadn't much choice: his men are starving, he has no ships to get food except these two, and that's that!"

"*And* he gave you both commissions."

"I think it shocked his Parliamentary soul when he realized that otherwise he'd be buying grain from vulgar smugglers!"

Clear of the land the wind freshened and Saxby gave the order to harden in the mainsheet so that the *Griffin* could comfortably follow in the *Peleus*'s wake, watching her closely as she turned from time to time when her lookouts spotted coral below the surface.

Slowly the sandspit dropped below the horizon but the mountains seemed to turn bluish-grey rather than diminish in size. Saxby gestured back to the anchorage they had just left, still known by its Spanish name of Caguas. "Must be the biggest harbour in the Caribbee!" he said.

Yorke nodded. "Perhaps Cartagena is bigger – that's the main Spanish base. People talk of huge forts there."

"Aye, that's true. Well, if we stay in Sir Thomas's company very long," he said cheerfully, "no doubt we'll see them!"

Yorke looked at the sun, now a few degrees above the eastern horizon and just lifting over the top of low distant clouds that always seemed to line the eastern horizon at dawn. "Time Burton was exercising his guns' crews."

"Yes, sir," Saxby said and turned to bellow, "Pass the word for Mr Burton. Oh, there you are. Guns' crews, Burton, where are they, eh? Still sleeping, I'll be bound!"

Burton hurried below while Yorke said quietly, "Give them a couple of hours at it. They'll be ready to drop, but one day we might be fighting for our lives and the ability to keep at it longer than the Dons . . ."

"Exactly, sir. Anyway, it's a sight easier than spending the day cutting cane."

Yorke nodded thoughtfully. "You know, Saxby, the fact is they've had an easy life since we left Kingsnorth."

"I know, sir; muscles are softening up. Mine, too."

"We'll have some sail training this afternoon after lunch. We can't delay the *Peleus,* but the men can get up the spare mainsail from below. We can spread it and inspect it for rat holes. And the jibs. Make sure we have sail needles, palms and thread ready to do any repairs."

"I've a good mind to tell Mrs Judd she's included in the sail handlers; she's getting mortal fat."

"You're the master," Yorke said with a grin.

"I've a mind to make everyone in the ship do some heavy manual work each day. They'll keep fit."

"He is right, Edouard," Aurelia said. "I do not get enough exercise." Then, as Ned stared at her she slowly blushed. "Just like Mrs Judd," she added, knowing that she was the cause of Saxby's bloodshot eyes. "One cannot have enough exercise just walking the deck."

"No, ma'am," said Saxby, who was obviously thinking that regular exercise might slow down Mrs Judd's demands.

"I think we should have some target practice with the small arms, too," Yorke said. "When we're ready – after lunch, I think – we'll close with the *Peleus* and have her drop some casks or planks of wood in her wake to give us targets."

Saxby nodded; he was thankful that Mr Yorke was beginning to take an interest in the running of the ship. No, that was not quite fair; he had always taken an interest. Now he was beginning to take part. He was, Saxby supposed, beginning to understand the workings of a ship. Not an ordinary merchant ship, because there was nothing difficult about that, but a smuggling or buccaneer ship. Saxby looked forward to the day when he would be the mate and Mr Yorke the master. Having all these lives dependent on you was a heavy responsibility or, rather, the responsibility was in trying to think ahead – like staying out of the trap they fell into off Cumaná. Certainly they escaped the *guarda costa,* thanks to that trick of cutting across the Don's bow, but Saxby knew he should not have been so close in to the shore. Sir Thomas had spotted that when first he heard about it, but he knew they were all inexperienced and had made no criticism. Still, Saxby looked forward to the day when Mr Yorke was as fine a seaman as Sir Thomas. Mrs Wilson – she had the same spirit as Sir Thomas's lady, and with these women it was the spirit that mattered. Like Martha Judd – and Mrs Bullock for that matter. They were just naturally loyal to their men, and that was all that governed their lives.

Just at noon four days later the lookout reported that the *Peleus* was deliberately luffing, slowing so that the *Griffin* would catch up. As soon as they were within hailing distance, Whetstone bellowed across: "Can you see land way over on the larboard bow? It's low; looks like a distant cloud."

Saxby could see nothing but called to the lookout aloft who finally allowed that yes, it could be a cloud or land.

"It's Cabo de la Vela," Whetstone shouted. "The mouth of the Riohacha is about sixty miles along the coast to the west. I deliberately made this landfall so we can get to the coast and then run back along it – it's flat all the way. The first we'll see of Riohacha will be the church on the west side of the river and some trees on the east side."

"What are we going to do when we arrive?" Ned yelled.

"As soon as we close the coast, I'll come over," Whetstone said. "It's very shallow all along the coast; a mile offshore you can anchor in three fathoms!"

By five o'clock in the evening, with a low sandy shore a mile away ahead of them, the *Peleus* rounded up, dropped her mainsail and jibs, and anchored. Saxby brought the *Griffin* close to leeward, listening to the depths being called by the leadsman, and finally anchored.

"Can't get used to anchoring so far out in such shallow water, sir," he commented to Yorke, gesturing at the *Peleus* to make sure he had seen the boat being hoisted out.

Whetstone brought Diana with him and was in high spirits.

"How was that for navigation, Ned! Always afraid of being too far to the north-east – then you miss this peninsula and the first you know is you're passing Aruba and arriving at Curaçao."

Diana was talking quietly to Aurelia, and from the French girl's blush and smiling face Ned had no doubt about what they were discussing: the last few days had been in effect Aurelia's honeymoon, and Diana was obviously curious.

"Now what?" he asked Whetstone, in case his thoughts were straying in the same direction.

"We've enough moon tonight to run along the coast to the town of Riohacha. We shan't miss it because it's built at the mouth of the river. A forest is conspicuous on high land at one side of the river, and the village is on the other. There's a church and close to it the jetty sticks out into the river mouth. It's damn shallow, though. If there was any north in the wind we'd have to wait because it kicks up a heavy surf."

"You seem to know this place!"

Whetstone nodded and grinned. "Yes, they know *La Perla* here. That's why you'll have to go in and do the bargaining. You'll have to bring out my 200 tons and I'll meet you out of sight down the coast: we'll transfer it by boat. It'll be tedious. Then you can go back to get your 400 tons and rejoin me for the return to Jamaica."

"I wish you weren't so popular," Yorke grumbled. "Transferring 200 tons of maize by boat . . . still, if we find there's no swell we can lie alongside each other."

"Yes – but we'd have to be lucky. Still, the price the governor is going to pay makes it worth it. And don't forget, we have commissions now!"

"Yes, I'm sure the Spanish mayor of Riohacha will be delighted to see them!"

"Now listen, Ned, the difficulty is going to be the language. Bargaining with these scoundrels and not speaking the language . . ."

"What did you do? You don't speak Spanish, do you?"

"No. I used Latin. The priest translated. It was all I could do to keep a straight face."

"What were you bargaining for?" Ned asked curiously.

"Oh, the lives of the mayor, a bishop who happened to be visiting his flock from Cartagena, a handful of businessmen – and the priest himself. I had them all on board the *Pearl,* in irons, of course. Always try and bargain with the other fellow in surroundings strange to him."

"I can just imagine a bishop in the *Pearl,* with Diana . . ."

"Yes, the poor fellow's eyes nearly burst. I think she overdid it, myself, but what with the priest and the bishop, the ransom was paid!"

"What happens now when these people sight a foreign ship? After a visit by someone like you, I'd have thought they would simply start shooting."

Whetstone gave a laugh which Ned knew would have made any bishop clutch his crucifix. "No, they're in a cleft stick. You forget the Spanish government doesn't send them enough goods from Spain and they're always short of everything. Felt for hats, nankeen for jerkins and breeches, calico and lace for dresses, pots and pans, olive oil and wine . . . Where do they come from? Dutch smugglers!"

"But why don't the Spaniards raise the alarm every time they sight a sail?"

"I'm sure they do, but if the ship anchors a mile out – not difficult because it's so shallow along here – and sends a boat on shore to negotiate, the Spanish can see there's no threat."

"Do you suggest I do that?"

"Yes. How's your Latin?"

"Aurelia speaks good Spanish."

"You'd risk taking her with you?"

Ned told him how Aurelia had disguised herself to be on the boat on their first – and only – smuggling expedition. "I don't think she'd be left behind this time."

Whetstone sniffed disapprovingly. "Don't let women run the ship," he warned.

"Diana always obeys you, of course." Ned was only teasing but watched the reaction.

"Well, yes, in her own way. I mean, she sees that what I say is for her own good," Whetstone said uncomfortably, running his fingers through his beard.

"But she does what she wants."

Whetstone grinned mischievously and said: "I suppose she does. The fact is, it rarely arises because she comes along."

"She does what you say as long as it coincides with what she wants to do."

Whetstone's grin, Ned thought, was one of the most pleasant he had ever seen; it seemed to spread all over his body, and was conspiratorial, drawing in the other person to share the joke.

Whetstone nodded towards where Aurelia and Diana were talking and laughing. "I'm glad they get on well. Diana was saying Aurelia loves this life."

"She hasn't had much experience of it."

"Enough, enough though; at least, Diana thought so, and that woman can see through a six-inch plank. I hope so, for Diana's sake: she needs another woman's company, and Aurelia has the same sense of humour."

Ned nodded towards the sun. "I don't look forward to creeping along unknown coasts in the dark, so perhaps we'd better get under way."

Whetstone waved to Saxby. "I'd better say this to the *Griffin*'s master, but the way you're going on, Saxby's going to be out of a job soon!" As soon as the master joined them, Whetstone continued: "I suggest you follow me because I know this coast fairly well. As soon as it gets dark I'll light a single poop lantern. But once we're off the entrance to Riohacha, I'll put up two lanterns: that'll be a sign for you to anchor. You'll be able to spot the town as soon as it's dawn and you can go in with a boat."

Saxby asked: "What sort of depths shall we be anchoring in?"

"Four or five fathoms, no more."

"And do you want us to signal to acknowledge your second lantern?"

"No. If you don't spot it I'll see you passing me! My lanterns couldn't be seen in Riohacha but yours could, and the Dons would be suspicious of two ships."

With that he called Diana, gave Ned and Saxby a cheery wave, and climbed down to his boat.

Chapter
Fifteen

The wind had eased considerably during the night so Saxby and Ned saw the *Peleus*'s second lantern only an hour before dawn and, without thinking what he was doing, Ned gave the order for the two seamen to put the helm down and the jibs to be dropped before realizing that it was Saxby's job. However, the master was already making for the mainsheet, calling to men to take in the slack, before going on to the fo'c'sle for anchoring.

Ned went to the ship's side and watched the black, inky water gradually slow down as the *Griffin* lost way. Overhead the great mainsail, with the wind blowing down both sides, rippled and occasionally flapped. Now he could see the waves were not passing the hull; the *Griffin* was dead in the water. In a minute or two she would be drifting astern, so that she would pull on her anchor and make it dig in.

"Let go, Mr Saxby!"

There was a thud from forward, then a clatter as the carpenter knocked the wedge out of the windlass. A bellow – "Don't stand in a bight, you fools; you'll lose a leg!" – was followed by a hissing as the anchor rope ran out of the hawse.

How much cable should he let go? That depended on the depth of the water. And he (and Saxby too, he noted thankfully) had forgotten to have a man in the chains heaving the lead and shouting out the depth. It was not too late now!

"Leadsman – to the chains and give me a cast at once!"

It took only a minute before the man was reporting three

fathoms and Yorke realized he had been standing by ready with lead and line, his heavy canvas apron lashed round his waist to keep off the worst of the drips as he coiled in the rope after each cast.

Three fathoms, eighteen feet. Two and a half fathoms, which was fifteen feet. Again two and a half, two and a half . . . obviously the bottom was level here.

"Snub her, Mr Saxby!"

He was not quite sure at what point Saxby normally gave the order, except the cable had always stopped racing out, and it entailed taking a turn round the bitts so that, with no more cable running out, the weight of the ship came on to the anchor and if it was going to drag it would drag at that point, otherwise it would dig well in.

"She's holding, sir!" Saxby shouted.

"Very well, veer away to thirty fathoms!"

That was 180 feet of cable, a dozen times the depth. It *sounded* enough. Anyway, Saxby would mention it if he thought they ought to have more.

"*Chéri,* you sound like a commodore!"

Aurelia, wakened by the change in the ship's motion, had come on deck and was standing beside him.

"I know, I'm treading on Saxby's toes."

"I do not think Saxby will mind," she said in her attractively precise English. Her grammar was almost perfect; her grasp of idiomatic English was so good that Ned rarely had to explain anything, but her accent was for him the most amorous sound he knew; more rousing than the rustle of silk on bare flesh. And these are fine thoughts to be having as a man anchors his ship in a couple of fathoms of water off the Spanish Main.

"Are we off this town now?"

"Riohacha. Yes. At least, Thomas showed two lights. I'm damned if I can see any sign of it, except a dark patch on the land. That may be the forest on the other side of the river."

"When do we go on shore?"

"Listen, I think I prefer to go in and fetch someone out to the ship, so you can translate here."

"And how do you explain this to the man?"

"Oh, that is not difficult," Ned said airily. "I find a priest and explain in Latin."

"Is your Latin good enough for that?"

"Yes, and Greek too. My Latin and Greek teachers both used leather straps as well as exercise books."

"There is, 'owever, one difficulty."

He loved the way she could never master the aitch in "however", and had never mentioned it to her.

"And that is?"

"How do you persuade a responsible Spaniard – a mayor, a dealer in grain, a priest even – that you are trustworthy? Why should they come out to the ship? I expect some of them in the past have already paid ransom to Thomas!"

"So they will trust me if you come on shore with me and speak to them in Spanish?"

"Of course! What pirate or buccaneer would have a woman on board? Obviously the *Griffin* is a very respectable ship!"

"Thomas has Diana!"

"But she never went on shore to translate."

"Oh, all right, you can come with us." He had not meant to sound so ungracious.

"You say that in a very grudging way, my darling. You make it very clear I am a nuisance but agree you need a translator." She sounded hurt, distant, a foreigner among people who barely tolerated her. Was it a passing hurt? He was not sure. In fact she was – with Mrs Judd – the most popular person in the ship, but did she know that?

"My dearest, the only reason I prefer you not to come on shore is that I don't want you to be hurt: I am frightened for you."

"There! I am a billstone. You wish you had never brought me from Barbados."

"Millstone. Surely it is no crime to want the person you love to be safe? You are not a millstone round my neck. You are all I live for –"

He broke off as Saxby shouted from the foredeck. "Very well, furl the mainsail." He turned back to Aurelia, wishing the moon had set, so he could hold her in his arms without everyone seeing.

"– everything. I want you to be safe."

"And me?" Her voice was softer. "How about me? If I stay on board while you go on shore I die a thousand times in case something happens to you. If you were killed, I should jump in the sea and drown myself."

It was said in a normal quiet tone but he knew she meant it. And likewise, would he want to live if – he deliberately stopped thinking and watched the men easing away the throat and peak halyards so that the heavy gaff was lowered, the mainsail being folded on the main boom by other seamen.

"It will be light in half an hour," she said. "I can just make out the false dawn. See how far west Orion's Belt is now."

"I wish we were married," he said suddenly.

"What difference would it make? Could we be more together?"

A gold band on her finger and bearing his name. She was right, that was all it would mean. And being his heir, but all he owned was the *Griffin*. Not even the ship, because of course it, too, belonged to the family. Certainly he had nothing to offer her, and since her talk with Diana she seemed quite content with the present situation. As he thought about it, watching the black line of coast, the sky overhead a shimmering mass of stars outlining the lace-like tracery of the *Griffin*'s rigging, he had to admit that his feelings were proprietary; he wanted them to be married so she bore his name. No children yet; a pregnant wife at sea, and then a bawling baby . . . He could wait a few years for fatherhood!

Daylight showed that Whetstone had been precise: the *Griffin* was anchored a mile off the river mouth and the forest on the higher land on one side made a dark mat, while opposite a scattering of white buildings were gathered round the church.

"Puts you in mind of the east coast of England," Saxby commented.

"Or the Kent coast from Folkestone round to Dungeness," he said.

"Aye, but it shows how right the old rule of thumb is: low land warns of shallow water; cliffs tell of deep water."

"The boat is ready?"

"Six oarsmen, sir, and a boatkeeper in case you need one. And Mrs Wilson, sir."

"Very well, let's get started, before the wind gets up."

"You saw the ship alongside the jetty, sir?"

"Yes. Laden, from the look of her. Doesn't look Dutch to me."

"Oh no, she's Spanish – just look at that sheer. Quite graceful, for a merchant ship. Hasn't that fat fishwife look of a Dutchman."

"What do you reckon she'll be carrying?"

Saxby shrugged and held out his hands, palms uppermost. "She may have come in just to pick up a small quantity, having worked her way along the coast from somewhere like Cumaná or La Guaira. Hides, tobacco . . . maybe even live cattle: shifting a herd up or down the coast to different pastures."

"I'll try and find out. In fact we'll smell it as we get close." With that Ned went down the ladder and gave the order to cast off. As the men began rowing and he pushed over the tiller to steer for the river entrance, he looked the length of the *Griffin*. She looked innocent enough; just the number of guns one would expect a merchantman to carry; just the worn paint; just the wear on the mast where the hoops of the mainsail chafed. Saxby would have men up there in a few minutes painting on linseed oil. More important, the wary watchers on the shore would recognize a peaceful scene: a merchant ship had anchored and her crew were going about their normal day's work.

Ned was thankful it was still cool: the sun had not yet risen over the horizon so the light was not harsh to the eyes. The whitewashed houses seemed pink, but before the boat returned to the *Griffin* the sun would have risen and the white would be a glare.

He spotted several men at the seaward end of the little town, obviously watching both the ship and the boat. No one was rushing about; no horses galloped from one end of the town to the other raising the alarm or carrying self-important men. The church bell was not tolling a warning. Obviously no one regarded the ship as a threat; instead she was a welcome smuggler, with olive oil and wine, nails and household articles, material for clothing.

He steered the boat towards the jetty and saw that the ship secured alongside it, her hull green and with a small figurehead of some woman wearing a crown, was the *Nuestra Señora del Carmen*. The men in the *Griffin*'s boat could read the name painted across the transom. Although most of the other paint was peeling or worn, the name was picked out in gold leaf on a red scroll that ran almost the full width of the transom itself. "Cor, look at it," one of the men muttered. "Fancy having to paint all those letters!"

"Fancy having to carve them in the first place," said a man Yorke recognized as one of the carpenters. "An' when you've finished it you step back to admire it and realize you've left a letter out."

The jetty was substantial, built of stone, and halfway along it, on the opposite side to the ship, steps were cut in. Ned steered the boat and gave orders to the oarsmen so that they stopped beside the steps.

The boatkeeper jumped up with the painter and Ned followed with the sternfast. By the time the two of them had secured the lines, three or four Spaniards, one carrying a musket over his shoulder and wearing what seemed to be a uniform, had reached the landward end of the jetty and were walking out towards them.

Aurelia, her hair hidden under a black, wide-brimmed hat pulled forward over her face, and wearing a loose-fitting grey dress, came up the steps and stood with Ned.

"We'll wait for them here," Ned said, "but while we're waiting we'll just walk across the jetty and see what the *Carmen* is carrying."

"I can tell you. *Maïs. Comment dit-on en anglais?*"

"Maize – how do you know?"

"It's scattered all over the jetty beside the ship – can't you see it?"

Ned grinned and admitted: "I was watching the men coming along the jetty, but I think you're right. They must have finished loading last night – as soon as the birds realize what's waiting for them they'll be along!"

"Some are here already – they drew my attention to the grain," she admitted. "Do you still want to walk over?"

"No. The deputation is nearly here so we'll go and meet them."

Ned noted that there were three whose elaborate dress marked them as men of authority while the fourth, with the musket, was a guard who kept several paces behind and had a couple of feet of slowmatch looped over the fingers of his left hand, a small trail of smoke showing that he was ready to fire the gun.

The three men stopped five or six paces short of Ned, who bowed and introduced himself in English, motioning Aurelia to translate.

One man stepped forward and, removing his large hat with a flourish which sent the feathers waving, bowed to Ned and then to Aurelia. He gave his name but spoke too quickly for Ned to follow any further.

"This gentleman welcomes you and says he is Don Alvaro de Estaban, and he is the mayor of Riohacha. He congratulates me on my Spanish!"

Before Ned had time to reply, Don Alvaro had begun to introduce the other two men. "The first one is the Collector of Customs, the second is the town treasurer. All three are men of trade, Don Alvaro says."

The hint was broad enough and Ned bowed to the other two. "Tell them they can see that my ship is anchored off the river entrance, and that I have come here in the hope of doing business."

Aurelia translated and Ned could see by their expressions that it was welcome news. "Tell them that I want maize – enough to fill my ship."

He deliberately did not mention the second consignment he would need for Whetstone; at this stage it might cause suspicion. The town mayor greeted Aurelia's words with a broad smile and gestured to the *Carmen*. Then Aurelia translated.

"This ship finished loading with maize last night. She belongs to the town treasurer – the gentleman on the left – and is due to sail with it to Cartagena where, Don Alvaro says, she will get a good price."

"Of course," Ned agreed, "because no doubt it is good quality maize."

"Of the best, the treasurer says," Aurelia reported.

"Ask him how much he would expect to receive for a quintal in Cartagena."

"A quintal fetches at least two pieces of eight, and the ship is loaded with 7,800 quintals. He mentions a measure called a *tonnelada,* which is 26 quintals."

Ned remembered a Spanish quintal was about 101 pounds,

less than a hundredweight, so the *Carmen* was carrying about 350 tons. He also knew that he had a very few good cards in his hand. He had not seen the grain loaded so he had to take the Spaniards' word for the quantity. Because the *Carmen* was smaller than the *Griffin*, he still needed another fifty tons for himself and 200 tons for Whetstone and the *Peleus*, and he had no idea of the current price of the grain in Cartagena. Yet to his advantage was the fact that the owners (he assumed the town treasurer was simply the shipper) would leap at the chance of selling all the grain here in Riohacha at a higher price rather than risk shipping it round to Cartagena, knowing that pirates might capture the ship or a glut caused by a good harvest knock the bottom out of the market. Hurriedly he changed hundredweights into quintals. Six hundred tons was roughly 13,500 quintals.

"Would you or the owners sell me a total of 13,500 quintals?"

The treasurer moved into the familiar Latin pose: shoulders hunched forward, hands held out, palms upward. "Who knows? It would depend on the price."

"The price," Ned said as soon as Aurelia had translated, "would allow for your saving in shipping charges, insurance, risk of the ship's capture, or the price in Cartagena dropping."

"What have you heard about the Cartagena price dropping?"

The treasurer's alarm was obvious but the mayor muttered something, obviously warning him not to give himself away.

"Oh, it is common knowledge along the coast that there has been a very good harvest and the Cartagena market has too much," Ned said airily, "but I am prepared to pay a fair price."

"In gold?"

"In Spanish dollars."

"And what price had you in mind?"

"I might go as high as a dollar for four quintals."

Ned had been forced to guess and from the sudden glint in three pairs of eyes he knew he had pitched the price too high. Still, the governor of Jamaica would pay more, and it gave a good profit.

The treasurer was shaking his head and Ned found himself

bored with the haggling that must follow: it was like two cockerels fluffing their feathers and shaking their wattles yet knowing they would not fight.

"That is my price," Ned said. "I cannot improve it. I know –" this was a random shot, but it might succeed "– that there is plenty in Santa Marta. I called in Riohacha to save myself the extra distance, but it is only a hundred miles. I can be there tomorrow."

The treasurer held up a hand to detain Ned, who was pretending to get ready to return to the boat.

"Señor, give me a moment to think. Supposing (I am not, of course, agreeing to your price, but supposing) you bought the maize, how do you propose to arrange it?"

The idea came to Ned so easily he was momentarily frightened: buccaneering presented no moral problems. "I suggest I bring my ship in to the jetty and first you load the extra, and I pay for it. I can then deliver that to my principals," (how easily this jargon comes to the tongue, he thought) "and then I will return and we will transfer the *Carmen*'s cargo to my ship."

The treasurer nodded but the mayor said: "You did not mention the name of your ship, señor."

"The *Griffin*."

The three of them repeated the name but obviously they had never heard of it.

The treasurer suddenly made up his mind. "Very well, you bring your ship in, and by the time you are at the jetty my donkeys will have started to bring the grain. Now, about the payment . . ."

"I will show you the gold and we put the bag at that end of the jetty." Ned pointed to the landward end. "You provide some guards and I provide the same number. When the cargo is loaded, I will withdraw my guards."

"Ah, it is a pleasure to deal with a straightforward man," the treasurer said, and obviously meant it. "Let us say three guards each?"

"Agreed," Ned said. "So if you will excuse me I will bring the ship in. I suggest when I return here from unloading, we use the same procedure while transferring the *Carmen*'s cargo?"

"Without doubt," agreed the treasurer.

An hour later the *Griffin* was secured on the opposite side of the jetty to the *Carmen*. Saxby had used the boats to warp the ship round so that her bow headed towards the middle of the river, and the *Carmen* and the English ship were lying side by side, bow to bow and separated only by the width of the jetty.

The first of the donkeys arrived with sacks of grain lodged on the wooden frames looking like sawing horses and used as saddles. A dozen extra Spaniards, obviously labourers, arrived to help unload the donkeys and carry the sacks of grain on board, where the *Griffin*'s men slid them down inclined planks into the hold and stowed them.

A Spaniard, obviously an overseer, stood by counting the sacks and marking down the numbers on his slate, and one of Saxby's men stood beside him with a similar slate.

Simpson, the mate, stood at the top of the hatch, clear of the dust being raised by the bags, shouting down orders to ensure the grain was stowed evenly so that the ship remained trimmed. At the end of the jetty Burton and two other men with muskets stood with three Spanish soldiers guarding a canvas bag filled with dollars, payment for the 250 tons. Saxby and the treasurer had earlier counted it and then secured the drawstrings on the bag. Saxby then produced a flat piece of sheet lead about two inches square, put the two ends of the drawstrings in the middle and folded over the lead as though closing a book. He hammered the lead until it formed a lump, an effective seal that prevented the drawstrings being slackened without breaking it. Saxby scratched three parallel lines on one side of the lump and the treasurer marked his initials on the other, and departed happily once he saw the money under guard.

Saxby went back on board the *Griffin* and joined Ned and Aurelia in the cabin. He reported what he had done and that the mules and donkeys were arriving regularly.

"You were right, sir," he said, "there's not a soul on board the *Carmen*. Her hatches are battened down and she's ready for sea. Perhaps the crew are having some leave. Or just being Spanish and not hurrying."

"I wonder if they're due back in a day or so," Ned mused.

Aurelia shook her head. "Surely, now that the treasurer man knows you are buying the grain, he'll tell the crew he does not want them. He does not seem the kind of man to pay wages unnecessarily."

"You're right, ma'am," Saxby said. "When we're back here and ready to transfer the cargo he'll send along these donkey drivers and slaves to help us carry the bags across."

Aurelia smiled at Ned. "It seems such a lot of trouble, doesn't it? We sail with 250 tons of grain and find Thomas and transfer 200 tons of it to the *Peleus,* so that she is fully loaded, and then we have to sail all the way back here to fill up this ship from the *Carmen.* . . ."

"Yes," Ned said, amused by the glint in her eyes, "it is a lot of trouble. It embarrasses me to bother the treasurer in this way. Now, listen, this is what we are going to do. First, send for Simpson and Burton."

As soon as the mate and the gunner had arrived, Ned spent ten minutes explaining his plan, another ten minutes listening to Saxby, Simpson and Burton choosing men, and then outlining his timetable.

"How many donkeys are they using?" he asked.

"Twenty, and each carries four bags."

"Our cargo will comprise 5,544 quintal bags, so that means about seventy loads for each donkey."

Burton said: "Each donkey is away about five minutes. I timed a few because I wondered where the grain was stored."

"Let's say ten minutes a load, so each donkey brings twenty-four sacks in an hour. Thus all the donkeys together are delivering 480 bags an hour. Our 5,544 bags will take nearly twelve hours. They'll stop work soon after nightfall."

Ned, whose mathematics were always weak, recalled that the first bags had thumped down on the jetty beside the *Griffin* at half past seven that morning.

"Yes, perhaps even earlier, because that treasurer will want his bag of dollars under guard in his own house tonight, and he knows the only way that will happen is to keep those donkeys trotting. So we will be sailing tonight, as soon as the moon has risen. That will be about half past nine." He looked at the three men. "You'll have the hatches battened down and your men ready by then?"

They all nodded cheerfully.

"The dust from the grain is making 'em all very dry,"

Saxby commented, "so I'm going to double the issue of water."

"No rumbullion, though," Ned said. "Steady hands and no Dutch courage, that's what we need."

"The rumbullion is locked up, sir, and the key's here," Saxby said, slapping his breeches pocket.

"Right, then I think you and I will take some exercise by walking up and down the jetty a few times, and perhaps we might stroll down towards the river mouth and see something of the town. It'll make Mrs Judd jealous if she thinks you'll be seeing a few beautiful señoritas."

"Some hope . . . They'll all be fat and they're kept indoors. You might see an eye round the side of a curtain, but that'll be all. Valencia – I was there once. The only women I saw were 'ores."

"Well, Riohacha is not quite Valencia, but put your hat on and let's inspect it."

Chapter
Sixteen

At exactly six o'clock, with the sun beginning to drop below the horizon, Saxby came to report that the last donkey had unloaded the last bags. "Both slates agree, sir, so we have 5,544 bags on board."

"We can start battening down now. Are there many Spaniards out there?"

"No, sir: the tallyman is waiting for us to agree on his figures – perhaps ma'am could tell him in Spanish. The donkey drivers have gone, so there are just the dozen labourers getting their last few bags on board. The Spanish guards will leave with the money when we give the word. Now and then a few people walk past the end of the jetty and look at the *Griffin* but none comes close."

Aurelia stood up. "Shall I see the tallyman and the guards?"

Ned nodded and Saxby opened the door and led the way on deck. Ned sat down on one of the two chairs, hot and weary and unwilling to admit that he felt very nervous. Or was it guilty? Perhaps apprehensive and guilty – the way he had felt as a small boy when he knew his tutor was going to discover some major misdemeanour.

How would Whetstone feel if he was in this position? He suddenly saw the bearded buccaneer – he would be roaring with laughter and probably hoisting a naked and giggling Diana into the bunk, shouting orders that he was not to be disturbed for an hour.

Ned knew he had to adopt the buccaneer's attitude. Most

tasks in life, he thought, involved individual attitudes. A man occupying a particular job adopted the attitude that went with it, as though it was a uniform. Did one ever see a cheerful-looking gravedigger? No, he would have a long face and mudcaked boots. A bishop had cope and mitre, round red·face and an unctuous voice. A butcher had plump, pink cheeks, smiling face and waved the steel back and forth across the blade of his knife while listening respectfully to a customer giving an order. Puritan parsons wore frowns in the same way as highwaymen wore masks. Buccaneers – well, Thomas Whetstone was the first he had ever met, and if he was typical Ned knew he would never fit in yet would always feel at home with them.

Ned knew he was avoiding thinking about the most important aspect of it. A buccaneer was free to choose his garb, his diocese (he chuckled at the choice of word), his ship and his mistress. How did *he* view his – was it a calling, a vocation, a habit, a weakness? By regarding it as privateering, and therefore as legally waging war against Spain, he found it affected him morally the same way as running a plantation: it was gambling. One planted seed and gambled that the weather would be good, that – in the case of sugar, for instance – the rains would come at the regular time and no hurricane would smash down the cane, or no drought turn the land into a scorched, brown and withered wilderness. With privateering you had a ship and a commission giving you permission to fight the Spanish, and (according to the law) any prizes or booty had to be legally condemned by an Admiralty court, with a percentage paid to the government. But if your ship was damaged, in battle or storm, you paid for the repairs; any seamen wounded were compensated on an agreed scale out of your pocket (or rather, the ship's pocket).

You were lucky or unlucky; like farming, buccaneering was a gamble. When it was compared with running a plantation, Ned found he could accept buccaneering as a similar sort of gamble. However, if peace with Spain was ever signed, he knew that would be when he and Thomas Whetstone would probably part company; to continue raiding and robbing the Spanish in peacetime would be simple piracy and no different from robbing one's neighbour.

Yet supposing the Spanish signed a peace treaty with England but still insisted that no foreigners had any right to be in the Caribbee, and sent to the mines any they captured. Supposing England was so weak, or France or Holland became so weak, that they had to agree to a harsh peace with Spain and could not insist that the treaty gave their own people the freedom of these seas? Would he then regard it as piracy? Or buccaneering forced on him by the behaviour of Spanish? "No peace beyond the Line" had been the rule, or slogan, from the day the English first started planting in Barbados and St Christopher; it had continued when the French and Dutch arrived and found that the Spanish harried them too.

It meant, he realized, that it did not matter what happened in Europe. England could be at war with France, France with the Netherlands and Spain could be at peace with all three, but out here in the West Indies, Spain was always at war with the English, the French and the Dutch. And likewise the English, French and Dutch out here for the most part remained friends, no matter what their governments were doing in Europe, because they needed to be allies against the common enemy, Spain. So if England signed a peace with Spain, he admitted, he would probably continue to sail with Thomas and Diana . . .

Aurelia returned to the cabin and put an end to the thoughts racing through his head like hens bolting through a hole in the hedge. She came over and held his face between her hands and then kissed him. "My man of two worlds!"

He pulled her down so she was sitting on his lap. "Which two worlds had you in mind?"

"Well, at first I knew Mr Yorke who owned Kingsnorth. A very quietly-spoken man who some thought shy and others withdrawn. A man of perfect manners, who seemed to have read more books than anyone else in Barbados knew existed. Yet a man who ran his plantation well and a man who rarely drank and had never been seen drunk. That was the gossip I heard. You were a man whose world comprised Kingsnorth. No hot waters – it was said you drank only the juices of fruit – and no wife or mistress, and an earl's son. You were the most discussed bachelor in the island: there was not a wife who was not planning to have a younger sister out from England to stay in the hope of landing you, or a cousin or a friend's daughter. In fact," she said with an impish smile and kissing him again, "you had six such young ladies introduced to you after they arrived here to find husbands, you being the first choice, but you were very polite to them and that was all."

"No one knew," he said, slipping his hand beneath her loose-fitting jerkin, "that I had long since fallen in love with a grey-haired, shrewish married woman!"

"Shrewish? Shrew?"

"*Musaraigne* is a shrew. We use it also to mean *une mégère*."

"*Merci!* A shrew, yes. But grey-haired?"

"In some lights your hair is so blonde it seems grey. The very light grey of an ash twig."

"Yes, I can see that a poor lonely young man could fall into the hands of such a woman. She was English, I suppose; the skin of her face like calico."

"No, she was French."

"Ah, a scheming old French *mégère*," she said. "No wonder those poor girls were turned away. That long voyage out here, and then back to England . . . what a waste." She was unlacing his jerkin as he pulled the cord of hers through the last eyelet. "Put the bar across the door," she murmured as she stood up and unbuckled her breeches.

"You didn't tell me about my second world," he said.

"Ah, that's the one I like. The world of Buccaneer Yorke, who robs the Spanish and seduces helpless young French *musaraignes*."

Yorke stood with Saxby and Aurelia in the darkness on the *Griffin*'s poop watching the slightly higher land to the eastward on the other side of the river. Beyond the low-lying forest the tops of the lime trees were beginning to show up as though there was a distant fire behind them; as though some farmer was burning the brush and old grass on a hillside to ensure a good new growth when the rains came.

The glow, more golden than red, spread as though worked by an artist's brush until they could see the upper edge of a full moon. Then, with an almost startling suddenness, the complete circle was above the trees, lighting the peaks of the distant mountains.

"They look like teats on a sow's belly," Saxby commented. "In daylight they don't seem so regular."

Yorke looked over the *Griffin*'s taffrail. There was no one on the jetty nor anyone walking along the track passing the end of it. The last light in the town of Riohacha had been put out half an hour ago. The town slept.

Below the level of the *Griffin*'s bulwarks next to the jetty there was an occasional movement. Finally Ned touched Saxby's arm. "Time you were going, old friend."

They shook hands and Aurelia kissed him on the cheek.

Saxby faced the men crouching inside the bulwarks and said hoarsely: "Carmens, follow me. Quiet now. Don't forget, halyards, sheets and cast off fore and aft. And the springs!"

He hurried barefooted through the entryport and Yorke watched him move deliberately across the jetty, disappearing against the shadowy Spanish ship as he went through her entryport. Behind him, like a snake, two dozen men followed. One went aft and another forward to stand by the ropes holding the ship to the jetty.

Yorke faced forward. "Griffins – man the halyards, see the sheets are clear for running. Get in both springs and stand by forward and aft."

The east wind, light as it was, blew the length of the jetty so that each ship could put her helm over the opposite way and sail off the jetty. Yorke saw that Saxby was luckier with the *Carmen* because although the river was not running very strongly it took the Spanish ship away from the jetty while pushing the *Griffin* against it. Still, scratched paintwork was to be expected; he could only hope he would not slam the *Griffin*'s stern into the stonework.

He watched Saxby's men hauling in the mooring ropes and saw the heavy gaff beginning to lift jerkily off the boom, halyards squeaking as they rounded blocks aloft. Then a flying jib raced up and was sheeted home, an almost perfect triangle with the flax pinkish in the moonlight. Another headsail went up as the gaff worked its way aloft, the mainsail unfolding beneath it, like a tailor displaying a roll of cloth. And he could see the *Carmen*'s bowsprit swinging away as the ship left the jetty and began to turn in the centre of the river, heading for the entrance.

Yorke looked astern along the jetty. No figures running

out with swords and pikes; no horses thundering up the track from the town.

"Cast off forward, cast off aft," he called to the two men standing on the jetty. Then, facing forward, he said: "Up mainsail . . . now, watch the throat halyard!"

For some unknown reason, despite plenty of tallow, the block on the mast through which the throat halyard first rendered sometimes jammed, and it was a type for which they had no spare.

Half a dozen men were pushing the *Griffin* away from the jetty using sweeps, and from the way the bow was trying to pay off to larboard the river was ebbing gently.

The moment the *Griffin*'s stern was clear of the end of the jetty he gave a series of orders, the first of which had the men hauling the sweeps on board out of the way while the second started the headsails soaring up.

He snapped an order to the helmsman to bear away another point, so that although the *Griffin* was heading away from the river entrance her sails filled better and she gathered speed. Yorke wanted to be sure that when he tacked the ship turned fast enough to avoid being caught in irons, stopped with the wind blowing down both sides of the sails. If that happened, it would take only moments to lose control and drift ignominiously aground on the far side of the river.

The moonlight showed the curving canvas of the sails and he could hear the water swept aside by the *Griffin*'s bow. Now was the time to tack, and as he gave the first orders he had a moment to glance over the larboard beam. Saxby had the *Carmen* abreast the town and in the middle of the channel, heading for the entrance. There was no flash of a musket or pistol.

Slowly the *Griffin*'s bow swung to larboard; the jibs thumped as they were blown across on to the other tack and sheeted home, and then the mainboom slammed across with a noise Yorke thought must be heard in Cartagena. The *Griffin* seemed like an excited horse galloping towards a fence represented by the river entrance.

"They sleep well here," Aurelia said, in a quiet voice which startled Ned more than a musket shot would have done: the concentration of sailing the *Griffin* out of Riohacha had driven every other thought from his mind.

"Yes. Saxby must have reached the open sea. It is difficult to judge distance in the moonlight: the shadows are deceptive."

Aurelia obviously waited until they had passed Riohacha and the *Griffin* was beginning to pitch gently as she reached the open sea before she said: "The treasurer was trying to cheat us, but we've ended up cheating him!"

Ned held out his hands in imitation of a Spaniard. "We intended to rob him, but as a buccaneering attack I think we failed."

Aurelia looked crestfallen. "Failed? In what way? You have all the maize you wanted, and an extra ship!"

"Yes, I forgot the value of the ship. But we paid the price asked for the 250 tons we have on board the *Griffin* – four times what that scoundrel could get in Cartagena, so he has made a handsome profit on that grain. Admittedly he has lost his ship – if indeed he owned her – and the cargo. But we could have rowed in during the night and cut out the *Carmen*."

"Well, we must be the only buccaneers who pay bills!" Aurelia said contentedly.

"I shall not make a habit of it," Ned said firmly. "Ah – Saxby's bearing away. We should meet Thomas in five or six hours' time. He's going to be surprised to see two ships."

"It saves us rowing more than five thousand bags over in boats," Aurelia said thankfully. "That would have taken weeks. I'm looking forward to telling Diana what we've done! We qualify as proper buccaneers now!"

"I think you really glory in that," Ned teased. "You would make such an elegant mistress of a great plantation. Now you are just the mistress –" he rubbed his hand over his chin "– of an unshaven buccaneer."

"I know which I prefer! Now every day is new and exciting and I look forward to it. In Barbados I dreaded going to bed because it meant waking up to the *ennui* of yet another day . . ."

Ned turned and said sharply to the men at the helm: "You are supposed to be following Mr Saxby!"

"Sorry sir," one of them said. "but the *Carmen* is yawing a lot. They're having to get used to the way she steers."

Ned walked aft with Aurelia. "It's the same with women; you have to get used to the way they steer."

The coastline was low, but suddenly Ned nudged Aurelia and pointed over the larboard bow. In the distance and well inland a group of mountain peaks were snow covered and the bright moonlight glinting on them made it seem that someone had thrown a handful of diamonds on to a piece of rumpled black velvet.

Aurelia sighed and alarmed Ned, but she explained: "They are so beautiful. Who knows when we shall ever see them again in the moonlight. What mountains are they?"

"The Sierra Nevada de Santa Marta, according to the chart. They must be a great help when making a landfall in moonlight or daylight."

Aurelia refused to go below: the moonlight flickering on the swell waves as they rolled past the *Griffin* in their endless procession to the westward, the curves of the sails making dancing shadows as the ship rolled, the excitement of sailing to find the *Peleus* – all this, she told Ned, meant she could not sleep anyway.

The *Nuestra Señora del Carmen* was just rounding up to anchor, with the *Griffin* in her wake, when there was a flash in the dawn sky as the *Peleus* fired a gun and a roundshot ricocheted close under the Spanish ship's bow.

Ned froze as the noise of a cannon firing echoed across the bay, but he relaxed as he realized that Thomas Whetstone was taking no chances: Thomas was expecting the *Griffin,* but when she appeared led by what was obviously a Spanish ship, from the shape of her hull and the cut of her sails, he assumed the worst.

It was still too dark to stand on the bulwarks and wave, so that Thomas would recognize individual people, yet to get closer to the *Peleus* would mean that Thomas would fire a broadside. Quickly he gave orders for the *Griffin* tó luff up and drop her mainsail and jib, and while that was done shouted to the bosun to stand by to anchor. But the wind and current were carrying the *Griffin* close to the *Peleus* and if Thomas had any sense he would suspect a trap; the *Griffin* would be just the sort of Trojan horse to drift alongside the *Peleus* and pour out Spanish soldiers.

The trumpeter! One of the carpenters could play a trumpet and often practised. Was he on board or had Saxby taken him in the *Carmen*?

"Neal! Neal! Send Neal aft!"

A moment later he was relieved to see a man running along the deck towards him and recognized the gawky shape of the carpenter.

"Quick, get your trumpet! Aim it at the *Peleus* and play some English tune!"

"What tune, sir?"

"I don't care!" Ned blazed, "but if you don't start inside a minute we'll get a broadside from the *Peleus*."

The man bolted below and a few moments later was back, scrambling up on to the bulwark. He balanced himself and the tune of "Early One Morning", strident and piercing, seemed to ricochet across the bay. Almost at once Ned saw a lantern on the *Peleus*'s deck and it began flashing as someone waved his hand across the window.

"Was he shooting at poor Mr Saxby?" Aurelia asked.

"He was ready to shoot at all of us!"

"But why? He must have recognized the *Griffin*."

"The *Griffin*, yes, but not the *Carmen*. It was our fault entirely; we should have made some signal, or anchored further away to leeward, where he'd know we could not attack him."

By now the *Griffin* was anchored and as soon as a boat had been hoisted over the side Aurelia said excitedly: "Come on, *chéri*, let's go over and see them!"

Ned called for the boat's crew and ten minutes later he and Aurelia were climbing up a rope ladder to board the *Peleus*. Thomas was waiting at the top, far from his usual exuberant self. "Ned, how can I apologize? I thought you'd been captured and the Dons were using your ship against me. That other vessel *is* a Spaniard, isn't she?"

Whetstone was so shamefaced that both Ned and Aurelia burst out laughing. "Yes, she *was* Spanish, but you were firing across Saxby's bow! She's our prize, the *Nuestra Señora del Carmen*, with 350 tons of maize."

"*Your* prize? But . . ."

"And we have another two hundred and fifty tons in the *Griffin*. Six hundred tons for Jamaica!"

Diana, who had been standing in the shadows beside the mainmast, came forward. "I apologize again for Thomas. He was so sure you were Dons springing a trap on him."

"We've a lot to learn," Ned said soberly. "It was our fault for not signalling to you somehow."

"Well, you did eventually – 'Early One Morning' sounded beautiful, though I must admit I had not heard it on a trumpet before!"

"And appropriate, too," Whetstone said. "About half an hour early, I should say. But the sun will be up by the time we get some hot drinks! Steward!" he bellowed. "Cook! Light that galley fire again since we shan't be going into action after all, and let's have a good breakfast. Will Saxby come over?" he asked Ned. "I'll send a boat for him."

He stumped off, giving orders right and left, and Diana linked arms with Aurelia. "You've had an exciting time!"

"No, it was all very quiet – at least, until Thomas made that big bang."

Diana was puzzled and just as Thomas returned she asked: "Why did you buy that other ship as well as the maize?"

"Oh no, we buccaneered that ship," Aurelia said matter-of-factly. "Can one 'buccaneer' a ship? Well, we stole it. First we bought 5,544 quintals of maize and loaded it on board the *Griffin*. There were another 350 tons in the *Carmen,* which was lying at the jetty. We were going to buy it but then we decided to take the *Carmen* as well as her cargo to make up the 600 tons and to save you, Thomas, the bother of transferring the maize to the *Peleus*." She winked at Diana. "And we know what a slow ship the *Peleus* is, Thomas; we thought that if we loaded her with maize we'd never get to Jamaica!"

"You are learning m'dear," Thomas said, "but remember, criticize a man's wife, criticize his manners, but *never* criticize his ship!"

With that he walked aft with Ned to hear the details, and the two men returned ten minutes later, by which time the smoke from the galley chimney indicated that breakfast would not be long, and announced that they would be starting for Jamaica at noon. They had agreed to leave Saxby in command of the prize, with Simpson as his mate. Whetstone's second mate would join the *Griffin* for the voyage to act as the navigator, teaching Ned the rudiments of navigation at the same time.

"Six hundred tons of maize and a prize ship! Ned m'boy, you'll be rich!" Thomas exclaimed.

"And so will you!"

"How so? I've just sat here at anchor, peacefully whipping rope's ends!"

"We go halves. We'd agreed on that."

"But that was assuming I'd do something towards it."

Aurelia said: "Just knowing you were here – that helped. And it was pure luck that we could sail off with the *Carmen*. If you'd been there you'd have taken the mayor, the bishop and the treasurer too and made them pay ransom!"

"You flatter me, but thank you: the Whetstone treasury is looking rather empty at the moment. It is a pleasant thought, though, that the Lord Protector's exchequer will soon be helping to fill it, through the governor of Jamaica."

Chapter Seventeen

Again light winds made it a slow passage to Jamaica and the three ships rounded the sandspit at Caguas six days after leaving the bay west of Riohacha. The great anchorage was empty but for four small privateers and a dozen fishing canoes, but the three ships had not been anchored for more than half an hour before a canoe brought out a fastidious young army lieutenant whose well-cut uniform was liberally encrusted with fish scales from his passage in the canoe. He came on board, walked uninvited down to the cabin, sat down in the chair and proceeded to brush the fish scales from his uniform. Ned walked over to him, lifted him out of the chair by the collar and ordered him back into the canoe.

"You can come on board this ship when you smell less like a fishmonger!"

"But I am an ADC to the governor! I have orders for you!"

"Will you go down the ladder or shall I have a couple of my men toss you over the side?"

When the lieutenant came back up the ladder ten minutes later, no fish scales were visible but his clothes still stank of rotting fish. The moment he set foot on deck Ned said quietly:

"Introduce yourself."

"But I say, I've had enough of –"

Ned pointed down to the canoe. "No one comes on board the ship I own and command and gives me orders, least of all army officers recruited in Billingsgate."

"Rowlands," he said sulkily. "Edward Rowlands, lieutenant, 48th Foot. General Heffer, the military Governor, has given orders that you –"

Ned raised his hand. "I am not interested in verbal orders from anyone."

"I have written orders here," Rowlands admitted. "I was–"

"You impudent rascal. Give me the packet and get down into your canoe!"

"But I need a reply."

"Send someone else for it; you smell too much and lack the manners to be allowed on board this ship again."

Protesting but nevertheless obeying, the lieutenant backed out the entryport as Ned broke the seal on the governor's orders. They were brief: the *Griffin* and the *Peleus,* which appeared to be laden, were to unload their cargo of maize at the Cagway jetty at once. Ned noticed the anglicized name of the port and went up on deck to wave across at Thomas Whetstone, indicating that he should come on board. The *Peleus*'s boat was already in the water, hoisted out as the canoe came in sight being paddled from the shore.

Thomas heard of Ned's insisting that the lieutenant brush off the fish scales in the canoe and bellowed with laughter. "Good for you – I'd have tossed him over the side. You're too soft-hearted!"

Ned handed him the general's orders and at once Thomas's manner changed. His face went grim, and he shook his head slowly. "I don't like this man," he growled. "For a start any sailor could tell him that the *Peleus* is in ballast; second, why isn't he inquiring about the third ship, which *is* obviously fully laden; and third, this reads more like an order to arrest a corporal for drunkenness. Starving Commonwealth generals don't order me about. We sell them goods for an agreed price, and that's as far as it goes."

Relieved that Thomas's attitude was the same as his own, Ned said: "The general probably wrote these orders days ago, ready for our return: that would explain why they refer to only two ships. Why don't you and I pay him – what's his name, Heffer – a visit? In the meantime the three ships stay at anchor."

Thomas nodded. "Treat him as though he is a Spaniard!"

They found General Heffer in his headquarters at the

large, airy house at Cagway, so built by the Spanish that from its balconies there was a fine view southwards over the sea and northwards across the anchorage to the mountain ridge.

Ned immediately recognized Heffer as a Cassius: anyone with any sense, let alone Caesar, would demand that the men about him should be sleek "and such as sleep o' nights". Heffer had the "lean and hungry look" of a man who thought and plotted too much. Tall, thin, gaunt of face and with eyes that were sunken and seemed to burn with a feverish zeal, he looked as though he would have been more at home as a Jesuit, ordering a few more turns on the rack.

He was sitting at a table writing when Ned and Thomas were announced and he continued for another three or four minutes before looking up to ask in a harsh voice: "Which of you is –?"

Ned nodded, for a moment startled before realizing this was only Heffer's way of distinguishing them.

"I want the maize unloaded at once."

"We shall want paying at once, too," Thomas said amiably.

"I am requisitioning your cargoes in the name of the Commonwealth."

"Are you indeed," Thomas drawled. "Well, that hardly concerns me because my ship is in ballast – in army terms that means she has no cargo on board – but I can't see my friend agreeing."

"What do you mean you have no cargo?"

"My ship is empty. The *Griffin* is carrying 250 tons of maize and her prize, the *Nuestra Señora del Carmen,* has 350 tons. So there are 600 tons of maize out there belonging to my friend."

Whetstone's voice was friendly; his face had the benevolent smile of a bearded friar. It should not, Ned thought, have fooled anyone, least of all a general.

Heffer looked up at Ned. "Your cargo is requisitioned."

Ned nodded as though agreeing. "The price is what was agreed before we sailed, of course."

"Price? Who is talking of price? I've just told you, your cargoes are requisitioned."

Ned nodded as though agreeing. "We understood your

problem; the garrison of Jamaica is starving. Still, you – or, rather your deputy, Major Slinger – did agree that if we could provide you with grain you would pay a certain price."

"We are at war," Heffer said. "The Spaniards might attack any moment."

"How true, how true," Ned said dreamily. "When we went into Riohacha and took the grain, I remember commenting that we are at war with Spain, and they might attack us any moment."

"Quite so," Heffer snapped. "Now, I want that grain unloaded at once."

"We can start unloading as soon as you have paid," Ned said, still in a dreamy voice. "Six hundred tons. Your tallymen will of course check, but we checked it too."

"I don't want to have to say this again," Heffer said angrily, "but that grain is requisitioned. I shall send troops out to take control of the ships. You are under orders from me to bring the grain ships in to the jetty, one each side. Now."

"Oh dear me," Ned said sadly, like a disappointed curate. "Troops in boats, eh?"

Heffer stood up and went to the door. "Rowlands! Send two platoons to each of those ships and two ensigns to take command."

With that he slammed the door and sat down at the table, picking up his pen and continuing to write.

"General," Ned said softly, "may I interrupt for a moment?"

Heffer looked up, obviously irritated and expecting Ned and Thomas to leave the room. "Well, what is it?"

"Just a slight difficulty. Before I came on shore to see you, I left orders for the mate of the *Griffin* (that is my own ship) and the acting master of my prize . . ."

"What the devil has that to do with me?"

"The orders were to prevent anyone from boarding and if soldiers came out in dugouts the ship's companies should sink them. If necessary they will also flood the holds of the two ships."

Heffer suddenly stood up, sending his chair flying. "You would never dare do that! You are bluffing! Why, you'd lose your ships. They'd just sink!"

This time it was Thomas's turn to shake his head. He had been silent for longer than he was accustomed. "General, we are rough sailors and know nothing about soldiering. Why, we couldn't tell a cavalry caracole from a pint of small beer. Still, we can be forgiven our ignorance because you know nothing about ships."

"Well, I don't see what this has to do with grain, but most certainly I know nothing about ships, which seem to me always to reek of bilgewater and swarm with rats."

"Indeed, how right you are. But do you appreciate that the cargo holds can be flooded without losing the ships? My friend arranged matters so that enough water would be allowed in to ruin the grain, but then the sodden grain could be thrown over the side."

Heffer looked wide-eyed at each man and then fixed his stare on Ned. "But why should you have given such orders? You had no reason to distrust me. After all, I am the representative here of the Lord Protector and Council of State."

Ned, scarcely able to believe his ears, shrugged his shoulders. "In business, one always has some security, or deposit. My friend and I thought we ought to have some sort of security because although you through Slinger struck a bargain with us before we sailed, who knows, some senior officer might have overruled you . . ."

"Senior officer overruled me? I *am* the senior officer," Heffer said crossly. "And I never break my word. You failed to make any arrangements for collecting the money. Now, what do you suggest?"

Ned said casually: "Well, if you really do want the grain, we will conduct it according to our normal rules of business."

"What are those?" Heffer said suspiciously.

"Full payment for the 250 tons is taken on board the *Peleus* and handed over to my friend here. Then I will bring the *Griffin* alongside and you can unload her."

"What about the Spanish ship?"

"Ah, we must be patient. As soon as the *Griffin* is unloaded, you deliver the full price for the Spanish ship's 350 tons of grain on board the *Peleus,* and then we bring the *Carmen* alongside and unload her."

"But what is to stop you bolting with her the moment you get the money on board the *Peleus*?"

"Nothing," Ned said bluntly. "But remember this: we sailed from here to the Main to get you the grain: we kept our word. You have no reason to distrust us. But the moment we arrived back with the grain, you decided to requisition it and not pay us. You did not keep your word. *We* have no reason to trust *you*."

Heffer banged the table. "I never gave my word!"

Ned stared at him. "Didn't you? I thought you did."

Heffer shook his head triumphantly. "If you recall the conversation exactly, Major Slinger never gave his word."

"In that case," Ned said, "we shall need the full price in gold, as agreed, to be delivered on board the *Peleus* before the *Griffin* or the *Carmen* come alongside and one bag is unloaded."

"This is ridiculous – why, I'll sink your ships!"

"That would be quite impossible for you, but anyway it would lose the maize." He turned to Whetstone. "You were right, Thomas, I can see why they never captured Santo Domingo. We'll find a better market in Havana." He gave Heffer an ironic bow. "Good day to you."

For a few moments Heffer looked desperate, finally running to the door and standing with his back to it. "I must have that grain! My men are starving."

Whetstone's voice cut across the room like a whiplash. "General Heffer, you are a thief but an incompetent one. You have the money to buy the grain, but you intended to persuade us to get it and then you'd requisition it. However, you'd report to the Council of State that you had to buy it at the current market price and you'd put the money in your pocket."

"How dare you – why, I shall –"

Whetstone waved aside the man's stammerings. "Heffer," he snapped, deliberately omitting his rank, "my friend and I deal with the Spanish. They are very cunning, very shrewd and very dishonest. But my friend and I survive; indeed, we flourish. We rate people like you as less troublesome than a cutpurse. You have the imagination of a pander. Now, yes or no; do you want the grain at the agreed price?"

"Yes, of course."

"Then send the full price out to the *Peleus*. Use a canoe with slaves rowing. Your fishy Mr Rowlands will be the only soldier and he will wait in the canoe until we have counted it."

"But —"

"Those are our terms. No grain until we have the money. By the way, you had better stop your soldiers going out in those boats: all that grain might be ruined!"

With an agonized screech Heffer ran out of the door, bellowing for Rowlands.

Ned and Thomas walked out of the building and along to their boat. "You know," Thomas said, "neither of us is a bully by nature . . ."

"No," Ned agreed, "but men like that bring out the worst in me."

"Not the worst; there's no rule that makes you carry your valuables where they can be taken by a pickpocket."

It took two days to unload the *Griffin* and five to hoist all the sacks of grain out of the *Carmen*. Much to General Heffer's annoyance, Ned insisted that no more than twenty-five soldiers be on the jetty at any one time, and had seamen armed with muskets and pistols to enforce the order.

By now Ned felt competent to command the *Griffin* providing he had a navigator, so that Saxby could remain in command of the *Carmen*. There was no Admiralty court in Jamaica and General Heffer had never mentioned her, so Ned and Thomas Whetstone had decided that the prize should have her name discreetly changed and Ned's forger should draw up a certificate of registry naming the four people each owning sixteen of the sixty-four shares in which ownership of a British vessel was vested. The owners would be Ned, Aurelia, Thomas and Diana. Giving her a new name had presented no difficulty: she had, in effect, risen from the ashes so she was called *Phoenix*.

The grain money from the general had been divided, with both Ned and Thomas agreeing that Saxby deserved a share, and from that had emerged a new plan: from now on the three ships would act together as proper buccaneers, with everyone serving on a shares basis.

Thomas and Ned had worked for several hours on the

plan. They had a complete list of the names and ratings of everyone on board the three ships, including the women. So far as was possible they rated the men in the way the Royal Navy did, with completely unskilled men put down as landmen, competent men as ordinary seamen, and very good men as able seamen. They did not appoint any petty officers except for three bosuns. Thomas kept his own in the *Peleus* and Ned had the *Griffin*'s regular one, but Thomas' finest seaman was made bosun of the *Phoenix*.

Finally, armed with the lists and their proposals, the two men had everyone in the three ships meet on board the *Griffin*, where Thomas addressed them.

With three ships, he told them, they could carry out some good buccaneering expeditions, and for that reason he and Mr Yorke were proposing that everyone went on to the accepted "no purchase, no pay" arrangement, with the regular division of the purchase.

Mrs Judd, who had never heard the word used before in this context, demanded to know what "purchase" was.

"It is the polite word for whatever we capture," Thomas said. "You could call it 'loot', but that is such a vulgar word."

He then went on to describe how it was customary to divide a ship's purchase into a hundred parts. Each person was entitled to a certain number of shares or parts, according to his rank. A certain number went to the ship, to pay for replacement of rope, sails, powder, shot and repairs.

"What about anyone who gets a leg knocked off, or a sword in his gizzard?" asked the indomitable Mrs Judd.

Whetstone waved a sheet of paper. "Here's the list of the most likely wounds – losing a leg, an arm, blinded in one eye, and so on. And beside each one is the shares such a man gets. Obviously the highest share goes to a combination like losing a leg and an arm and the sight of one eye.

"Now, the wounded are always the first to be paid out. That means if we have a lot of wounded in a particular attack, there will be less of the purchase left to share among those who escaped without injury. But that's fair, you'll all agree?"

Everyone murmured his approval.

"So this is what happens. With all your approval, I shall be the leader of the squadron. Mr Yorke and Mr Saxby will agree to this because I've been buccaneering a few years.

Very well, I decide where we shall attack. In fact this will be done in agreement with everyone. If someone does not want to stay on board his ship for a particular attack, he's free to leave the ship and go on shore."

"And get beastly drunk, I suppose," Mrs Judd declared.

"Perhaps," Whetstone said with a grin. "Anyway, we attack, and it doesn't matter whether one ship, two or three get purchase, we all meet together later and share it out, a third to each ship. Then each ship divides her part into a hundred shares."

Whetstone then described how they were proposing to change some of the men from one ship to another. "Some of you who have been with me for three years or more will be going to one of the other ships. There's no compulsion, though. Some less experienced will be coming to the *Peleus*."

"What about the lady, sir?" a voice asked.

Whetstone grinned. "There are several ladies now, Bennett, but as you are a Peleus I can guess who you mean. She'll be staying in the *Peleus* with me."

"Ah," the man said, obviously now quite satisfied. "Wouldn't want to change our luck!"

Whetstone then read out the names from the three lists, indicating in which ships they wanted the men to serve. When he had finished, Ned stepped forward.

"There's no compulsion; no one has to change his ship if he does not want to. Indeed, once everyone is fully trained, there's no reason why we don't have another meeting to change round again. The whole point of the present change is to spread the experienced men evenly among the three ships."

There were no complaints. Ned and Whetstone had been very careful with the list and changed the least possible number of men. Ned and Aurelia found themselves saddened by the switching of Mrs Judd from the *Griffin* to the *Phoenix*, but Saxby would be lost without her, and the Bullocks were staying in the *Griffin*. The mate, Simpson, went to the *Phoenix* while two women transferred from the *Griffin* to the *Peleus*, where they could help Diana and amuse the men.

The next day was spent changing round the ships' companies and their possessions. Few owned more than could be packed into a small canvas bag. An exception was

Mrs Judd, who had managed to bring the set of her favourite copper cooking pots from Kingsnorth, and her carvers and bone saw. She watched the pots being lowered into the boat with such care and such threats to the seamen should they drop one that Saxby was finally exasperated enough to growl: "You never guarded your virginity with such care."

"I didn't," she admitted bluntly. "What damned good did it ever do me?"

The day after the change, the twelfth since they had arrived back in Jamaica with the grain, saw the masters of the three ships, Thomas, Ned and Saxby, arranging their watch and quarter bills, which were lists telling each man his task in the various sailing evolutions like weighing anchor and tacking, and his post when the ship went into battle.

Aurelia, Mrs Bullock and the remaining two women decided they would be responsible for the wounded if or when they had any, and sheets of nankeen and calico were cut into strips of various widths and then rolled up for use as bandages. Small earthenware jars were filled with pitch, ready to be warmed over the galley stove so that the stump of a limb could be pushed into one to stop the bleeding and protect it while it healed: most buccaneers swore by the method, claiming that many fewer had gangrene and it was the surest way of staunching the blood, even if agonizing. Aurelia had nearly fainted when Diana had mentioned the jars, but when she described how she had herself been forced to use them, she told Aurelia in no uncertain terms that her determination might save men's lives in the heat of battle.

Ned walked round the ship with his new mate, John Lobb, the former second mate of the *Peleus*. By an extraordinary coincidence Lobb was a man of Kent; he came from Little Chart, a tiny village a few miles south-west of Ashford and a dozen miles from Godmersham. He knew the Yorke estate there; indeed, he admitted that he and his brother and their father regularly poached over it until John Lobb came to sea, and the remaining Lobbs no doubt still continued the habit.

"Best place in the county for hares, sir," he said with all the enthusiasm of a man trying to persuade Yorke to buy it.

"I know," Yorke said wryly. "Deer, too, but you would never have taken them!"

Lobb's young face went crimson and then he went white: poaching deer meant transportation if you were caught.

Seeing how upset the mate had become, Yorke slapped him on the back and laughed. "We no longer own the estate! One of Cromwell's favourites lives in it now! I hope the Lobb family are taking all his deer!"

"You mean the Roundheads confiscated it? The land and the house?"

"All of it. And the estate down at Saltwood and the small one at Ilex. My father and my brother have escaped to France."

"He caught us once, the Earl did. Your father, sir. Dad had two hares and I had a rabbit. He was out riding and had stopped to watch something so we didn't spot him. But he spotted us and while we was netting some rabbit holes (my brother had a ferret in his pocket) his lordship was on us!"

"What did he do?" Yorke asked, curious.

"Well, he asked us what we'd caught so far, and we said, two hares an' a rabbit. So he pointed his riding crop at the nets and when he found the ferret wasn't in, he said to put him in, and he'd take a hare for every three rabbits the ferret raised. Well, the ferret raised six, so we gave him our two hares and he let us keep the seven rabbits."

"Then what happened?"

"Well, sir, he just rode off. He warned us against taking deer, because he said if his gamekeepers caught us with one they'd take us straight before a Justice, and no meat was worth transportation. So we never did. We kept on poaching his rabbits, but they were so thick they were ruining the crops and hedgerows."

Ned was amused at this poacher's view of his father, yet not surprised. The Earl was a kindly man with a sense of humour. The idea of trading two of his own hares with poachers in exchange for seven of his own rabbits would amuse him, and to avoid having the gamekeepers going racing round the estate to catch these impudent poachers, he would have told some tall story when he gave the hares to the kitchen staff.

John Lobb was a good seaman. As the two of them walked round the ship he suggested several alterations in the way ropes were led, all intended to make it easier to handle the ship in action. He had already talked to Burton about the guns, explaining their experience in the *Peleus* and describing how their actions were rarely against ships; more often than not they were on shore, acting as soldiers and attacking a small town.

Yorke had listened to Lobb's discourse and realized that this was a part of buccaneering that Whetstone had not described. Ned decided that Whetstone, this enormously cheerful, confident and competent man, had one failing: he assumed that everyone was as confident, competent and knowledgeable as himself. But for Lobb, neither Ned nor Saxby would have started training their ships' companies in land fighting. Fortunately there were exactly a dozen former soldiers among the men taken as prisoners of war by Cromwell, Irishmen at places like Drogheda and Wexford, and Scots after Dunbar.

Ned and Lobb assembled the eight still remaining on board the *Griffin* and explained that they were needed as instructors and that two of them should go over to the *Phoenix* so that each of the two ships had six soldiers who would be responsible for training the others.

Burton, as the *Griffin*'s gunner, was anxious to start at once and Yorke put the six soldiers in his charge. Within the hour men were racing across the *Griffin*'s decks clutching pike, musket, cutlass or pistol, and Lobb was teaching three or four of them the finer points of swordplay, using cutlasses made of wood and showing them the advantage of holding a dagger in the left hand, ready to stab an opponent who could be spun to leave his right side exposed. A couple of sacks, filled with sand from the beach and slung from the shrouds so that they hung at the height of a man's chest and belly, made targets for pikemen, although Lobb kept a man busy sweeping up the sand as it trickled from the holes made by the pikeheads.

Aurelia, standing at the poop with Ned and watching jabbing pikes, slashing cutlass blades (even if they were made of wood) and yelling men leaping over guns and running along the bulwarks holding muskets and pistols, said quietly: "I think this is more like real buccaneering than stealing grain from Riohacha."

"Different shopkeepers sell different sorts of goods," Ned

said. "It seems to me, though, the buccaneer is the kind of shopkeeper who has to have everything in stock, though he might never sell all of it."

Aurelia said, matter-of-factly: "Diana can use a pistol and a musket, knows how to load a cannon, and can use a cutlass and pike."

Ned could see what was coming next and tried to avoid it. "She can do these things perhaps, but I doubt if she has ever killed a man yet!"

"She has, five. One she shot with a pistol just as he was going to cut Thomas across the head from behind with a cutlass."

"Five, eh?" Ned said nonchalantly. "Who looks after the wounded?"

"Oh, she does. But," Aurelia pointed out with chilling logic, "there are never wounded to attend to until *after* the fight. As she says, they don't fight pitched battles; it is always a quick raid. There aren't enough of them to fight companies of soldiers. Thomas says the buccaneer has to be like a mosquito – fly in quickly, sting and get out quickly."

"You are becoming quite an expert on buccaneering," he said, and was ashamed of the hint of a sneer in his voice.

Even if Aurelia noticed it, she ignored it. "There are not many of us," she said simply, "and one mistake over the size of the enemy could kill us all. Diana saved Thomas with her pistol; I would feel more confident if I had a pistol and could be close to you."

Ned had no intention of ever letting Aurelia land with a raiding party, but obviously now was not the time to tell her. Now was the time to be enthusiastic; to encourage her. This was not the moment to tell her that she was the only thing in the world that he valued, and having her translate Spanish a couple of times was the limit of the risks he was going to let her take.

"Yes, I'll have a word with Burton. You won't bother with muskets, will you? They are very heavy and even though you fire them using a rest, they give a terrible kick. A pistol will be fine."

She thought about it. "Yes, Diana said she doesn't carry a musket after the first time because it was so heavy and bruised her shoulder when she fired it. So pistol, pike and cutlass."

He could imagine her saying to Mrs Bullock at the plantation house in the same tone of voice: "The master will be late for dinner tonight, so I shall eat alone."

By next day the hold had been swept clean of grains of maize and the sweeping had yielded enough to fill two sacks. One of the men was hammering the grains before putting them into a pestle to make fresh maize bread as a welcome change from the usual black bread and occasional white. All Lobb's suggestions for improving the rig had been adopted and most of the men on board had blistered hands and bruised shoulders from drill with various weapons.

Thomas and Diana came over in the late afternoon, Thomas admitting as he climbed up the ladder that he was intrigued by all the bustle that had been going on in the *Griffin*. Instead of answering him, Ned led him forward to where Burton was watching avidly as Aurelia sorted out the pieces of a matchlock pistol spread out on a blanket and began reassembling them, naming each part and its function as she did so.

Thomas, who had stopped so that she could not see him, said gruffly to Ned: "You know, for a couple of peaceful fellows we seem to have chosen a pair of warlike women. I don't believe in it, but ever since Diana shot a Spaniard stone dead just as he was going to cut me in half like a wheel of cheese, I've had to let her land with us."

"Aurelia has the same idea, but I shall refuse."

"I'm sure you will. Won't make a dam' bit of difference, of course. It's a sign they love you, or want some exercise on land. Diana would be doing a far more useful and important job staying behind in command of the ship, but it's hopeless: I have to leave – rather, I used to leave, until he came to you – young Lobb. Thanks for reminding me; I'll have to pick someone else."

At that moment Lobb came up, nodded cheerfully to Whetstone and said to Ned: "Sir, there's a fishing canoe coming alongside. It's from the jetty and there's an army officer in it."

"That fellow Rowlands," Thomas growled. "Still smelling like Billingsgate fish market, I'll be bound. Wonder what he wants."

"Shall I let him on board, sir?" Lobb asked. "He was very particular that I should ask."

Ned nodded and then smiled at Thomas. "You know, I think these soldiers are more scared of our ability to bargain than our fighting skill!"

"They've reason," Thomas said with a broad grin. "You've won all your victories so far without firing a shot. You're the hero of the Peleuses after that Riohacha affair."

Together the two men walked over to the entryport in time to see Lieutenant Rowlands pause on the top step of the rope ladder and give himself a hurried last brush down to get rid of fish scales. As soon as he saw Ned and Thomas he gave them a smart salute.

"General Heffer's compliments to you both, gentlemen. I have letters to you both from the general."

Thomas held out his hand, took his letter and tucked it down in front of his jerkin. Ned took his and did the same, saying: "There's no reply, I suppose?"

"Well, sir, there is. You see, the general is asking if you would both call on him – at once, gentlemen."

"Why, has he found some of the maize unripe?" '

"Oh no, sir, he is delighted with it," Rowlands hurriedly assured Thomas. "It's just – well, the Spanish are coming!"

"Are they now," Ned said with a casualness he did not feel. "Well, if we go round taking their islands and their grain, they're bound to turn snappish sometime or other, eh Thomas?"

Whetstone nodded. "Mind you, it hasn't worried me because of course we have the army here as a garrison to defend us. A couple of thousand men, didn't the general say? Seasoned campaigners – they all survived the Santo Domingo affair."

"The general will explain, I am sure," Rowlands stammered. "May I tell him you will call?"

Thomas ran his fingers through his beard and turned towards Diana, who was on the other side of the poop talking to Mrs Bullock. "M'dear, when do you want to go over to the jetty and try to buy some lobsters? Will tomorrow be all right?"

Diana guessed what was going on. "Or the next day, there's no rush."

Rowlands had crushed the brim of his hat in his agitation. "I think the general was hoping sirs, that you could both come over now."

Thomas gave a sigh which seemed to start in his boots. "It's devilish hot for traipsing round in all that sand. What do you say, Ned?"

"I suppose we need some exercise," Ned said, "and I'd do anything to get away from this smell of fish!"

Chapter Eighteen

The general was a man who thrived on worry and bad news; like a drunkard reaching for rumbullion or mobby, he could not have enough of them. They made his already cadaverous face seem thinner and longer, like a sheep's skull, an effect emphasized by his protruding teeth which dried in the heat and made his lips catch on them, so he had to lick them frequently to avoid his lips sticking like skaters run out of ice. Ned wondered if he was married and thought sympathetically of a wife having to look at that face each morning.

The general greeted them with a heartiness which required a good deal of physical effort: rearranging his face into a smile put a strain on facial muscles unused for months, if not years. Ned and Thomas were among the half dozen men in the island whom he could not bully or command. He was indebted to them for the grain; he knew he might have to ask them to go for more if storeships did not arrive from England. But he had more pressing problems than grain.

"You saw the four privateers which have arrived since you were last here," the general said. "Splendid fellows, privateers; we owe them a great debt."

"What have they done," Thomas asked amiably, "and why haven't you paid your debt to them?"

The general looked puzzled, obviously repeating to himself Thomas's sentence. "Oh, they haven't *done* anything for us yet; in fact, as you know, they have only just arrived. I was referring to privateers in general."

"Yes, yes," Thomas agreed. "There's bound to be a bad

one in any dozen you chose, but no doubt that is also true of the army. I'm sure the Lord Protector has had to dismiss more than one in every dozen generals and colonels . . . wives are the same. Not for the Lord Protector, of course, but less than one in a dozen are satisfactory."

The general, lost in Thomas's booming and cheerful voice, shook his head with what Ned felt was resignation and said: "I didn't know; I have only one."

Thomas looked puzzled, realized what the general was thinking and decided not to enlighten him: it would make a good story for Diana and Aurelia.

"Thank you for coming over," the general said. "We face a grave emergency –"

"Who is 'we'?" Thomas interrupted.

"Well, strictly speaking, I suppose the army in Jamaica. You see, some fishermen have just come in from Santiago de Cuba, or near there, with news that the Spanish are preparing a fleet to retake this island. Ten thousand soldiers were mentioned."

"Have they sailed yet?" Thomas asked innocently.

"Er, no, not yet. At the end of next month, I understand."

"Six weeks' time. Well, at least you have time to build a fort or two and some batteries to protect the anchorage. Remarkable how the end of this sandspit forms the doorway to the harbour. The Dons used to hang their victims there."

The general looked startled. "Hang who? Where?"

"The end of the point – they called it *palizada*, which means 'palisade' in English, or 'stockade'. The Dons strung up Protestants captured at sea, privateersmen, prisoners of war . . . Never very fussy, the Dons. Still, you can use it. Call it Gallows Point."

The general nodded. "Gallows Point. Yes, that is a good idea. A few skeletons hanging in chains from gibbets there will frighten off unwelcome visitors."

Ned managed to repress a shudder and just avoided commenting: "And welcome ones, too."

"This Spanish army at Santiago de Cuba," the general said. "We have no defences against it."

"I was just saying, General, that you will have to build a fort or two and some batteries."

"But I have no guns to put in them!" His tone was that of a

man whose misery always triumphed over the optimism of others. "I have men and nothing with which to feed them; men with no weapons to defend themselves; men dying from the fevers these noxious night vapours bring with them."

Thomas nodded sympathetically. "The Lord Protector is going to be very upset when he reads your dispatches. A general whose army has neither guns nor food . . . no, that wasn't how he ran the New Model Army . . ."

The general looked even more lugubrious; like a condemned man accepting that his plea for clemency had been dismissed. "It was Venables, of course, who left us in this mess; he was in such a rush to get back to report to the Lord Protector that he took one of the frigates. That led to the admiral going with the rest of his fleet, to look after his own interests, and the few storeships that had arrived to stay without protection. That was about the time you came."

For two or three minutes no one spoke: Thomas and Ned were deliberately silent, determined not to make it any easier for the general, who in turn neither knew what to suggest nor how to draw ideas from the two men who had been quick enough to provide grain – at a price, the general noted – when he asked them.

Finally Ned said in the saddest voice he could produce: "A Spanish army carried here by a Spanish fleet. Well, you could charter one of those small privateers to sail to England with a dispatch. Providing it arrives safely, at least the Lord Protector will know what happened to his – what was it called, 'The Western Design'?"

Heffer nodded miserably. "It was a grand conception. Never before have the English tried anything like it. Just imagine, the whole of Hispaniola would have been English."

"Just as well it failed," Thomas said brutally. "What the devil would we have done with an island like that! How would we have defended it? We can't even defend Jamaica, and you could lose half a dozen Jamaicas in Hispaniola!"

The general looked startled and Ned was reminded once again of a sheep's head: the man's eyes were wide now, and he looked as though any moment he would start calling the lambs.

"You think Jamaica is an important capture?"

"The finest anchorage in the whole Caribbee," Thomas said

flatly. "If you had a few guns to defend the entrance, you could use it as a base to attack the plate galleons when they sail up from Cartagena to Havana; you can raid the Greater Antilles – Cuba, Hispaniola and Puerto Rico; you can raid Mexico and the Moskito Coast; you can raid the Main – just as we did to get your grain. Why, I'm almost tempted to stay a few weeks myself, and I know my friend feels the same."

The bait was in position but for a moment Ned thought it had too subtle a taste for the general. Then, like a man waking with a start, he said: "Why don't you stay, then? There's plenty of fresh water, and once we get the cattle and hogs down from the hills, you can put down fresh salt meat."

"And what do we use to pay for that, General? We are privateers," Ned said. "Which reminds me, we need a commission signed by you for our third ship, the *Phoenix*." .

"Of course! In whose name?"

"The master, William Saxby."

"Rowlands!" the general bellowed, and when the lieutenant appeared ordered him to prepare the commission at once and bring it in for signature.

"You still owe me twenty guineas for the other two ships," he commented.

"We undercharged you on the grain, so I suggest there is no charge for them or the *Phoenix,* which carried the most grain."

"But only two of the three ships carried grain," the general said fretfully.

"Then call Rowlands back and don't trouble yourself with a commission for the *Phoenix*," Ned said easily. "The Spanish certainly don't ask for them; they'd just as soon fire a broadside. I had an idea you were going to make a proposal, and a commission would give everything an air of – how shall we say, dignity?"

"No, no, think nothing of it; the *Phoenix* must have a commission. Now, I am no sailor; I am a simple soldier who is now also the governor of Jamaica. I also realize that we should have a fleet to protect us, but – well, I am not of course blaming Admiral Penn, because his orders were to return to England with his fleet as soon as his original orders were carried out. I do not think the Lord Protector ever visualized this situation, where a fleet would be needed to protect a captured island."

"He must have been an optimist, the Lord Protector – and his Council of State – if he thought the Spanish would not counter-attack."

Heffer was not to be trapped into anything that could be reported to Cromwell as criticism. "No doubt he assumed all their ships would be sunk."

"Of course," Thomas said and Ned found it hard to keep a straight face. "But forgive me, you were saying that you felt you need a fleet to defend you."

"Don't you?" Heffer said cautiously. "If this Spanish army, ten thousand strong, lands on the north side of the island and marches against us here . . . I have three thousand men, no artillery, precious little cavalry and more than five hundred men sick. What shall I do?"

"If it was me, I'd go to England in a privateer and report to the Lord Protector," Thomas said unsympathetically.

"I cannot desert my post," Heffer said, his right hand on his breast.

"Of course not," Ned said. "I suppose the Dons will string you all up on gibbets along the Palisades."

"Yes, I fear so," said the general miserably, "unless you gentlemen can do anything to help."

"Oh, you want more grain, eh?" Thomas said.

"Well, I had in mind a more active role."

"We can't possibly evacuate three thousand men," Ned said. "And anyway, where would you take them? Back to Barbados? The island would be hard put to feed them for the months needed for the dispatch to reach England and transport ships collected and sent out here. A year, eh Thomas?"

"At least, not that we could carry a tenth of that number from here to Barbados. Seven hundred miles to windward – can you imagine it? The men would die like flies. Yellow fever, typhus . . ." he shuddered. "What would happen to my own men? Sons to me, every one of them. And daughters."

"Mine, too," Ned said mournfully. "More of a parish than a ship; prayers twice a day and always before we go into battle."

"Very laudable, very laudable," the general said hurriedly,

realizing that fatherhood and prayers were quickly driving him into a corner. "But I was wondering if you could be persuaded to take the other four privateers under your command. That would give you a squadron of seven vessels."

"Still not enough to evacuate three thousand soldiers," Thomas said firmly, determined to force Heffer out into the open.

"No, let us for the moment leave aside the question of quitting the island. With these seven ships, I was wondering – that is to say, given I am only a soldier – whether you could sail for Cuba and, ah, make some sort of – well, a *demonstration*. Not at Santiago, of course!" he said hastily, "but close to some other big city, so that the Spanish will fear an attack . . ."

Both Ned and Thomas said nothing for a full two minutes. The silence pressed down on Heffer, who closed his eyes and put his elbows on the table and joined the tips of his fingers as though to make a tent into which he could crawl.

Thomas coughed a few times, as if clearing his throat would help him think, and then said slowly, apparently ruling out the idea: "If we demonstrate with seven ships for seven days and still don't land an army, the Dons are going to guess we are trying to fool them."

"But they are not fools," Ned commented. "They will ask themselves: 'What are the English doing that they try to mislead us into thinking they are going to land *there*?' When they see there is no landing anywhere, they'll guess we are trying to draw them away from where we really fear an attack, like a lapwing pretending to be lame to draw you away from her nest."

The general opened his eyes and nodded and both Ned and Thomas suddenly realized that Heffer was being the lapwing: he had been leading them away from what he really wanted to propose in the hope that instead one of them would suggest it.

"Well," Thomas said finally, "so that's that. We must be getting back to our ships. If the Spanish fleet is coming, we don't want to get trapped in this anchorage. Do you – er, have you a family you would like us to take? We can't guarantee where we'll go but almost anywhere will be safer than here."

The general shook his head. "Thank you, I am alone. If you would spare me just a moment, I have just one more – well, hardly a proposal, but . . ."

"But what?" Thomas asked impatiently.

"A sudden attack on Santiago de Cuba. It's our only chance!" Heffer said it in such a rush that it came out like one long word.

"*Your* only chance," Ned said. "For us it would be suicide."

"One sudden attack. You keep every penny of the purchase. The other four privateers, too."

"Purchase!" Thomas exclaimed. "If what you say is true there'll be no purchase! Santiago with the Spanish fleet anchored there with an extra ten thousand soldiers on top of the normal garrison. And we have seven privateers, every one of them built as a merchantman. It would be like a company of one-legged soldiers, led from behind by a pot-valiant Falstaff, attacking your garrison of three thousand!"

"There is no way you can be persuaded to change your mind?"

"You could charter the seven ships, put a couple of hundred soldiers in each of them, and we could land the troops – say 1,400 of them, if the other privateers can carry that many, which I doubt – twenty or thirty miles from Santiago so that they can make a flank attack."

"How do they get back here?"

"We could arrange a rendezvous," Thomas said bleakly, "but they might find the Spanish fleet waiting there, laying buoys to mark where we've sunk."

"So you cannot help? You have a fantastic opportunity to render the Lord Protector a great service. You could be the saviour of his Western Design. He would never forget you, you can be sure of that."

"I am sure of that," Thomas said, "but we must go back to our ships, I am glad we could help you in the matter of the grain – help the Lord Protector, perhaps I should say."

Back on board the *Griffin,* they had to describe to Diana and Aurelia what the general had said and how he had said it. Ned had several questions to ask Thomas, but he had waited until they were all in the cabin. Some of the questions might come better from Diana and Aurelia: he had no wish to antagonize Thomas, who was in a curious mood. He seemed to be half drunk, yet his breath showed he had not touched any hot waters today.

Diana made no comment until Thomas had finished his story; then she said: "Whetstone, you may be Oliver Cromwell's nephew, and he may be your least favourite uncle, but why are you so cruel to this poor wretched General Heffer? It seems to me you should sympathize: Venables, his own commander, bolted for London to make his excuses to the Lord Protector and blame the navy, and then the admiral followed, taking all the ships."

Thomas grinned sheepishly. "Why should I help the Roundheads?"

"I'm not saying you should. I'm just chiding you – chiding, I emphasize; not nagging – for being hateful to a frightened old man."

"Old be damned," Thomas snorted, "he's my age or younger. I remember the Heffers – a grumbling discontented set of Puritan scoundrels from Wiltshire. Still bearing a grudge because they did not get a penny piece from Henry at the Dissolution of the Monasteries, unlike our friend's forebears."

Diana and Aurelia looked at Ned and the French girl said: "That is true?"

"One estate. We should have had more."

"I was not criticizing," Thomas said. "Not a penny for Papists or Puritans, that's my motto."

"Yes, but it wasn't General Heffer's fault his great grandfather was not in favour at the court of Henry VIII, any more than it's any credit to Ned that his ancestors were!"

"Your sympathy, my dear, is entirely misplaced. That two-legged sheep had the impudence to suggest we attacked the Spanish fleet in Santiago and was kind enough to say we could keep any purchase."

"He meant well," Diana said, "but you did not!"

Ned, puzzled by her words, said: "Attacking the Spanish fleet with seven little privateers seems – well, even a soldier can see that the odds are ridiculous."

Diana smiled, and it was a smile that Ned mistrusted at

once. It was sweet, understanding, affectionate – was everything that a smile should be, except for the look in her eyes.

"Dear Ned – Thomas knows something that you do not. He has not told you yet (though obviously he intends to within the hour), and he tried to use it to part the general from his gold, except that apparently we've already taken it all for the grain."

"Dear Diana," Ned said. "What is it that your scoundrel of a lover knows that I do not?"

"There is no Spanish fleet in the West Indies, Ned; no frigates, no galleons, just a few *guarda costas*. One fewer of them now, thanks to Mr Saxby."

The captains of the four privateers were, in Ned's view, just what he expected pirates to look like. At the moment they had commissions from General Heffer, pieces of parchment with which he had hoped to persuade them to serve under Whetstone. One of the captains was French, another Dutch, and two were English, and Ned was startled, as they climbed on board the *Griffin,* to find they knew Whetstone well and obviously liked him.

"The general had us over at dawn," one of the English captains, Morgan, told Thomas. "He asked if we would serve under 'Mr Whetheread' in the *Peleus,* and we said no, we wouldn't. Then we realized you'd been changing your name. Anyway, when we found out what he was going to propose to you, we said we'd go if you went, and he'd better give us commissions so we'd be ready. We knew you wouldn't have anything to do with it but we thought we might as well get ourselves commissions."

"Did he charge you for them?"

"The twenty-guinea fee? He tried," Morgan said with a grin, "but after we had them drawn up and in our hands we said we hadn't any money with us, and anyway we didn't care about Jamaica; that we couldn't pay twenty guineas for it, let alone for the privilege of getting ourselves killed for the Lord Protector."

"What did he do then?"

"Oh, said it was a standard fee, a sort of stamp duty, but he could waive it. So we said he'd better wave 'em, and offered him the parchments to wave, but he said it was another sort of wave. So, Thomas, we're not rascals any more; we are privateers!"

"Not wave," Thomas said, "but W-A-I-V-E. It means to – well, make an exception. If he waives the twenty-guinea charge, you don't have to pay it."

Morgan pointed at Ned. "Who's your friend, Thomas?"

Thomas introduced him by his proper name. Morgan nodded and as he shook Ned's hand said: "You had the plantation at Barbados, didn't you? Kingsnorth, or some such name. Chased you out, did they?"

When Ned nodded, Morgan commented: "The general has no idea who he's asking for help – five English Royalists, a Frenchman who did in a priest who seduced his sister, and a Dutchman who was born hating Spaniards."

Whetstone gestured for them to sit down in the shade provided by the taffrail now that the ship had swung to the east and the sun was beginning to dip rapidly. Ned found it natural to sit beside them, the only clean-shaven face in the row.

"Well, lads," Thomas said, pausing as he walked across the deck in front of them, "does anyone want to come with me and visit the Dons?"

"Where?" asked the Frenchman. "We are new to these islands, Thomas. We have only just arrived from the Moskito Coast."

Thomas ran his hand through his beard and grinned slyly. "A safe place. Rich, I reckon. Somewhere no buccaneer to my knowledge has ever waved a cutlass or tossed a pot."

"Where, Thomas?" the Frenchman asked again.

"Not so fast, *mon ami*. Choosing the right target is the most important part of buccaneering: choosing the right comrades is the second. But third is agreeing on the terms."

"Surely dividing by seven is the fair way."

"Has any of you more than thirty men?"

When they shook their heads he said: "I have more than fifty, and so has Mr Yorke. Half for us, a half for you four: that's only fair to our own men."

The four privateersmen murmured their agreement.

"So half and half it is," Thomas said.

Ned said: "There's just one thing we might do for our friend the general."

Thomas and the four men looked startled, and tried to guess what Ned had in mind.

"There should be plenty of guns lying around, wherever we go. If we can carry any away with us, especially bronze pieces, I suggest we make a present of them to the general. Or give him any iron guns we have that we'd prefer to change for bronze."

Morgan was obviously far from happy at the idea. "Why should we provide the bloody Roundheads with guns? Once you give 'em guns it'll be a constant 'We want shot' because English shot won't fit Spanish guns."

"We won't be giving them to the Roundheads," Thomas said delightedly. "That's why it is such a splendid idea. We provide the guns and shot, and the Roundheads provide the powder and gunners!"

"To fire at us, I suppose," Morgan said.

"No, to defend our new base! The general told me that the reason he is not building forts or batteries to defend this harbour is that he hasn't any guns to put in them. Now, Cromwell or not, that's a pity. We can use this harbour for refitting and repairs, and before long, you'll see, there'll be plenty of shops and taverns. Providing there are some guns protecting that entrance from any stray Spanish privateers."

The Frenchman held up his hand. "I agree, Thomas. Your motives are so devious I think you must have French blood in your veins!"

The other three quickly agreed and the Frenchman said: "For the third time, Thomas – *where*?"

"Santiago!"

"*Sacré bleu!*" the Frenchman exclaimed, and Morgan muttered some oath that was drowned by the exclamations of the other two.

"We'll never sail in," the Dutchman said. "The entrance is too narrow. And we'll never tow in with boats without being shot to pieces by the fort. I was taken there once as a prisoner."

"But you escaped," Thomas said. "Shall I tell you how? You broke out of the prison somehow – the details don't matter – and you made for the hills to the eastward. You climbed over the ridge and came down the other side, to where there's a long bay with fine beaches. You stole a fishing boat, and sailed to the north side of Jamaica. You crossed the mountains to here, cleaned yourself up, and managed to get on board a Dutch ship smuggling in slaves or goods."

"How do you know? I never told you!"

"Alternatives," Thomas said crisply. "You had no others. The only safe way of escaping from Santiago is eastward over the hills; the only place you could find boats is that bay; the only place you could reach is Jamaica, with the wind just abaft the beam . . ."

"What has this to do with us now?" Morgan asked.

"Old Gottlieb here found the best way out of Santiago. It is also the best way in. That bay is well out of sight of Santiago. Let's get to sea before too many people guess what we're up to. We'll sail in company, but if any of us are separated, we'll rendezvous at Caimanera. That's on the east side of the Bahia de Guantanamo. Anyone not there a week from today will be left out: we daren't risk raising an alarm along that Cuban coast; those ports and towns are plump pullets that have been fattening for us."

Eight days later the sun was within two hours of setting when the squadron, led by the *Peleus* and followed by the *Griffin,* the four privateers and the *Phoenix,* sailed close along the Cuba coastline, occasionally having to curve round isolated cays or the ominous brown patches in the clear water that warned of coral reefs.

The ships were making about five knots; the sky was clear but there was a good deal of haze blurring the coastline. Thomas Whetstone had come on board the *Griffin* with the Dutchman, Gottlieb, who had offered to leave his own ship in the hands of his mate for this last part of the voyage.

Thomas tugged his beard from time to time as he walked impatiently between the mast and taffrail, looking forward over the starboard bow and occasionally examining it with his battered telescope, whose brass tubes looked as though they had been used frequently to drive a nail flush or knock the top off a bottle whose cork had stuck.

"Several red cliffs, you said?" he asked Gottlieb.

"Yes. There's a sugar loaf hill, then about four miles beyond it a hill three times as high. Then there's a beach with a river running into it, the Rio del Bacanao."

Thomas closed the telescope. "Well, that seems to fit, so we should now be off the mouth of the Rio del Bacanao, but I'm damned if I can see any red cliffs beyond, nor Punta Berracos."

"It's the haze," Gottlieb said. "You'll see them soon, and Punta Berracos. You can't miss that; it has a curious round hill on it."

Ned said: "There's one thing about this haze – if we're having trouble identifying the coast, any sentries in there probably won't notice the ships."

"Better rely on them having too much wine with their meal than the haze." Thomas pulled the telescope open once again. "Hey – there's an odd-shaped hill! Yes, it's a headland with a round hill on it. And . . . damn this haze . . . yes, the cliffs are – well, not red, but . . . well, perhaps they are."

Gottlieb nodded confidently. "Beyond that is Bahia Daiquiri, and from there a series of sharp hills run about four miles to Siboney, where we anchor. The nearest hill has a flat summit, and each gets higher as you approach Siboney."

"I hope you're right," Whetstone said.

"We pass Siboney and find a small village just beyond, Aguadores. We anchor there. Then we land and walk over the hills to Santiago. Not such a climb, really; once we're up on a ridge of hills it's level until we reach the castle."

"Let me go over it again," Ned said. "Santiago is like a big slot in the cliffs, the entrance only sixty yards or so wide. A castle, the Castillo del Morro, is high on the east side, and the Catalina battery low on the west side."

"That is correct," Gottlieb said in his precise English. "And we shall arrive off Aguadores just after it is dark. There is no chance that we shall cause an alarm because, as I was telling Thomas, any ship arriving when there's not enough light or the wind is too fluky to try to enter Santiago, always anchors in the bay at Aguadores to wait."

"Don't make it sound too easy," Thomas grunted. "There's always something that goes wrong. Something unexpected."

The Dutchman gave a harsh laugh. "I lead the march to Santiago – with you, of course, Thomas – as the guide."

Chapter Nineteen

Whetstone estimated from the position of Orion's Belt that it must be about midnight. With the ships anchored off Aguadores and most of their men landed by boat clear of the village, they found the beginning of the climb not too arduous because the hills became steeper after the first couple of miles. The worst problem was the cloud of mosquitoes; next worst was the narrowness of the path leading up through first forest and then thorny scrub. Finally they were high enough to look down at the ships floating like toys on a village pond.

Ned was thankful both he and Thomas had been able to persuade the women that for once (if they had said "for once" a single time, they must have said it a hundred) they could be much more use helping sail the ships round than scrambling over hills and perhaps spraining their ankles.

With three hundred men slithering and sliding, tripping and cursing as they followed the rough path, Thomas said to Ned: "I think we'll light the torches: we're going to have broken legs otherwise, and we're out of sight of Santiago."

The column halted and flints struck against steels as the men blew gently into the tinderboxes until they glowed enough to light the rough torches they had made. The weak lights showed up a fearsome crowd with unshaven faces scratched and bleeding from branches springing back as one man followed another, and swollen grotesquely by mosquito bites.

Soon the column was on the move again. As he climbed,

his shin and thigh muscles aching, his clothes sodden with
perspiration and his ears ringing with the incessant buzz and
hum of insects, Ned found he was beginning to have doubts
about the Santiago raid. Not Santiago as such, but because
this was his first buccaneering raid. The descent on Riohacha
could be explained away because Jamaica needed the corn. At
least, he thought so. Three thousand men were starving. Yet
if he was as honest with himself as Thomas was, those three
thousand men were the enemy: they were Roundheads who
had stolen his family estates, forced his family into exile,
confiscated his own plantation and forced him to flee
Barbados. Now they wanted to arrest him just because he was
who he was. Why was he helping them, then? Because the
general had promised a good price for the grain and said he
would pay in gold! In the end it had taken threats to make the
fool pay up, but that was understandable now that they knew
he had used the last of the money in his treasury. The troops
were lucky they had nothing to spend their money on; it
made less of a problem for the general not to pay them.

So, he mused, why had he this doubt about Santiago? A
successful raid by the buccaneers would certainly alarm the
Spanish. It would either frighten them off any thought of
attacking Jamaica – and thus do Cromwell's work for him –
or make them realize Jamaica had to be recaptured if the
Spanish possessions were to be safe, which meant the
buccaneers would be doing the Spaniards' work for them. Or
doing their thinking, rather; drawing their attention to a
dangerous threat. Yet without the buccaneers and their ships,
the threat to the Spanish did not exist.

Either way, he realized, the buccaneers were helping
Cromwell or the Spanish. This conclusion so startled him
that he stopped and Saxby, next behind, bumped into him
with a muttered apology but a warning that three hundred
men were following in the darkness.

Thomas Whetstone dropped back, telling Gottlieb to go
on ahead, and fell into step with Ned. "Are you feeling all
right?"

"Yes, I was just thinking."

"Ah, indeed. No good comes of it," Thomas said
seriously. "Good men can go mad doing that." He stumbled
over the root of a shrub and cursed. " 'What am I, an honest

man, doing here behaving like a footpad . . .? Shall I have the strength to steal a doubloon when I see one . . .?' That's it, eh Ned?"

"Something like that!"

"Well, console yourself that if they catch you they'll stretch you six inches longer on the rack, then crack your spine at the neck with the garotte, and generally be hateful. So grab those doubloons and admire the perfect cross-crosslet embossed on one side. Or is it the cross-potent? I always get 'em mixed up: heraldry is a black art. Give thanks to Philip IV and remember that he mined the gold free in Mexico, and he'd only waste the money paying his army in the Spanish Netherlands or building ships to drive us out of the Caribbees."

"All right, as long as His Most Catholic Majesty *does* realize we are only saving him trouble," Ned said, his voice now considerably more cheerful. "His armies in the Netherlands will be better off back behind the Pyrenees, and if he sends a fleet out here, it'll only sink on reefs!"

"Remember Ned," Thomas said soberly, "here it's been 'No peace beyond the Line' for more than a hundred years, and it is the Spanish who say it."

"Yes, don't worry about me. I was just sad that what with your uncle and the King of Spain, there's not much chance that Aurelia and I can ever settle down on a plantation and live peacefully . . ."

"You're looking at Diana and me, I suppose."

"Obviously. I know you are happy together, but . . ."

"You'd be wrong if you went on after the word 'together'."

"How do you know what I was going to say?"

" '. . . but if only you could settle down on your estate in peace and start a family,' and so on . . ."

"Yes. What's wrong with that?"

Thomas cursed as a branch brushed aside by Gottlieb swung back and hit him in the face. "Everything's wrong with it, Ned. The last thing that Diana and I want is to settle down. Oh yes, we did once, at the beginning. Sailing round in the *Peleus,* we felt like tinkers, or gipsies, every day a different anchorage, at least once a week a different country, French, Spanish, Dutch, English – we never knew which language we'd be trying to use. We got to hate the *Peleus*; she was like a prison. Then slowly we realized it wasn't the *Peleus*, it was *us*. Diana and me. We woke up to the fact that the *Peleus* was both our home and our escape.

"You see, Ned, it doesn't matter a damn where the *Peleus* is, at anchor or at sea. If she's anchored in Curaçao, very well, then our home for a while is in Curaçao. But it could be Barbados, some bay along the Main or, as it is now, Aguadores. Tomorrow – later today, rather – it should be Santiago de Cuba. Freedom, Ned, that's what Diana and I have. Who cares what my damnable uncle does next? He won't live for ever, and his son is a ninny, so as soon as they bury Uncle Oliver the Council of State will be quarrelling – but I don't care. Just so long as they don't make peace with Spain!"

All that Whetstone ·said made sense; in fact, as Thomas described how he and Diana had begun to feel like tinkers and then slowly the ship had become their home, Ned realized that Aurelia had already reached that stage; that she already regarded the *Griffin* as her home. In the last two or three weeks, when he had been apologetic about bad weather, rough seas, the monotony of the food, she had been more and more dismissive about whatever it was. He realized that she had not been trying to reassure him that she did not mind; she was trying to convince *him* that the life of a buccaneer was an interesting one, to persuade him that they should be like the snail, carrying their home around with them.

Gottlieb had stopped, and by the time Ned and Thomas reached him they could see that they had just climbed over the edge of a great flat ridge: ahead of them the ground was level and in the starlight they could see a bulky building on a lower slope.

Thomas turned to face the oncoming column and bellowed: "Stop. Ten minutes rest. Pass it back!"

Ned had the feeling that he could see through the darkness; that like some bird he could hover over the far corner of the ridge and look down on Santiago sleeping in its valley at the end of the narrow channel leading from the sea. On the eastern side the great Castillo del Morro stood at the end of the precipitous cliffs that they had been skirting most of the way from Aguadores; on the west side the Catalina battery was built into a flat ledge more suited to ospreys. In the town the *alcaldia* would be locked up on one side of the *plaza*; the mayor would be sleeping peacefully. Would there be an *alcaide,* a governor of the Castillo? Presumably Santiago was big enough to have its own *gobernador*. In fact it must be the main town of a province, so somewhere down there the governor slept soundly too, unaware that three hundred buccaneers were approaching, a column of cutthroats escorted, so it seemed, by an aerial column of vicious mosquitoes, each with a sting sharp enough to fell an ox.

"We'll split up when we're closer to the Castillo," Thomas said. "Are you sure you want to tackle the castle? It looks enormous. The town will be easy. No troops down there, and the rule of thumb is simple – the rich and the important live in the largest houses. Ransack the homes and ransom the owners!"

"The castle suits me. I'm new to all this. It's best that you have the most men. My fifty should be enough for the castle, as long as we can get to it without raising the alarm."

Thomas looked back along the column. "At least they had the wit to douse the torches without being told."

"They just burned out. They don't last forever."

"True, true, Ned! Ah well, these sorry poltroons have had enough rest. If we wait too long, some rascal who managed to hide some hot waters will get drunk. Still, we searched 'em thoroughly."

"Do you remember that passage from Shakespeare, where Falstaff is leading a column of men he has just pressed into the King's service . . ."

"Yes, but we've better bargains! You're not comparing me with Falstaff? I haven't such a belly!"

Chapter
Twenty

Ned and Thomas stood side by side as the column trudged past them. "Griffins this side," Ned said, counting them off. As soon as fifty had passed he called softly; "Stop and wait."

Now Thomas was counting out eighty of his own men and grouping them to one side and then calling for Saxby, who stood beside him as another eighty were counted and then led them a hundred yards ahead and halted. "Burton?" Thomas called and as soon as the *Griffin*'s gunner stepped forward had the rest of the column follow him, counting as they went. The last man was given a slap on the back as Thomas said: "That's nearly three hundred of us! Not a man fallen by the wayside."

The Castillo seemed black and menacing, heavily shadowed by the light of the stars in a clear sky. The entrance was on the north side and Ned could see a long path zigzagging up the hillside from the town below.

Thomas came and stood beside him. "Santiago de Cuba..." he said quietly. "Down there they're all sleeping – prelates and pimps, treasurers and trollops, rich and poor." He looked up at the sky. "Our people will be weighing anchor at Aguadores about now. I'll be glad to see the *Peleus* coming in through the channel. Look." He pointed down at it; they could not see the entrance from this angle but the main anchorage was clear enough, reflecting the stars and showing how sheltered it was. "We can go alongside those jetties and load the purchase; aye, and hoist on board your dam' guns."

"You'll be glad to see them when they're installed in batteries on the Palizadas."

"Aye, but you don't expect me to admit it, do you?"

The two men stood together for another couple of minutes, and then Thomas turned and Ned saw he was holding out his hand. "Good luck, Ned. Two or more pistol shots, and we'll know you're having to fight for it, and we'll go ahead and attack the town."

"And if there's a big explosion," Ned said, "you'll know some fool fired a pistol in the magazine!"

With that Thomas laughed and strode off towards the groups of men waiting at the top of the track leading down the steep side of the valley to the town.

Ned's men were still squatting behind a big wedge-shaped rock, out of sight of the castle but less than three hundred yards from it. He stood in the midst of them and said quietly: "The entrance is on the other side from here – the landward side. There'll be sentries. I want a couple of men to come with me now: we've got to silence those sentries. Then you can all come in and secure the rest of the garrison. Find the governor of the castle – take him alive, if we can. Roberts – you pick five men, and your job will be to find the magazine and seize it. The governor will probably have the key. Raven – you have the nails and hammers? Right, pick your men and you'll be responsible for spiking the guns if necessary. The rest of you will be with me but you stay outside until we've dealt with the guards. Who's coming with me for the sentries? Ah, Day and Lloyd. Right, we'll start. Now, remember, everyone: no shots unless it is to save your own lives: we don't want to raise the alarm down in the town and make it harder for the others."

He led the way to the eastern side of the castle, the three men creeping from one great boulder to another and managing most of the time to stay out of sight of the castle battlements. The rock forming the whole ridge was criss-crossed with splits and crevices which slowed them up, but when Ned looked behind from time to time at the rest of the men he was hard put to distinguish them at fifty paces.

Then they were close up against the castle walls and Ned led the way round to the side. There was no path, indicating how often the garrison inspected the place, and he had to push through low brush, thankful that, like the rest of the men, he had lashed strips of canvas round his shins to keep out the painful thorns and prickly pear spines.

Suddenly he was at the north-east corner. From here he could look down on the town and distinguish the path up to the castle which led to the doorway halfway along the north side. He stopped and took out his pistols and felt in his pocket for the spanning key. Putting down one pistol he fitted the key on to the other and turned it until he could feel the tension hard on the spring. Putting that pistol in his belt he fitted the key on the other one, conscious that Day and Lloyd were doing the same. The three men then drew their cutlasses. The sword seemed heavy and clumsy in his hand and Ned suddenly realized that drawing it was the last act before tackling the sentries in the sequence that started in Jamaica. Before killing the sentries. He felt dizzy for a moment. What about Day and Lloyd, did they feel squeamish? He doubted it; both had been transported and although they had been good workers at Kingsnorth and enthusiastic members of the *Griffin*'s crew, Ned had always guessed that the crimes for which they had been transported had been serious. That, he realized, was an advantage at a time like this: he needed men about him that would not hesitate to cut a throat.

He began creeping towards the path, keeping as close to the castle as he could, but over the years masonry had fallen from the walls, stones that were rectangular and still as sharp-edged as when the masons had chiselled them to shape a hundred years ago. Now the blocks, two and three feet long, were often hidden in low bushes and forcing Ned and his two men to walk three or four yards away from the shadowy shelter of the wall. Were there snakes in Cuba?

Suddenly he was on the path, realizing that his concern to avoid cracking his shins on the stones had led him to walk with his head down. The doorway of the castle was now only five yards away and he was standing in front of it like an obelisk!

He promptly crouched and turned slightly. The doorway was enormous, a great black square studded with bolts to blunt the axes of attackers. Inset at the side of this door was a much smaller one just large enough to admit a man. It was open, but beside it Ned could distinguish a black bundle, as though someone had left a sack of potatoes for the garrison cook.

He turned and gestured to Day and Lloyd to follow as he crawled towards the door. A yard or two to one side of the worn path, the rock showed up lighter than the surrounding dried grass and scrub. Ned realized that a sentry looking out through the door would see three black tortoises coming towards him.

It was painful: every shrub seemed a hedgehog of thorns, every stone as sharp as the point of a knife. And now he could hear a strange noise, as though a child was blowing up and deflating a pig's bladder. He stopped warily. It was coming from above so he lay down and rolled over on his back to be able to peer up at the top of the door. At once several thorns stuck into his shoulders, but now the noise appeared to be coming from ground level. He rolled over again and raised his head. It was coming from both sides.

He moved another couple of yards towards the door and listened again, and Day crawled up alongside. "It's that sack thing by the door, sir. I think it's the sentry sitting there asleep and snorin'. Shall I . . .?"

The man was holding a knife in his right hand, as well as the cutlass in his left. Ned hesitated a few seconds and then thought of Thomas and the other 250 buccaneers descending on the town. "Yes," he muttered.

Day moved slowly and evenly towards the sentry and stopped beside him, obviously sizing him up. Then he put a knee against the man's left shoulder and pulled his head towards him. The knife winked a moment in the starlight, there was a hoarse intake of breath, and then the snoring stopped.

Lloyd immediately jumped up and helped Day pull the man's body to one side, away from the door, and leaving it beside a helmet and pike. A moment later Ned was through the door and, expecting to find himself in a dark cavern forming the inside of the castle, was startled to see stars above him. The building formed a hollow square, the inside being a parade ground. Just inside the doorway a staircase spiralled up, obviously leading to the guardroom and the garrison's quarters at a higher level.

Ned knew that the rest of his party, who must have been watching the grisly affair of the sentry, would be streaming in through the door at any moment. The magazine entrance would be somewhere out there in the square, and there might be another staircase, but this one was, for the moment anyway, the most important.

Day hissed at someone and the men filed in as Ned took a cautious few steps up the staircase. It began spiralling to the left in the usual fashion, so that a defender retreating up the stairwell (or attacking coming down) kept his body covered with the sword in his right hand, while the man below had his left side open, being forced to use his sword across his body and shortening his reach.

Treading on stone was better than wood: there was no risk of a plank squeaking. Yet it was not as dark as Ned had expected. He paused for a moment and, glancing up, he saw there was a light above – a lantern in the guardroom? He sensed that Day and Lloyd were close behind and resumed climbing. Down below, somewhere at the bottom of the stairwell, there was a metallic click as a careless buccaneer's cutlass caught the wall.

Now it was much lighter – and again he heard snoring. He stopped and counted. He could distinguish at least four men, perhaps five. If there was always a sentry at the castle gate during the hours of darkness, the men would probably do four hours on duty and eight off. Oh, what did it matter? Suddenly he was in a corridor going to the left; facing him, opposite the top of the stairs, was the guardroom door and he saw seven men asleep on simple truckle beds, naked because the room was hot, both from the sun's heat held in the thick stone walls and the lantern hanging from a hook in the ceiling.

The thought of slaughtering seven sleeping men made him pause, but without thinking he moved to one side as he felt Day trying to pass him, followed by Lloyd. The two men moved as silently as shadows, passing from one bed to another like priests bestowing blessings, and each time a gasp told of a throat cut.

First Day and then Lloyd bent down over the last man to wipe the bloodstains from their knives before sliding them back into the canvas sheaths.

By now Ned, sick with the knowledge that he had hesitated when he should have acted swiftly, and feeling faint at the sight of the dark pools of blood spreading from the head of each bed, had reached up and unhooked the lantern.

"We must find the governor of the castle," he whispered. "We want him alive. Ransom," he explained.

"What about the officers?" Lloyd asked.

There must have been a couple of corporals or sergeants among the seven whose throats had just been cut. The governor might be a major – perhaps retired from the King's service in Spain and sent out here to end his days quietly as the garrison commander at Santiago. He might have a captain or a lieutenant under him. A captain or a lieutenant, Ned realized, could provide information: the whereabouts of the key to the magazine, for instance . . .

Ned led the way along the corridor towards a distant door. He drew his cutlass and, motioning Day to lift the wooden latch, pushed the door open and walked into the room. A man was asleep on a considerably more comfortable bed; an officer's uniform was draped over what seemed a model of a man made of wicker, a hat with a large plume rested on a ball-shaped stand. At that moment Ned realized there was an archway leading to another room.

"Secure him!" he whispered to Lloyd, and nodded to Day to follow. He held the lantern long enough for Lloyd to wake the man and keep him down on the bed by the simple method of holding his cutlass blade horizontally across his windpipe. Through the archway was a similar room, complete with sleeping officer, well-tended uniform and hat with plume. "Secure him and bring him into the other room," Ned said, taking a leather belt and a wide sash from the uniform.

In a couple of minutes both officers were sitting on the bed in the first room, blinking in the lantern light and looking absurd in their nightshirts. Both began talking in Spanish until Ned threatened them. Swiftly Day tied the wrists of one man behind him, using his sash, and Lloyd secured the other.

"I'll need the lantern. Capsize them both onto the floor, put them face to face, and then buckle the belts together and use the length to secure 'em back to back. Lloyd, you can guard 'em. You can get a grip on their hair and they'll be too scared to try anything in the darkness. Come on, Day!"

Ned hurried along the corridor just as he realized the rest of his force was hurrying along. There was one more door, and, afraid the men would make a noise, he flipped up the latch with the hand holding his cutlass, and burst in holding the lantern to one side.

It was a large room with a bed on a raised dais. There were two people asleep on it, a bald man in late middle age, and a young woman with long black hair. She was naked, with large breasts, and the mascara had run down her cheeks and smeared to give her an absurdly debauched appearance. As she opened her eyes, wakened by the light, she gave a shriek which owed nothing to modesty and snatched the sheet from the bald man, who woke with a grunt.

She looked like a whore and obviously more accustomed to bedroom dramas than the man. She ran towards Ned and Day, expertly manipulating the sheet and obviously intending to knock the lantern from Ned's hand.

Day appeared to do nothing, but suddenly the woman sprawled across the floor, sheet flying and once again revealing a splendid but over-ripe body. A moment later Day, who had tripped her, was sitting on top of her as she lay face downwards, and had one of her arms bent up behind so that she could not move.

"I'll look after 'er if you'll see to the old scoundrel, sir," Day said, grinning. By now several of the party were crowding into the two rooms and, after exclaiming at Day's prisoner, who was trying to turn her head round far enough to spit at him, they hurriedly obeyed Ned's order to secure the man.

"We've found the magazine but it's locked, sir," Roberts reported. "No sentry on it. Terrible great key it needs."

Ned bent over the man with a lantern, concerned first with confirming that he was the garrison commander, although the fact that his was the last door seemed significant. Damnation, he needed Aurelia's Spanish. Still, many Spanish officers had served in the Netherlands and spoke French.

Ned aimed the lantern at the man, who was still waking slowly, rheumy-eyed, and even now reaching out with his left hand, as though trying to find the woman.

Did he speak French? A little. What was happening? Why did the woman scream? Where is she? The best *puta* in the town, and she screamed like a cat!

Ned waited a few more moments for the man fully to

recover his senses and then with a hard bark in his voice began his questioning.

"Where is the garrison commander?"

"Commander? I am the *gobernador* of the castle, Major Luis de Torres."

"How many officers have you in the garrison?"

"Two, a captain and a lieutenant."

Ned snapped his fingers to attract Roberts' attention and pointed to a huge key hanging on a nail in the wall beside the bed.

"The key to the magazine – where is it?"

"I shall not tell you," the old man said defiantly, although he could not resist a glance sideways.

Ned told Roberts: "Try that key in the magazine lock. If it fits secure the lock again and bring the key back to me."

He turned back to the major. "How many men do you have?"

"Eight non-commissioned officers and men and two officers. The rest of my men are at the Catalina battery."

"How many?"

"Why should I tell you all this? Who are you? Go away and leave me in peace!"

"*Boucaniers,*" Ned said crisply. "English buccaneers. If we go away, we leave you dead – unless you answer our questions."

The man now was very wide awake and suddenly aware that he was naked and that outside the ring of lantern light was not just one man but a dozen or more.

"How many at Catalina?"

"An ensign, sergeant, corporal and six men."

"How many guns there?"

"Three."

"You are lying about the men. Nine, including an officer, for three guns? Rubbish. How many really, eh?"

"Twelve men. But it is true for the rest."

"Why do you have such a small garrison up here in the castle?"

"Last year we had the *vomito negro*. Twenty-two soldiers died. I ask Spain for more, but none come."

"Why do you not ask for some from Cartagena or Vera Cruz?"

"My requests have to go to Spain," the major said stiffly. "I am not under the Viceroy's jurisdiction."

"Are there troops here in Santiago?"

"No, of course not. They are here in the castle and at Catalina. Why should my troops be in town?"

Ned looked at the seamen round him. "Burne, help the major put on breeches, coat and boots, and then tie his hands behind his back."

Then he remembered the woman who, from Day's curses, was now trying to bite him.

"Major, tell your woman that unless she is quiet we will cut her throat. She has to put on her shift and then we will tie her hands. But if she continues . . ."

"You – you wouldn't dare! You –"

"Major, the only men you have left alive in the castle are yourself, the captain and the lieutenant. Now, time is short!"

Five minutes later the buccaneers had the major, captain, lieutenant and the whore standing against the great door of the castle. In front of them the ground fell away steeply to Santiago nestling in the valley. Ned fingered one of his pistols. One pistol shot – that was the agreed signal. Then the 250 buccaneers would be breaking down doors, trying to explain to the sleepy burghers of Santiago that the buccaneers had arrived for their gold and silver.

There was a better way of waking and warning them.

"How many cannon have you here?" he asked the major.

"Only three."

"Bronze or iron?"

"Iron. The rest – nine – are down at the jetty over there," he pointed across the channel. "We are going to build a new battery to support the Catalina. This castle is not well placed – enemy ships can creep along too close to the coast for us to depress our guns."

Three iron guns: they were of no consequence. He called for Roberts, gave him instructions, making sure all the buccaneers heard, and then followed him through the door back into the castle, warning Day and Lloyd to keep a tight hold of the prisoners, using as many buccaneers as they needed.

Roberts led the way to the magazine and when Ned gave him the key, unlocked the door. The dim light of the lantern showed steps going down and as Ned hesitated, Roberts said:

"If you just want to *see* how big the magazine is, sir, I'll stand up here and shine the light down the steps so we keep the flame away from the powder. I went down in the dark and felt my way round. S'enormous, sir, there's enough powder in there to blow up all o' Cuba!"

Ned went down the steps. It was like descending into a crypt, except the air seemed unnaturally dry, and instead of coffins on shelves there were hundreds of bags of powder. Then, in neat rows, were barrels of powder, each as high as his thigh and about three feet in diameter in the middle. Enough powder to blow up Cuba – well, Roberts was hardly exaggerating.

He walked back to the foot of the stairs. "Very well, Roberts, I'm going to start now."

"Good luck, sir," the man said, and Ned was glad to see he came down another step and held the lantern to throw more light.

The fuse was not very long: about eight feet, and no one was too sure how reliable it was. It had been made on board the *Griffin* on the voyage from Jamaica, according to a method that Burton had once heard about. The fuse was made of the bark of the mangroves growing at the water's edge and the men had sliced off as much bark as they could reach. For the next four days, while they were at sea, the reddish strips had been kept in the sun, drying. As soon as Burton – and everyone else on board it seemed, who now took a sudden interest in the experiment – reckoned it was dry enough it was hammered and hammered until the fibrous strips could be cut as narrow as line, and then plaited into a long fuse. Burton tried a foot length as an experiment and it sputtered and crackled, but it burned steadily from one end to another, taking eight minutes. No one but a foolish optimist would rely on that rate, though.

Ned pulled over a bag of powder and rested it against the bottom step. He made a small slit in the top, pushed a few inches of fuse into it, and then put a second bag on the step above, overhanging it sufficiently that when he made a slit the powder poured on to the lower bag, partly burying the end of the fuse. Carefully he walked up the steps, paying out the fuse as he ascended. He ran out of fuse four steps from the top. He looked up to see perspiration pouring from Roberts' face. The man was shaking and embarrassed.

"Don't worry," Ned said, "being so close to so much powder and holding a lantern is enough to turn your hair white."

"Oh, it ain't for me," Roberts said apologetically, "I was all right when I was feeling around in the dark!"

"What's the matter now, then?"

"Well, sir, I got to thinking what'd happen if you fell and broke a leg or something, and there's no one to hold the lantern while I get you out."

Ned laughed and thanked him. "We can start now. Go and tell the party to start making their way down to the town and give a whistle when they've started. You follow them and I'll be along soon."

"Right ho, sir. You want to step up here for the time being with the lantern?"

"No, give it to me here: I'm afraid of pulling the fuse out of the bags."

Roberts disappeared into the darkness. Ned shone the lantern at the stonework. The magazine was a good twelve feet down, made of thick stone blocks which fitted perfectly. How many tons of powder? Roberts had counted the bags and barrels, so they would be able to make a guess afterwards.

Supposing an hour goes by and there is no explosion?

Should he come back? This mangrove fuse – it could take an hour to burn, or fifteen minutes. Or it could go out. He pictured himself coming back through the castle door after an hour and heading for the magazine to find out what happened to the fuse, and suddenly seeing a flash. That would be the last thing he would ever see. Where the devil was Roberts' whistle?

At that moment a hoarse voice said: "Sir – everyone's on their way down the hill. That whore's making a fuss."

"Roberts!" Ned said crossly. "You're supposed to have gone with them!"

"Yes, sir, but I got frightened when I thought of you holding the fuse in one hand and the lantern with the other. You need a third hand to open the lantern door and with me here we've got a hand to spare."

Ned grinned at him and passed up the lantern, holding the fuse which looked like a thin, reddish snake.

"Now, set the lantern down on the ground where I can reach the candle with the fuse. I want to keep the fuse flat on the step, so there's no strain on it."

Roberts put the lantern down, moving it until it was level with the fuse.

"I hope there's no loose powder on these steps," Ned said.

"Wait, sir," Roberts said urgently. He went up to the magazine entrance, put the lantern down on the ground outside, then came back down the stairs and, crouching down, blew vigorously where he had been standing. "Now, sir, if you'll just give me a bit of room." He then blew vigorously until he was sure there were no loose grains on the four steps over which the fuse passed. After that he went up and brought the lantern back, positioning it carefully.

"Open the lantern door, then," Ned said.

It swung open easily, showing it was in regular use, and Ned held the end of the fuse over the candle flame. For a minute or more nothing happened; then the plaited mangrove began to sputter and glow.

"It's like a bad-tempered snake," Roberts said, shutting the lantern as soon as Ned took out the fuse and put it down gently on the step. Both men watched the fuse like rabbits caught by a stoat.

"It's burning evenly. But faster than I expected. Come on Roberts!"

At the top of the steps Ned carefully shut the magazine door and locked it. He was far from sure why he did that but said casually to Roberts: "There might be a draught."

"Yes, sir," Roberts said politely, "I was thinking the same thing."

The two men then marched to the main door and set off down the hill after the rest of the party. Although neither of them realized it, they slowed down gradually as they left the castle behind them, but they were almost at the bottom of the valley, close to Santiago itself, before they caught up with the party, all of whom were sitting beside the path.

"Thought I'd better halt here, sir," Day explained. "Didn't want us marching into the town without the drums beating!"

"You were quite right," Ned said, cursing himself for having forgotten the chance that they would get down so quickly. "We'll wait here," he announced to the rest of the men. "But try and find some boulders to shelter behind, because when the magazine goes up . . ."

The whore was arguing with the major, but Ned interrupted, tapping the major on the shoulder. It seemed only fair to warn him.

"Major, your castle might explode soon, so you and your officers and your, ah, friend, will have to lie down behind some boulders. For your own safety," he added.

It was difficult to estimate the time. The moon, now waning, rose while they were lying on the ground behind their boulders, and moved quickly on its westward path. Ned guessed as the time dragged past. Fifteen minutes, half an hour. . . . He almost dozed.

"How long do you reckon it's been, sir?" Roberts whispered.

"More than an hour. It's gone out."

"Well, not our lucky day," Roberts said philosophically.

"Give me the lantern."

"Why – where are you going, sir?"

"I'm just going to check that fuse. You stay here in charge of the party."

"Indeed, I don't, sir," Roberts said angrily. "If you're going back, then I'm coming with you."

"You'll do as you're told and stay here, Roberts."

"My bloody oath, I –"

The flash lit distant mountain peaks before almost blinding them; the land trembled so violently that Ned thought the whole ridge was going to collapse on top of Santiago. It was not so much the sound of an explosion but a vast noise, a massive thunderclap that rumbled, reverberated and echoed, and as it stopped thousands of frightened dogs began barking, startled gulls mewed and wheeled below, and landbirds fled with shrill cries. Then the Castillo, its walls blown into separate blocks and chips, angled pieces and coping stones, began tumbling out of the sky, and the whore began a shrill chant which seemed to be one enormously long word but was every prayer she ever knew strung together.

Chapter
Twenty-one

At first light Ned saw the *Griffin* making the turn into the narrow entrance, her mainsail slamming as she occasionally lost the wind. Close astern were the *Peleus* and the *Phoenix,* but the cliffs hid the other four privateers he knew would be waiting their turn to come in.

Standing here on the Catalina battery with Roberts and Day and looking up at the still-smoking pile of rubble that at sunset yesterday had been the Castillo, Ned found it hard to believe. Most if not all of the town's most important citizens were now assembled in the *plaza*; three bronze guns here at the battery and nine more at the jetty would ensure the defence of Jamaica's harbour; and Thomas and Saxby with their men were rounding up everything of value in Santiago that could be carried away as purchase.

He knew Aurelia would be standing on the *Griffin*'s foredeck, excited, perhaps frightened (but he thought not), and maybe worried at the sight of the grim pile at the cliff top. The ships at Aguadores would have seen the flash and heard the explosion and she would be fearful for his safety until the *Griffin* could see the Catalina battery. Now the sight of a white flag flying at each end (linen sheets from the *Griffin* and, Aurelia had said emphatically, to be returned as soon as all the ships were in the port) might reassure her: they showed that Santiago had been captured by the buccaneers. He imagined Diana, too, standing at the bow of the *Peleus,* a brunette Viking, anxious to see Thomas. Last night might well have been the first time they had slept apart for some years, and sleeping alone was the ultimate solitude, as he had just learned.

"We must get back to the *plaza*," he told the three men. "Sir Thomas will want to know that the ships are coming in."

With the sun still below the horizon it was cool, but the stench in Santiago was appalling; piles of rotting garbage scattered every few yards along the streets were being raked over by dogs and hogs. Once the sun was blazing down the smell would become almost unbearable.

In the *plaza* at least half the buccaneers were standing at intervals round the four sides holding muskets and pistols trained on a couple of hundred men and women who were sitting or lying on the flagstones, most covered with blankets and many moaning as if mourning at a funeral. In one corner of the *plaza* Ned saw the reflection of metal and realized it was a pile of gold and silver objects, presumably plates and goblets, cutlery and probably articles from the cathedral, which formed half of one side of the *plaza*.

From time to time four or five buccaneers walked into the *plaza* from side roads and added more items to the pile, handling the precious metals as nonchalantly as foresters might pile up logs for the winter.

Ned then realized that one of the three men slowly walking across the *plaza* and talking to the assembled Spaniards was Thomas, whom he found in excellent spirits.

"The *Griffin* is coming in, with the *Peleus* close astern."

"Excellent, Ned. Let's hope they can get alongside the jetty without stoving in a plank or two!"

"I checked the guns: twelve bronze altogether, and 1,500 shot to fit them."

"That should protect the anchorage for a while and old General Heffer is going to be pleased. Now, I must get on. Some of these people are not being helpful. In fact you and your men can stay with me to scare them."

Thomas had managed to find a privateersman who spoke passable Spanish, and once he had taken Santiago he discovered a Spaniard with good English. Now Thomas was checking the identities of his prisoners, and the more important were being sent to one corner of the *plaza*: they would not be freed until a good ransom was paid.

"Who have you found up to now?" Ned asked.

"Most of those that matter: the town governor was in his bed – he's over there now, in the special corner. The bishop of Santiago, the *Intendente,* who is in effect the town treasurer, the mayor, some important officials from Havana who were visiting the governor . . . I'm just checking these people to find a few wealthy business men."

"And the town treasury?"

"That was the first place we captured after your bang! No time to count the gold but there are bags of coins, ingots . . . I've never seen so much in my life. I have twenty men guarding it. We'll carry it out to the *Griffin* and *Peleus,* but we'll include men from each of the privateers in the guards, just so they'll rest easy in their minds."

With that, Thomas pointed and asked the translator: "Who is this man?"

The portly Spaniard sitting with a gaudy blanket round his shoulders stood up nervously and bowed. He listened to the translator, who then gave his reply. "He is a dealer in slaves."

"How many does he import a year?"

"Not many because he buys most of them from the market in Havana and resells in this part of the island."

"How many does he sell a year?"

Ned noticed the cunning look in the fat dealer's eyes. The translator was speaking slowly when he translated into Spanish, giving his fellow countryman time to think. Ned tapped the translator on the arm. "Talk faster when you translate. I speak Spanish, and one mistake by you means your throat will be cut. And you are responsible for people answering honestly."

Thomas immediately understood what was in Ned's mind, knowing he did not speak Spanish.

"Ned! I'd forgotten you speak Spanish – and French, of course. Anyway, let this fellow exercise his tongue, but I'd be grateful if you'd listen."

"But señor," the man protested. "I am doing my best. This man is very wealthy and very cruel, and when you go he will probably have me bastinadoed for helping you!"

"Most unfortunate," Thomas said. "When we go, I suggest you move to the other end of the island. Now, how many slaves does he sell a year?"

Day had taken out his knife and was absent-mindedly stropping it against the leather sleeve of his jerkin, and the slave dealer was watching the blade nervously as it turned over and slid along, turned over and slid back.

"He says five hundred a year, but he is lying. Ten times as many."

Ned nudged Day. "Scare him a little, but don't hurt him."

Day gave a truly diabolical laugh, tossed his knife in the air, caught it without looking and then prodded the fat Spaniard's stomach with his finger, as though seeking a soft place to insert the blade. The Spaniard fainted, collapsing beside his wife like a poleaxed steer.

Thomas wrote on the slate he was carrying. "I'll put him down for the value of five thousand slaves. Who's next?"

It took him two hours to select forty-one of Santiago's leading citizens and put a price on their heads. In each case the husband was released to go off and find the money while the wife and children were kept in the *plaza*.

"Every one of them a married man," Thomas commented to Ned. "I'm not sure of the significance."

"It's a bad place for bachelors," Ned said. "By the way, how are these people going to pay ransom if you've already looted their homes?"

"You are new to the game," Thomas said. "When we looted the houses we took plate, any jewellery we could find, and money. But as usual we found very little money. They hide their coins – bury them in the garden, put them up a chimney, under a stair . . ."

"But they were not expecting buccaneers – we know that."

Thomas bellowed with laughter, a roar which made mothers and daughters clasp each other in fear that it was the preliminary to a massacre. "Not buccaneers, Ned; they're frightened of the Spanish tax men!"

"Do they pay such heavy taxes?"

"I don't know what they pay, but they are *charged* heavy taxes. These islands, and the Main and Mexico, have to support themselves with local taxation: they get nothing from the gold and silver mining: that goes direct to the Spanish crown." He glanced up at the sun, which was now heating the *plaza*. "Well, now we wait for the ransom to arrive. Let's go over and see our womenfolk and make arrangements to start loading the ships."

By dawn next day each of the seven privateers was loaded.

The *Griffin* had three of the brass culverins stowed in her hold, the *Peleus* three, the *Phoenix* two and the other four privateers had one each. Thomas Whetstone had found five brass three-pounders on ordinary carriages, owned by the army and left in the town, while in the town hall were stored ninety breast, back and headpieces of armour. Neither he nor Ned were very sure how much use armour would be – anyone wearing them would be assumed to be Spanish because of the design, but Ned suggested that for a particular occasion they could be painted an unusual light colour.

The Catalina battery had a bigger magazine than anyone expected: Ned guessed that much of the material stored in it had been brought down recently from the castle, in anticipation of building the second battery mentioned by the major. Anyway, the *Griffin, Peleus* and *Phoenix* were each carrying five hundred roundshot for the cannons, while the *Griffin* had thirty barrels of powder, the *Peleus* seventy-five Spanish muskets and twenty-five barrels of bullets, and the *Phoenix* had three hundred empty grenade cases and ten barrels of brimstone. She also had two hundred bundles of slowmatch, although Burton's verdict on it was that the plaited mangrove was more reliable.

The gold, silver and pewter plate, flagons, tankards, candelabra and cutlery had been listed, stowed in sacks and finally distributed in the holds of the seven privateers; the jewellery by common consent had been locked in a thick blanket chest and stowed in the *Griffin* with four armed men guarding it. The money, in sacks and boxes, was in the *Peleus* and the *Griffin*.

Except for twenty-two wives still under guard in the *plaza* awaiting ransom payments by their husbands, the buccaneers were ready to sail, and Thomas had been rowed over to the *Griffin*.

"Those damned women," he said. "Or damned husbands, rather. I shouldn't have been so soft-hearted and sent them mattresses to sleep on, and blankets. What sort of husband would leave his wife in the *plaza,* captive to buccaneers?"

"Tightfisted ones, obviously!" Ned said. "You put such a high ransom on those husbands that when you let them go to get the money and kept the wives as hostages, they decided their wives weren't worth that much!"

Thomas stared at him incredulously and, after a minute's thought nodded. "Either that or they think we'll get impatient and go, leaving them behind. Well, we'll soon see if they're bluffing!"

"You can't call on them," Ned teased.

"No, but I can bring those women out to the ships! They – the husbands – will think we are taking them with us. Yes, we'll distribute the women in the *Griffin, Peleus* and *Phoenix,* send the children home and prepare to sail. I'll bet we'll get results!"

"How will the reluctant husbands pay? Shall I stay in the *plaza* with a couple of dozen men?"

"No – let Saxby; he looks fiercer than you. A dozen weeping husbands swearing they don't have a doubloon to their names will break your heart!"

With that Thomas was climbing down to his boat to collect the women, calling to Ned to give the orders to the four privateers, making sure that they spent half an hour or so making obvious preparations to sail.

When he went down to the cabin to explain Thomas's plan to Aurelia and warn her that eight or ten tearful Spanish ladies would be coming on board soon, he had expected her to be angry because of Thomas's apparent ruthlessness. He was not prepared for her to storm round the cabin in a fury, cursing the delinquent Spanish husbands and using many French words that Ned had never heard before. As he prided himself on his ability to curse fluently in French, he made a mental note to insist on translations later. The sight of this wildcat striding round the cabin naked – she had been sleeping in the hammaco – was in one sense alarming (in case one day he should be the cause of a similar outburst) and in another very rousing.

Husbands! Her tirade was against husbands, and suddenly Ned realized that these Spaniards were attracting all the anger and hatred she had been bottling up in the years of her marriage to Wilson: he had bullied, scorned, belittled and ignored her, and she had borne it as she imagined a dutiful wife should. Then she had escaped and now saw more than a score of wives – wives, it was irrelevant that they were Spanish – abandoned by their husbands. She could see Wilson doing precisely the same thing. Pay a ransom of ten thousand doubloons for her? Oh no!

She turned on Ned: "What do we do with these women if the husbands don't pay us? Are we supposed to take them to Jamaica? Then what – put them in brothels? Are you and Thomas mad? What does Diana say? She knows nothing of this, I am sure. Perhaps Thomas has his eye on one of them. You men!"

"Listen," Ned said firmly, "if you scrabble around the deck in bare feet like that you'll get splinters . . ."

"Never mind that, we sometimes make love on the deck! You don't worry about me getting splinters then!"

Ned sat in the chair, his head between his hands, and waited.

Finally, in a calmer voice she asked: "Well, what are you going to do with the women when we get to Jamaica?"

"We are not taking them to Jamaica. You were so excited you did not listen properly." Once again he explained the bluff, and she shook her finger at him.

"You see, you deliberately upset me by not explaining things clearly. You think I am a man –" she broke off when she watched Ned's eyes surveying her body. "Well, you think I *think* like a man, but . . ."

"Darling," he said, "Thomas won't be back for an hour."

"Yes," she said, "I missed you last night."

Two hours after the last of the four privateers had sailed down the channel and out of Santiago, and while seamen were climbing the shrouds of the three remaining ships and generally obeying the order to "Look busy", Saxby sent a message by boat from the Catalina battery with a list of eighteen names. Burton explained that the names were of the wives whose husbands had come rushing to the Catalina battery as soon as the four privateers had begun to weigh, and paid their ransom in full. A second boat left the *Griffin* and went with Burton to collect the women from the three ships and restore them to their husbands.

Aurelia, still angry with the dilatory husbands, explained in detail to the wives who had been detained in the *Griffin* exactly why they had been held, adding that if their husbands had paid the previous day like the others, the women would not have been forced to spend such a distressing time on board a ship. To her surprise she found that the eleven wives kept on board the *Griffin* had, after the initial tears, enjoyed the experience. The six youngest undoubtedly basked in the lecherous gazes of the *Griffin*'s crew, who were feeling the full effect of the hot nights and several days away from the release offered by the Cagway brothels.

Thomas was soon over to discuss plans with Ned. "Five wives left, according to my list. What unfeeling brutes their husbands must be," he complained, unconscious of the irony.

"Perhaps those five husbands are not happily married . . ."

"That could be so," Thomas admitted.

"So if you want to punish them, free their wives. Once those women know their husbands would not pay for their release, they'll realize their husbands are villains!"

"You have a pleasantly devious mind," Thomas said, "but let's see how much ransom we are asking those five husbands to pay." He looked at his slate, where all but five names had been crossed out. Against each name was a figure, indicating the amount of ransom owing.

"Would you believe it!" Thomas was disgusted. "These fellows were priced about the lowest, too. Well, considering the purchase we already have, we'll wait another half an hour and if the husbands haven't called on Saxby to pay, we'll turn the wives loose. That'll mean five unhappy husbands. If I did a thing like that, Diana would kill me!"

"If it was Diana and up to you to pay, you'd pay like the rest of the husbands. But you are probably doing these five a good turn. We have only one of those wives on board the *Griffin* and she's as broad as she is long."

"I have three in the *Peleus*. Dull but not shrewish, I should say. By the way, did I tell you the bishop was the most helpful of all the citizens?"

"No. In what way?"

"When we found him in his house we made him show us where his own money and plate was kept, and then we took him to the cathedral. I had an idea he had a good deal of church plate hidden away – and I don't know why; it was just a feeling. Well, he denied it and shouted and yelled and prayed so loudly that when we cleared the cathedral, I decided to search the crypt – and that was when I found the rack."

Ned shivered at the thought of that gaunt metal contraption with its sweat-stained leather straps, looking like an altar made of iron by a mad blacksmith. Having it in the crypt of the cathedral meant that the screams of the heretics being racked would not be heard outside, would not disturb the peaceful days and nights of Santiago's true believers. "Did you find any more treasure hidden down there?"

"I didn't, but the bishop did."

"You mean he fetched it for you, eh?" Ned was only teasing but Thomas nodded, unsmiling.

"Yes. We strapped him down on the rack and gave it a few turns to take up the slack. Then I asked him. I found we had to let off a turn or two so that he could speak. The sight of this rack made me so angry I put the turns back on again, so that he'd have some idea what it's like when his men torture someone. When I finally let him go he was very helpful. He produced half a dozen solid gold candlesticks, for instance, each four feet high and as much as one man could carry. They were used for funerals; special candles to put round the coffin as it lies in state."

Aurelia joined them, greeting Thomas, who looked at her knowingly. "You were glad to have Ned back, I'll be bound."

She nodded without blushing and once again Ned was impressed at the change taking place in her. "Was Diana glad to see you?"

Thomas shrugged his shoulders. "She is still angry with me for not taking her over the hills."

"You've only yourself to blame then," Aurelia said unsympathetically. "I enjoyed bringing the ship round with Lobb. If Ned ever makes *me* angry I shall simply put him on one of the cays and sail away."

"I believe you would," Thomas said and turned to Ned. "We'll have to keep an eye open for each other. If you don't wave to me before sunset I'll board, and you do the same for me!"

"What are you going to do for these poor women?" Aurelia asked. "How many are left?"

"Five," said Thomas mournfully, "and their future will be dreadful, I must admit."

"Why? What are you going to do with them?" an alarmed Aurelia demanded.

Thomas shook his head. "Men . . . there'll be violence . . ."

"Oh no! Why, they're not young. That . . . sort of thing . . . it could kill them!"

Ned turned away, doubting that he could keep a straight face, but Aurelia thought he was avoiding her anger.

"Please, Thomas," she pleaded, "let them go. We have an enormous amount of purchase. Show mercy!"

"I can't do both. If I let them go, I'm not showing mercy."

"Riddles, Thomas, you are talking in riddles!"

"You are thinking the women's future will be dreadful. I'm concerned about the husbands. Imagine what it will be like when the wives storm into the house and demand to know why their husbands did not value them highly enough to pay ransom. Think how shamed they will feel in the company of wives whose husbands *did* pay!"

"Was that why Ned asked me to explain to the other wives?"

Thomas nodded cheerfully but then said seriously: "Aurelia, if you have any doubts about all this, come on shore with me and we'll walk through to the cathedral. It has some fine stained glass windows. In the crypt is a rack. It is used regularly. The leather straps are stained too – black, from the blood and sweat of victims."

"Yes, Thomas, I understand," she said softly. "I am a Huguenot, you remember. Barely twenty-five years ago Cardinal Richelieu was destroying us at La Rochelle. Our people exist only by the Edict of Nantes, and no one but a fool would trust the king not to revoke it soon and the church will start the massacre . . ."

"Well, don't have too much sympathy for these Spanish wives," Thomas said. "They're all staunch Catholics and they'd all sit round in their best clothes, rosaries in hand, watching you being broken on the wheel or stretched on the rack."

Aurelia nodded contritely. "You are right as usual, Thomas, and Ned too: I should not interfere."

"You caught the habit from Diana," Thomas said amiably. "It's my fault; I don't beat her enough. Well," he said turning to Ned, "we might as well put these women on shore. The sooner we get back to Jamaica the sooner we can divide the purchase."

Chapter
Twenty-two

The *Griffin* led the way past the Palizadas into the great anchorage and Ned was just going to give the order to Burton to fire off a few guns to make sure that General Heffer knew the buccaneers were back, when he saw a strange ship anchored at the far end of the anchorage. Her ensign was flying at half mast, and the flag hoisted on the general's headquarters was also at half mast.

Who could be dead? Was it someone in Jamaica – the general, perhaps – or Europe, the news being brought by the newly-arrived ship? It would do no harm to cover the ship, Ned decided, and gave orders to Lobb to tack up the harbour and anchor ahead of the merchant ship. He could rely on Thomas and Saxby anchoring the *Peleus* and *Phoenix* on each side, and the other four privateers would be close.

The anchor was hardly down before Ned saw a canoe setting out from the jetty near the general's house, and a careful inspection through the glass showed that Lieutenant Rowlands was sitting in it, a piece of canvas protecting him from the splashing of the paddles as the slaves sped the boat towards the *Griffin*.

Ned looked over at the *Peleus* and saw that she was hoisting out a boat, so that Thomas would be over in a few minutes. This fool Rowlands seemed to come to the *Griffin* because she was the largest . . .

The lieutenant came up the ladder, gave Ned a cautious but correct salute, and handed him a letter with a large seal on it.

"So the Spaniards did not come to attack from Santiago," Ned said solicitously, waiting for Thomas to arrive.

"No, sir, but we have later information that they have a fleet of seven ships and three or four thousand soldiers preparing: a fisherman arrived yesterday who had actually seen the seven ships at anchor in a bay near Santiago. Aguadores, I think the place was called."

Thomas came up the ladder and strode across the deck. "Ha, it's the general's potman! How are you, Oarsman?"

"Rowlands, sir. Very well. If you'll excuse me, there's no reply."

Thomas waved him back to the canoe. "What news has the general's potman brought us?" he asked Ned, who waved the sealed letter and led the way down to the cabin.

Ned broke the seal, read the four or five lines of writing, and handed it to Thomas, who read it twice, his face a mask. Aurelia watched both men anxiously; she had never seen such expressions before. She looked questioningly at Ned.

"Cromwell has died and his son Richard – Thomas's first cousin – has succeeded him."

Thomas gave the letter back to Ned. "And the general wants us to go over to see him urgently. Well, he may have more news. He doesn't say when Uncle Oliver died but it must be two or three months ago, and by now I expect the country is heartily sick of Richard. I can't see the army putting up with *him* for long."

"Yes, allowing for the time it took for that ship to get here, anything could have happened in England. Still, we're more concerned with what's happening here!"

"I'll tell you one thing, Ned, the general and everyone else here is squatting nervously on a fence. The next ship to arrive may bring a new governor, orders to abandon the island, to capture Cuba, return to England, place the general under arrest . . ." Thomas's eyes glinted as he tugged at his beard in his excitement. "Now these poltroons know what the Cavaliers have been going through: the dreadful uncertainty of going to bed at night and never knowing what misery the morning will bring. Come on, Ned, let's go and discomfort the general; it'll be better than bear-baiting at Vauxhall because *we* have a talking bear!"

"By the way," Ned said, gesturing to make sure Aurelia

was listening, "your Lieutenant Rowlands says they've just received more news from a fisherman: he reports seeing a Spanish invasion fleet of seven ships anchored at Aguadores."

Thomas bellowed with laughter. "Certainly he saw a fleet of seven ships! If he'd looked closer –" he winked at Aurelia "– he'd have reported they were commanded by two women admirals!"

"Wait a moment, Thomas. Let's think what we are going to say to the general, whatever he might have to tell us."

"How do you mean?"

"Well, Cromwell may be dead, but there's still a Council of State. Out here we must remember Jamaica is an isolated island surrounded by Spanish ports. It has no defences, but we've just brought enough guns and powder from Santiago to defend Cagway harbour."

"You're not proposing to *give* the guns to the Roundheads, are you, Ned? Make them pay for them!"

"But we know the general has no money, and we've already decided that Cagway and the Palizadas are a perfect base for all the buccaneers. Yet we need it to be defended. We want to be able to anchor here in safety and do repairs, for example. And we don't want always to be worrying that a few Spanish privateers might sneak in round the Palizadas on a dark night. Don't forget, they've only just been driven out, so they know every reef and every rock. *We* want the defences; the devil take what the Roundheads want!"

Thomas nodded his agreement. "I still don't like the idea of *giving* them all those guns, shot and powder. Certainly the guns will defend us, but they'll defend Roundheads, too."

"We'll bargain," Ned said, suddenly getting an idea. "The guns have to be mounted in forts or on batteries, and I'm damned if we want to use our people as masons and labourers. If the general will agree to use his soldiers to do the building, we'll supply the guns, powder and shot."

"And we'll make sure that every time we raid a place we'll bring back more guns and shot."

"Come on, Thomas, let's go and bargain with the general. Let him report on the Spanish fleet at Santiago!"

The general was very agitated. The bottom had just dropped

out of his world professionally because he owed his
promotion entirely to service with the late Lord Protector.
Politically he was exposed because he had many enemies in
England and had never met Richard Cromwell. He had
powerful enemies here, too, even among his own officers:
many of them wanted to return to England before they were
struck down by yellow fever or typhus, and the last ships to
leave for England carried letters to influential friends,
accusing their general of everything from corruption to
inefficiency, and saying that Jamaica was a useless possession.
And this morning the news had come from the fishermen
about the Spanish fleet at Aguadores.

The only good news was that the buccaneers had come
back, sailing in as silently and unexpectedly as they had left
several days ago, and he only hoped that Rowlands had
delivered his letter safely and not antagonized them. A good
young officer, Rowlands, but one of his brother officers had
called him a psalm-singing hypocrite and the general found it
hard to quarrel with the verdict.

He heard footsteps and voices and then the bellowing
laugh of Whetheread, the bearded buccaneer leader.
Suddenly Heffer felt less lonely. The buccaneers were an
independent crowd, but at least they were not cowards, like
half his officers, who were so scared that they would lie, cheat
and probably mutiny in their mad rush to get out of Jamaica,
and who had shown their worth at Hispaniola.

"Hello, General Teffler," Thomas bellowed, and Ned
realized that he had quite deliberately made a mistake in the
man's name to throw him off his stride. "Flags at half mast,
eh? The Lord Protector found the Lord finally withdrew His
protection! Ah well, it'll happen to us all."

"Please, please, no blasphemy."

"That's not blasphemy!" Thomas exclaimed. "He was a
scoundrel and his son is a ninny. Left *you* out on a limb, hasn't
it? Don't know whether you're still a general or reduced to a
trooper. You'd better join us now; there'll be a rush once
Richard fools around with the army, and we've only a few
vacancies!"

"Ah, Mr Whetheread, you will have your joke. The news
arrived from England, as you probably guessed, in the
merchant ship that came in yesterday."

"Did it bring fresh orders for you?"

"Not exactly," Heffer said cautiously. "They had some private mail and, of course, the master had sailed from London, so he had the latest news."

"Up to what date?"

"The Lord Protector died twelve weeks ago. I am not sure when the ship sailed."

"So no official news, no orders, nothing for you. You're just acting upon rumour and gossip from the ship." Thomas said it without malice but Heffer, suddenly realizing how another interpretation could be put on his activities, went pale.

"I'm *not* acting upon gossip," he said primly. "I'm not doing anything. Or, rather, I am continuing to carry out the last orders I received."

"Ve-rree wise," Thomas drawled. "One mistake at a time like this and you could end up with a noose round your neck!"

"Oh, come, come, you exaggerate."

"I assure you, I don't," Thomas said. "The King had his head chopped off. However, what you do is none of my affair, but if the Lord Protector's been dead three months, the chances of Richard still having any authority are negligible. It needs only one of your enemies to be in power – or even someone who has never heard your name . . . Still, it's a disagreeble subject, and you'll have to wait for another ship to bring you orders."

"Yes, quite," Heffer said, glad to change the subject. "You had a good voyage?"

"Yes, the weather was good but fishing was poor. Trailing a line over the stern never brings me luck."

"Ah yes. Well, I asked you to call on me so that I could confirm the news I mentioned in my letter about the Lord Protector, but also I have fresh intelligence about the Spanish at Santiago!"

"You mentioned that place before, I remember. In Cuba. Something about a Spanish fleet was it not?"

"Yes, and I have impeccable information which arrived this morning that a Spanish fleet of seven big ships was anchored at Aguadores, close to Santiago, two days ago, and the Spanish army in Santiago is ready to embark."

"You need defences," Ned said sympathetically. "Batteries at the end of the Palizadas to cover the harbour entrance. A fort on the seaward side. Another battery on the Palizadas and also one on the other side."

Heffer swallowed hard, obviously trying to be patient. "I told you, Mr Kent, that I have no guns; they are still in the storeships that have not yet arrived."

"I'm no soldier," Ned said, "but how many guns and forts and batteries would you need to defend the harbour? Not the island, just the harbour and its entrance."

Heffer's brow wrinkled. "To defend the harbour you must prevent an enemy landing on the Palizadas, because it is so flat. They could put carriage guns ashore on the seaward side in calm weather and get them across the sand. Men could haul them; they would not need horses. So – a strong fort on the shore opposite this house with a minimum of four guns; a battery at the end of the Palizadas with, say three guns, and another on the opposite side with another three guns. Ideally one would like another fort with three guns covering the Palizadas to the eastwards, where the peninsula begins, in case the enemy landed farther up the coast. So that's a minimum of ten guns, and preferably thirteen."

Ned nodded thoughtfully. "You have no guns, no shot, general. How about powder?"

"Sufficient for the two dozen shot that the musketeers and cavalry have."

"But you are not short of men – I mean, if you had the guns you'd have enough men to build forts and batteries."

Heffer looked both hungry and wistful. "If I had the guns, I'd have the forts and batteries built in a month!" he exclaimed. "Plenty of stone, plenty of sand for mortar . . ."

"Such a pity," Ned said sympathetically. "We buccaneers like this anchorage, but of course with no defences it becomes a trap, which is why we did not stay last time, and now you have more confirmation that the Spaniards are coming, we shall sail as soon as we have more provisions and water."

Clearly Heffer could have bitten off his tongue for having mentioned the Spanish fleet. If only he could persuade the buccaneers to stay, he had a little squadron of his own. Or anyway, a squadron whose interest was similar to his own.

Ned leaned towards the general and said casually: "We could strike a bargain with you."

"What bargain?" the general replied suspiciously. "I can't bargain with buccaneers, you know!"

"The other day you were trying to get us to defend you for nothing; a few days before that you were only too glad to buy grain which saved your garrison from starving."

"Oh well, what are you offering?"

"A dozen bronze cannon – they're culverins – with plenty of powder and shot, and a couple of hundred grenadoes and brimstone. And some three-pounder carriage guns."

Heffer's eyes looked as though they would pop out of his head. "What, what . . ." he stammered, "what are you asking in return?"

"That you build two forts and two batteries in the positions you've just described, along with the appropriate magazines, cookhouses, and cisterns where they can't sink wells."

"Where are those guns coming from?" Heffer asked cautiously. "How long will it take for you to get them?"

"An hour or two," Ned said in a bored tone. "The guns, powder, shot, grenadoes and brimstone are all loaded on board our ships."

"But – well, you didn't have them when you were last here, did you?" Heffer asked incredulously.

Ned shook his head.

"May I ask where you found them?"

"First, do we have an agreement that you will build the positions if we supply the guns?"

"Indeed, indeed," Heffer said eagerly. He held out his hand first to Ned and then to Thomas, and when they had shaken it, repeated his question.

"They are Spanish guns," Ned said. "In excellent condition. I doubt if any one of them has fired twenty-five rounds."

"Spanish? Then what about shot? No English or French shot will fit."

"We shall supply one hundred roundshot with each gun, and later we will make sure you get more when we raid other Spanish ports and towns."

"But where did these come from?"

"Santiago," Ned said.

271

"Santiago de Cuba? Why that's impossible! The Spanish fleet is at Aguadores . . ."

"Seven ships, you say? We have seven ships. We were anchored at Aguadores two days ago."

"But you can't have been to Santiago! Why, it has an enormous castle defending it!"

"The Castillo del Morro?"

"Yes, that's it."

"Just a hole in the ground and a pile of stones," Ned said.

"But how do you know?"

Thomas said in a bored voice, "Because he blew the confounded thing up on Friday night."

"Goodness me," said Heffer. "Goodness me!"

As Ned and Thomas walked back along the jetty to board their boat, Thomas said: "You know, we might as well pay a call on that ship. It'll be good hearing some gossip from England."

"We might be recognized," Ned said cautiously.

"With seven ships we have little to fear. The general is on our side because he wants those guns – and we could secure this merchant ship without a word of complaint from him. He certainly couldn't interfere."

"You know, Thomas, you think like a buccaneer; there's none of the old Huntingdon squire left."

Thomas slapped Ned on the back. "Finest compliment you've ever paid me. That's why we all stay alive. If you're going to catch wolves you must think like a wolf: otherwise the wolf catches you. You're learning too, you know."

Intrigued by this piece of information, because he had been depressed over the last few days, thinking that he was slow to take the lead and remembering how Day and Lloyd had seemed to be acting instinctively at the castle, Ned said almost angrily: "All I've learned is how to navigate, thanks to your man Lobb."

"Whoa there!" Thomas said, stopping in mid-stride and turning to face Ned. "Not feeling confident, eh? Don't be fooled by my beard and my loud laugh, Ned; you'll be the leader of all the buccaneers in a few months and I'll be glad to serve with you as second-in-command. Diana says three months but I reckon six would be better."

A completely flabbergasted Ned said: "Why? What on earth makes you say that?"

"Ned, my boy, there are two kinds of buccaneers: the leaders, who think and plan for the next year as well as this. And there are the cut-and-thrusters, good hands in a fight but not thinkers. We need the leaders. Who decided on the spur of the moment that blowing up the castle would terrorize Santiago so no Spaniard would argue with us? It wasn't me. Who brought the cannons back and bargained with the general so that the army builds our defences? It wasn't me!"

These had been such obvious things that Ned was embarrassed by Thomas's praise. But it was scorching hot standing on the jetty, and the men in the boat had come back after sheltering from the sun on the shady side of an old shed although it was almost noon, with the sun nearly overhead.

"Let's get into the boat."

Thomas held his arm. "A moment more. We have three ships that we own, and those four buccaneers came with us. When the word gets round how much purchase those four are sharing, we'll have a couple of dozen more privateers, English, French and Dutch, coming in here and wanting to join us. They'll hear that I led the Santiago raid. Well, I'm going to tell them the truth, that you led it. They'll elect you their leader. If you choose me as your second in command I'll be more than content. I know many of these men and I'll warn you against the scoundrels. But all the boats who've been using Tortuga will come over here now – particularly if Heffer gives them commissions."

"Where is Tortuga?"

"I can't think why I haven't mentioned it before. It's an island at the north-west corner of Hispaniola – at the other end of the Windward Passage – with a good anchorage. The Spaniards can't get at it: they haven't the ships to attack by sea and that corner of Hispaniola is just thick jungle. They even have a name for themselves, 'The Brethren of the Coast'."

"They're just a collection of pirates, then?"

"No. Outcasts, yes, like you and me: persecuted by the English for being Royalist or Catholic; by the French for being Protestant; by the Dutch for not being Dutch; and by the Spanish because they are 'Beyond the Line' as well as not being Spanish."

"Come on, let's pay a call on that ship," Ned said, his mind already beginning to spin at the thought of what could be done with twenty ships and a thousand men, using Jamaica as a base.

The merchant ship was the *Emerald* of Bristol and her master was a portly Devonian, William Parker. He greeted them warily at first, recognizing their boat as coming originally from the *Griffin*. It was obvious that he had guessed they were buccaneers and was nervous with their seven ships surrounding him.

In less than five minutes he had fallen under Thomas's cheery spell, was calling both men "sir", and was completely won over when he warned them that there was a great danger of a Spanish fleet from Santiago recapturing Jamaica and was told the seven ships had just come from destroying the defences.

"A good purchase, eh?" he said jokingly.

"Not enough to cover our expenses," Thomas grumbled. "Still, we brought back great guns for the general so he can build some defences here. Now, enough of that; tell us what is happening in England?"

Parker looked gloomy. "The news was not good when we sailed from London. The Lord Protector had died the week before. The country – well, London anyway – seemed stunned."

"His great strength was in London. Not many tears were shed down in the west country," Thomas said, making it clear he was not a Parliamentarian.

"No, quite. Well, there was not a great deal of enthusiasm at the thought that Richard was succeeding him."

"What brought you to Jamaica?" Ned asked.

"A dozen or so people want to settle here. Granted land by the Lord Protector. They took passage with me because I was going to Barbados and Antigua. Now they don't know whether to stay or come back with me."

"What worries them?"

"Well, are their land grants still any good?"

"Of course, as long as they were signed by the Lord Protector or someone he appointed legally. Otherwise everyone would lose his land every time a lord protector or a monarch died."

"Ah, I'll tell them that. It sounds good sense. Trouble is, they couldn't get any reassurance from the general here."

Ned gave a dry laugh. "Tell me, what news from Barbados?" he asked casually.

"A very unhappy island, it seemed to me. I hadn't been there for three or four years, but now . . . every man's hand seems to be turned against his brother. There was a nasty duelling episode while we were there; one of the island's biggest landowners was killed."

Ned nodded. "A small island, everyone knows everyone else – perhaps too well – and heavy drinking is a habit. What happened?"

"There was a gambling party in Bridgetown, I understand. Two or three dozen people there and gambling for high stakes. One man was cheating – five or six people had been watching him for an hour or two. Then one of them accused him. He had marked cards in his hand but he denied everything and in a terrible fury challenged his accuser to a duel. They fought at dawn next day. He was shot in the stomach and died before sunrise. A young man, owned two big estates, but he had a wild temper, people said."

"Did you hear his name?" Ned asked, casually trying to disguise his interest.

"Oh yes. I've met him a few times and brought out goods for him this voyage. The rate was agreed but he refused to pay it all. Paid me exactly half. A bad man, really; no one was mourning him, as far as I could see."

"What *was* his name?" Ned repeated.

"Wilson. He had a plantation near Bridgetown, and recently he bought Kingsnorth, so people said. I delivered his goods at Bridgetown and he cheated me, standing on the jetty and calling *me* a scoundrel."

"We mustn't speak ill of the dead," Thomas said piously. "Well, we have some work to finish on board the *Griffin* so we will bid you a good day sir. You will not be sailing for some days? Good, then you must visit us."

In the boat Ned sat on the thwart, Parker's words repeating in his ears like a jungle drum. "A bad man, really; no one was mourning him, as far as I could see . . . Wilson, Wilson, Wilson . . . marked cards in his hand but he denied everything . . . challenged his accuser . . . shot in the stomach and died before sunrise . . ."

Thomas gripped his arm. "Stop feeling sorry for Wilson; it should have happened years ago. Start thinking about how you tell Aurelia. She won't be grief-stricken, but it'll be a shock. Would you prefer that Diana . . .?"

"No, I'll do it. I'm not sorry for him, Thomas; he challenged me, you know."

"And you refused?" It was Thomas's turn to be shocked. Refusing a challenge invited the accusation of cowardice.

"If I'd fought him, I'd have killed him, sword or pistol."

"That'd have been no loss!"

"Yes, but I did not think Aurelia would ever marry the man who killed her husband, much as she hated him. Every time my right hand touched her, she might remember . . ."

"You're right, I suppose; women can be unpredictable. But you took a big risk. The island would have loved to call you a coward, and Aurelia might have thought you were too frightened to risk your skin on her behalf – I presume she was the cause."

"Yes, she was, but she understood. And now someone has done the job for me. For us, really."

"You'll be able to marry now," Thomas said cheerfully. "Oh, what a wedding we'll all give you! After the usual period of mourning, of course!"

By then the boat was coming alongside the *Griffin* and Thomas said: "I'll leave you to it. Diana will want to hear the news. Gently does it and don't rush things, Ned." He shook him by the hand and Ned stood up on the thwart and jumped for the rope ladder.

Aurelia was waiting on deck and she walked towards him and clasped his hands in hers. "Did everything go well?"

"With the general? Oh yes, he has agreed to build the forts and batteries if we provide the guns, powder and shot."

"And then you and Thomas visited the other ship."

"Yes, we went over to hear any further news."

"She came through Barbados." She said it as a statement, not a question, and she was looking past Ned as she spoke, to a point in the distance measurable only in time, not distance.

She gripped Ned's hands tightly. "You heard some bad news."

Again, a statement, not a question, Ned noted. Was it bad news really? Yes, a death always had to be regarded as bad news; it was the kind of hypocrisy that was necessary among civilized people.

"Yes, my darling. It concerns you. And me, too, I suppose."

"Something has happened to Walter." Again a statement; somehow, he felt, she had known all along. He led her to the companionway and down to the cabin, conscious that seamen on deck had guessed that something unusual was happening.

She sat in the chair, quite composed, and clasped her hands. The skin of her face had tautened, emphasizing her high cheekbones, but there was no expression, no fear, anger or relief.

"How did it happen?"

"A duel. He made the challenge."

"He challenged you, and you refused for my sake although you knew he would put it about that you were a coward."

Ned knelt before her and took her hands in his. "You are a widow, now."

He was not quite sure why he said it because it was a banal, unnecessary remark, but she suddenly pressed his head to her breasts. "I've been a widow for a long time, Edouard; from the day I fell in love with you. You can only be married in your heart if you have a true husband. I was married only in the eyes of the church."

"So we are free," he said. "Free to be together with no one to deny us."

She looked down at him. "Can we be more free than we are? Can we be more together than we are? For a buccaneer, *chéri,* you still worry about the laws made by men in remote places which do not apply to us."

He grinned and admitted it. "I want us to be married, yes. You are right, it will not affect us really, not to make us happier or more free. But it will make a difference to me. I can't explain how or why, but it will."

"I know," she said gently, "I know and understand. It is the difference between a man and a woman. I am yours; you realize that. But you want a marriage ceremony because you are not certain that I know you are mine."

"I don't know the reasons; I just want us to be married."

"Then we shall be – when you ask me, of course, and we must have proof of Walter's death."

"Parker, the master of the ship, will swear an affidavit, I'm certain. That would be enough."

"Edouard – you realize what Walter's death means?"

There was something in the tone of her voice which made him think quickly to see if there was some awful snag that he had not considered, but there was nothing.

"Well, we can marry . . . but what else?"

"I am Walter's widow. *La veuve*. I will – no, I *have*, inherited all his possessions. My wedding present to you, my darling, is Kingsnorth. Will you accept it?"

*If you have enjoyed this book
and would like to receive details
of other Walker Adventure Fiction titles,
please write to:*

*Adventure Fiction Editor
Walker and Company
720 Fifth Avenue
New York, NY 10019*